World Broadcasting:
A Comparative View

The Ablex
Communication, Culture, & Information Series
Eileen Mahoney, The George Washington University,
Series Editor

Communication, Organization and Performance
by Tom Dixon, Queensland University of Technology

Unglued Empire: The Soviet Experience
with Communications Technologies
by Gladys D. Ganley, Foreword by Marshall I. Goldman

Writing in a Milieu of Utility: The Move to Technical
Communication in American Engineering Programs 1850–1950
by Teresa C. Kynell, Northern Michigan University

News Media and Foreign Relations: A Multifaceted Perspective
edited by Abbas Malek, Howard University

World Broadcasting: A Comparative View
edited by Alan Wells, Temple University

Forthcoming:

Diplomatic Discourse: International Conflict at the United Nations—
Addresses and Analysis
by Ray T. Donahue, Nagoya Gakuin University, and Michael H. Prosser,
Rochester Institute of Technology

Mass Media and Society
edited by Alan Wells, Temple University, and Ernest A. Hakanen,
Drexel University

Telecommunications Law, Regulation, and Policy
edited by William H. Read and Walter Sapronov,
Georgia Institute of Technology

World Broadcasting:
A Comparative View

edited by

Alan Wells
Temple University

Ablex Publishing Corporation
Norwood, New Jersey

Copyright © 1996 by Ablex Publishing Corporation

All rights reserved. No part of this publication may be reproduced, stored in a
retrieval system, or transmitted, in any form or by any means, electronic,
mechanical, photocopying, microfilming, recording or otherwise, without
permission of the publisher.

Printed in the United States of America

Library of Congress Cataloging-in-Publication Data

World broadcasting : a comparative view / edited by Alan Wells.
    p. cm. — (Communications, culture, & information studies)
    Includes bibliographical references and index.
    ISBN 1-56750-245-8 (cloth). — ISBN 1-56750-246-6 (paper)
    1. Broadcasting. 2. Broadcasting policy. I. Wells, Alan, 1940–
II. Series.
PN1990.8.W67   1996
384.54—dc20   96–27566
                                                            CIP

Ablex Publishing Corporation
355 Chestnut Street
Norwood, New Jersey 07648

Contents

About the Contributors

OSABUOHIEN P. AMIENYI has a PhD in mass communication from Bowling Green State University, Ohio, and is currently an Associate Professor in the Department of Radio–Television, Arkansas State University. Has worked in the U.S.A. and Nigeria at various times as a radio and television writer/producer/director, advertising copywriter, information officer and lecturer. He conducts research in developmental communication, international communication, media and society, and media education.

HUSSEIN Y. AMIN holds a PhD from Ohio State University. He is a professor in the Department of Journalism and Mass Communication and a senior associate of the Adnam Center for television journalism at The American University in Cairo. He is on the Board of Trustees of the Egyptian Radio and Television Union, and a consultant to many Arab and international television networks. He has written extensively on Middle Eastern and international communication in both Arabic and English.

JOSEPH K DIEMER holds a Masters degree in Communications from Temple University. He is a former journalist, and has written articles for trade publications in Australia and New Zealand.

ERNEST A. HAKANEN holds a PhD from Temple University. He is Director of the Undergraduate Communication Program, Department of Humanities and Communications at Drexel University, where he also serves on the Honors Program, Graduate Program in Technical and Science Communication, and Graduate Program in Electrical Engineering Faculty. He is an advisor to the Pennsylvania Humanities Council.

HSIANG-WEN HSIAO is Associate Professor at the Chinese Culture University in Taipei, Taiwan.

GERARD IGYOR holds a PhD from Temple University and is an Assistant Professor of Communication at Millersville University. He has worked in Nigeria as a Film and Television Producer with the Nigerian Television Authority. He does research in international telecommunications, telecommunications technology policy, and transborder satellite broadcasting.

VENICIO A. DE LIMA is Professor of Political Communication at the Universidade de Brasilia (Brazil). He holds a BA in sociology and political science from the Univeridade Federal de Minas Gerais and a PhD in communications from the University of Illinois, Urbana. He is the author of *Comunicacion y Politica en America Latina: El Caso Brasileno* (1993). He is an editor of *Comunicacao & Politica* (Brazil) and is on the Editorial board of *Critical Studies in Mass Communication* (USA).

SUNIL MISRA holds a PhD in Anthropology. He is a senior consultant on research and evaluation to the Population Foundation of India. He was formerly Director of Audience Research at All India Radio, and Professor and Head of the Department of Survey and Programme Evaluation at the Indira Gandhi National Open University.

JANIS E. OVERLOCK holds an Institute for International Education Professional Development Fellowship, and is completing a doctoral dissertation entitled *The Development of the Business and Economic Press in Hungary and its Impact on Market Reform, 1968–1994*. She holds a Masters in Journalism degree from Temple University and a BA in History and German Literature from the University of California at Riverside. Her current position is Curriculum Development Coordinator at the SIMBAH Journalism Center in Budapest, Hungary.

KENNETH C. PETRESS received a PhD in Political Communication from Louisiana State University. He teaches rhetoric courses at the University of Maine at Presque Isle. He has lived in China, and taught at three major universities there.

DONNALYN POMPPER is an Instructor in the Department of Communication and English at Cabrini College in Radnor, Pennsylvania. She has 12 years of experience in public relations and journalism working with the Campbell Soup Company, Tasty Baking Company, Lewis Gilman & Kynett Public Relations, and the *Philadelphia Inquirer*.

MATTHEW J. RUSHER holds a Masters degree in Journalism from Temple University.

JULIO SOLER-BURGUILLOS has an MS degree in mass communication from Arkansas State University. He is currently an Art Director at Rainbow Educational Concepts, Inc., and has worked as a film and television producer/director/editor and advertising creative executive in Madrid, Spain.

HIROSHI TOKINOYA is Professor in the Department of Mass Communications at Tokai University in Tokyo. He has published numerous research studies on Japanese and cross cultural mass communication.

ALAN WELLS is Professor of Communications at Temple University. He has been Director of the university's London program, and a Visiting Professor at the National University of Singapore and Temple University Japan in Tokyo.

Preface

Mass communication is justifiably a major topic of interest in American colleges. Students of journalism, mass communications, sociology, political science, and psychology are sensitive to the far-reaching impact of the mass media on individuals and society at large. Courses quite naturally focus on current practices in the United States. This volume is designed to put such material in comparative perspective and thus shed new light on American media practices. It is designed as a resource for the growing number of courses dealing with international media and is also recommended as a supplement to texts for basic mass communications courses that attempt to provide a global perspective.

There is also a growing interest in comparative mass media in other countries. In fact, this book was written while I was teaching American students in England, native Singaporeans in their own country, and predominantly Japanese students at Temple University Japan. Many of the contributing authors are not Americans, or have spent time living outside of the U.S. They have contributed their expertise and perspectives to the book. Although there is probably no such thing as a purely "international" perspective, we have attempted to make the book useful for university students both within and outside the United States. Perhaps no single volume can do justice to this topic; what is attempted here is the presentation of a sampling of geographic regions and issues, with the understanding that course instructors may provide supplementary reading of their own choice.

The mass media in the United States are almost entirely commercial enterprises. Television is dominated by large corporations, and newspapers are increasingly concentrated in chain and multimedia conglomerate operations. Both the electronic media and the press rely heavily on advertising for their revenues. This pattern of ownership and source of funds shape the product that is presented to the public. Thus, financial imperatives determine the type of programming offered. Government regulation by the Federal Communications Commission and the Federal Trade Commission may on occasion inconvenience the electronic media, but it seldom threatens their basic structure and practices. The writings in this volume indicate that the American pattern is not the only, or necessarily the best, mode of operation.

The book is intended to be an introduction to the world's broadcasting and its organization. It is not meant to be an encyclopedia, so although all of the world's regions are covered, there is only brief information on the smaller countries and a few countries with low populations have been omitted. The individual country chapters focus on those with the largest populations in their regions. Together they contain well over half of the world's people. Statistics are provided in each region chapter that give comparable population and economic figures, and radio and television set numbers. Although the accuracy of such statistics can certainly be questioned, it appears that both the distribution of wealth and the access to broadcasting is very uneven: Much of the world population is too poor to have really entered the broadcasting age, much less the information age of high technology.

I am of course indebted to the authors who have permitted me to include their work: This is in essence their volume. My thanks also to Linda B. Pawelchak, who did wonders with some very rough draft copy, and to TUJ biologist and administrator Jonathan Wu, who teased area maps from his computer. Last, thanks to my students, who have demonstrated to me that the mass media in the United States cannot be studied in isolation and that the study of overseas media is both interesting and fruitful.

—Alan Wells
Tokyo, June 1995

Chapter 1

Introduction

Alan Wells

Broadcasting is a major component of the mass media in most of the world's countries. Because of their technological similarities, radio and television are often run on similar lines, frequently by the same people. In the United States, for example, the major television networks developed out of the major radio networks. They are still involved in radio but diversification of that medium has muted their preeminence. Both radio and television in the United States are regulated by the Federal Communications Commission under the same broadcasting statutes, and with the exception of public broadcasting stations, are funded by commercial spot advertisements.

The media systems in a country usually reflect the economic, social, political, and even geographic conditions of the country. The study of media systems would be sterile, however, if it merely demonstrated how well they "fit" their social environments—for media systems are designed by people and can be changed (within limits). The central task in studying media systems is to determine how the type of system adopted influences the way the medium is used and how this in turn shapes its social impact. With this in mind, I turn first to the ways in which media systems have been classified. Several characteristics relevant to a more detailed analysis of such systems are then suggested.

MEDIA SYSTEM TYPOLOGIES

Despite the complexity and variety of mass media systems, media experts in the past often urged the adoption of a simplistic scheme of classification—a bipolar view with the "free" U.S. system at the desirable end of a continuum and totalitarian systems at the other. This approach has been a strong ideological weapon in the spread of American media enterprises overseas. As Skornia (1965) noted concerning television, this view was most evident in the trade journals:

> An editorial in *Broadcasting* magazine in March, 1955, told of the alleged victory of the American broadcasting plan, which has "prevailed in all democratic nations," over the so-called British Plan. The editorial concluded: "Henceforth the lexicon will change. It will be the 'American Plan' versus the 'Totalitarian Plan' until the latter collapses." Similarly, *Advertising Age* in November of 1959 observed that "Nations that have resisted commercial TV have made little progress. Nations that have not resisted commercial TV have made rapid strides." (pp. 181–182)

The quote from *Broadcasting* magazine assumes that commercial television has a monopoly on democratic virtue. Publicly financed systems, such as that in Britain, are labeled "totalitarian." *Advertising Age* implied that commercial television was causally related to national progress. There is little evidence that fully commercialized media are so beneficial, although this view is as common today as it was 30 years ago.

The choice, however, is not limited to either free (private commercial) or totalitarian (one variant of public) systems. Various alternative means of sponsorship (e.g., by political parties in multiple party states, labor unions, churches, etc.) may widen the choice beyond that between business and government control. Some forms of public control of electronic media may be possible that could produce cultural and informational programming that would be relatively free of either political or commercial interference. Broadcasting, therefore, can theoretically be controlled by public, commercial, or political forces. Actual broadcasting organizations are usually influenced to varying degrees by all three. Thus, the U.S. system is not entirely free of political constraints and its Public Broadcasting System introduces the possibility of some inputs to the system that are responsive to the public. Even with political domination, some commercial and public uses are served. In the former Soviet Union, for example, advertisements for consumer goods were broadcast and cultural and information programming was at least partially independent of political directives.

Adding a third control dimension to the bipolar continuum refines it considerably but still leaves us with a simplistic classification scheme for entire media systems. Other classifications in the literature are therefore examined for a more useful one. Merrill and Lowenstein (1971) proposed a three-stage classification based on the differing characteristics of media audiences. They claimed that

> "media in any nation grow from *elitist* to *popular* to *specialized*. In the elitist stage, the media appeal to and are consumed by opinion leaders, primarily. In the popular stage, media appeal to and are consumed by the masses of a nation's population, primarily. In the specialized stage, the media appeal to and are consumed by fragmented, specialized segments of the total population. (p. 33).

Media systems, they believed, pass through this orderly progression. Thus, most systems in less developed countries are still in the initial elitist stage. When literacy is widespread and a large segment of the population has escaped abject poverty, the media shift to the popular variant, as they have in Europe, North America, Japan, Israel, and Australia (Merrill & Lowenstein, 1971, p. 36). With higher education, affluence, leisure, and sufficient market scale, the final stage is reached. Somewhat ethnocentrically, Merrill and Lowenstein claimed that the United States was currently entering this stage, the first country to do so (p. 39).

This typology, of course, fails to take into account organizational factors or the way the media are used. It is based primarily on the pattern of growth experienced in North America and it seems most appropriate for categorizing the print media. The electronic media even in many poor countries never really had an elitist stage because cheap transistor radios, collective listening and viewing, and the importation of mass television fare make such a stage unnecessary. Alternatively, as in China, ideological imperatives may ensure a mass audience (or none at all) from the outset.

Perhaps the most commonly used typology of media systems is that

Table 1.1.
The Siebert–Peterson–Schramm Typology

Type (Name)	Control of Media	Programming Policy	Representative Countries
Soviet–Communist	Government, Communist party	Emphasis on transmitting Communist doctrine, mobilizing support for government, and raising cultural tastes of masses	Soviet Union, and other Communist countries
Libertarian	Nongovernment	Emphasis on freedom from restraints on programming	Anglo–American and other Western countries
Social responsibility	Organizations responsive to public	Emphasis on transmitting public information and discussion of social issues, and the avoidance of harmful material	Anglo–American countries
Authoritarian	Public and private subordinate to state	No criticism of government, censorship of programming	Early European countries, less developed countries

developed by Siebert, Peterson, and Schramm (1956). As interpreted by Wright (1959), they "view the communication systems of the world as operating—more or less precisely—under four major theories" (p. 24), or perhaps *styles* would be a better term. These are the Soviet–Communist, libertarian, social responsibility, and authoritarian patterns. Their characteristics are depicted in Table 1.1.

This typology failed to discriminate among the wide variety of Communist and non-Communist systems (although in part this is inevitable in any typology); its social responsibility type is only emergent and there is no consideration of transferred systems of a colonial or neo-colonial nature (e.g., extensions of international commercialism). The typology also ignores the crucial fact that some media systems are organized to make money, whereas others are organized merely to communicate to a public.

In his examination of European systems, Paulu (1967) began with a Western–totalitarian continuum in mind. To him, "the Western theory is that within practical limits all points of view should be heard, under the assumption that the best ideas finally will prevail." Censorship is used, he noted, to exclude "dangerous" material, which apparently includes any democratic questioning of commercial domination: "The totalitarian point of view is that the press should be used, as the Soviet Constitution declares, 'in conformity with the interests of the working people, and in order to strengthen the socialist system'" (p. 51).

Such a typology was of little use in analyzing the European media systems. Paulu (1967, pp. 51–76), therefore, turned to the classification scheme developed by Namurois (1964), which outlined four types based on different modes of control: (a) *state operated*, by government ministry, department, or administrative agency, including most Communist countries; (b) *public corporation*, operated autonomously under state charter, as in Britain, France, West Germany, Belgium, and the Netherlands; (c) *public interest partnership*, operated by legally private corporations with state stock interests, as in Italy, Sweden, and Switzerland; and *private enterprise*, operated by private corporations with weak government regulation, as in the United States, Japan's private stations, and Luxembourg.

While the Siebert–Peterson–Schramm typology depicted in Table 1.1 stressed the underlying philosophy of the media, Namurois the stresses the *control* of electronic media. This produces a much more discriminating set of criteria, merging the Soviet–Communist and totalitarian types but separating out elements of both the libertarian and social responsibility categories. The usefulness of the Namurois types is in projecting program style from the type of control. The private enterprise operation is unlikely to produce costly educational programming or curb the "consumption now" exhortations of advertising. The state-operated station or public corporation appears best suited for those tasks.

This classification, however, fails to take account of important differences within each type, as Paulu's (1967) exposition of media systems indicates. It is possible for a state-operated system to be either more or less centralized, either shrill or low keyed in its programming. Thus, stations in the former Communist Yugoslavia, for example, had considerable autonomy in programming and budget allocation (p. 57). Among other state-operated systems, China's revolutionary use of the media contrasted with Russia's more quiescent and comparatively decentralized style of media use. Public corporations vary in their organization and programming imperatives (cultural, informative, educational, entertainment) and the degree of government intervention. They may prohibit or permit advertising. Partnerships exist between government and private entrepreneurs or, as in Sweden, between government and a variety of political, commercial, and cultural organizations.

Several variations of these media classification schemes have been developed in recent years. These have been usefully summarized by Mundt (1991) and include an updated typology by Lowenstein that includes three forms of press ownership and five philosophies. Also discussed are the more complex schemes devised by media scholars John Merrill, William Hachten, J. Herbert Altschull, and Robert Picard. To avoid many of the difficulties of classification, the approach used in this book is simpler. Each of the major countries is treated separately with a consideration of all or some of the dimensions.

THE FIVE KEY ASPECTS OF MEDIA SYSTEMS

The Namurois (1964) classification by control appears to be adequate on this dimension. Control is a key factor in describing and analyzing media systems. Linked to control are the questions of finance, programming, target audience, and feedback mechanisms, and these, it is argued, are the other essential elements distinguishing media systems.

The options for financing the media range from advertising revenue to some form of subsidy, either private or direct government tax support or a mixture of the two. License fees on electronic media receivers are commonly used to pay for broadcasting service. Almost half the world's countries (including most of Europe) employ this method.

Advertising practices vary widely in countries that raise revenues from this source. The U.S. pattern of commercial domination, in which up to one third of broadcast time is used for advertising, is by no means the only style. Most European countries finance broadcasting with some advertising revenue; however, commercial announcements are strictly controlled and program sponsorship is often preferred to spot announcements. There are often fixed time limits for advertising that are more binding than the National Association of Broadcasters' code provisions in the United States. In Germany, for example, only 20 minutes of commercials are permitted per day. When advertising is limited in these ways, program content is influenced less by the advertiser.

Programming may be directed to commercial, educational, cultural, or political ends or simply to entertainment. Usually, of course, the broadcaster has a combination of such goals. All programs must be minimally entertaining if they are to hold the attention of their audience. Following the formulation of Merrill and Lowenstein (1971), target audiences may usefully be classified as elite, mass, or specialized.

The need for feedback is particularly crucial in educational programming. It may take the form of fieldworker reports (which have been found most effective for specific projects), audience participation and local control, polls or rating systems, and evaluations by critics or sponsors. The latter two methods are most common in commercial systems for which raw size of audience is often crucial. The former methods, although more cumbersome, are most useful where the main concerns are education and change.

A realistic classification of media systems, therefore, probably goes beyond the typologies of three or four categories. The five key dimensions of media systems outlined earlier are summarized in Table 1.2 and systems may combine these dimensions in dozens of ways. The primary questions to ask about a system, therefore, are the following: How is the medium controlled? How is it financed? What is its purpose? Whom does it serve? How does it ascertain the effect it is having?

Table 1.2
Key Dimensions of Media Systems

Dimensions	Options
Control	State operated, public corporation, partnership, private enterprise (with varying degrees of government regulations), institutionally sponsored
Finance	License fees, general taxation, advertising and tax combination, advertising, private subsidy
Programming goals	Entertainment, education, sales, culture, political ideology, cheapest possible imported material
Target audience	Elite, mass, specialized
Feedback mechanism	Field reports, audience participation, polls and ratings, reports from critics and sponsors

THE VARIETY OF MEDIA SYSTEMS

The mass media system in the United States is commonly characterized as private and commercial. It transmits useful information and entertains its audience but its main task, the one for which it is rewarded, is to "deliver" audiences to the advertisers. Despite the presence of some outstanding journalists and creative artists, and the occasional educational and cultural use of the media, they are run overwhelmingly as profit-making enterprises. Given this set of economic constraints, there is probably no real alternative to current practices: The context in which media personnel work must change if the nature of their product is to be upgraded. The United States and Canada are not included for detailed treatment in this book because it is assumed that most readers already have more knowledge of their systems than could be contained in a single chapter.

The commercial pattern in the United States is, of course, of global importance and is often the standard used to judge other countries' media, particularly because it is by far the largest exporter of television programming. American-style commercial broadcasting systems are sometimes claimed to be "natural" to politically free countries. Evidence supporting this claim is not very strong. When we examine the media of other countries in the Western world, we find a variety of systems, each reflecting the traditions and institutions of its country. Newly independent and developing countries, which are often politically neutral, seldom have time to develop their own media traditions. Therefore, usually they imitate one of the existing systems of the free world. The model chosen may be that of the United States but it is equally likely to be the British or French pattern, partly because those two countries once ruled widespread empires and partly because they demonstrate a viable alternative to the American commercial operation.

For Americans who are seriously interested in reform of media operations, the study of successful Western media systems (even if they obviously could not be adopted in whole) can suggest many alternatives. In addition, they provide the key to understanding Canadian media sensibilities because that country's communication patterns and traditions closely resemble the British (or French), even though most Canadians can receive and are avid consumers of U.S. broadcasting.

COMMUNICATION AND DEVELOPMENT

The purpose of this last section is to investigate global communication theory in the context of today's changing world. The investigation begins with a brief summary of world events and their current ideological and theoretical explanations, which I believe make a new perspective necessary. This is followed by an examination of macroexplanations of the world economy, which provides a backdrop for addressing global media and development theories, most notably those of the "cultural imperialism" school. In the conclusion that follows this discussion, suggestions are made for new empirically based theories of communication and development.

New World Order or World in Crisis?

The last decade has been marked by both the complacency of the postmodern West and the near collapse of the Communist world. The ideas of the information society and postmodernity convey a notion of a qualitatively changed world. Intellectual attention in the United States has recently focused on "the end of history" thesis. This thesis does not deny that historic events are occurring but that the world ideological debate is now over. To be sure, ideologies that propose humane solutions to world problems do appear to be in decline. In both the East and the West, a single ideology seems paramount, a somewhat mean-spirited faith in a market economy. This vulgarized revival of 18th-century Adam Smithism applauds corporate power and private greed and many of the tenants of social Darwinism. In Britain and the United States, governments have reversed their welfare state momentum. Presidents Reagan and Bush relaxed controls on corporations and Thatcher's "revolution" freed capitalist enterprise and privatized state industries. Their successors have not reversed the trend and both countries have reverted to the income inequality of the 1940s.

In the East, the "democratic" revolution has ushered in a period of chaos in the former Soviet Union and Eastern Europe as new states emerge and cultural irredentism threatens renewed European carnage. With the abandonment of Communist economic planning in the East, many of the new leaders (to the applause of the optimistic Western press) have opted for a market economy. Boris Yeltsin and Lech Walesa, for example, both appear to subscribe to a market ideology despite the massive dislocation it is causing. No alternative model for economic organization seems to be available, except begging for aid. It is ironic that Welesa, as the former champion of what capitalists would surely regard as overpaid, underworked, welfare-coddled Polish workers, went to the United States and asked for a new Marshall Plan from the world's largest debtor nation. He went home honored but empty-handed. The countries of the former Soviet Union also appear to be putting their faith in the benefits of a market economy and their hope for massive foreign aid. However, the Western economy is stagnant and not in a generous mood. The East hopes to join the so-called First World of prosperity. With the exception of the former East Germany (which had a ready and able buyer), most of the old Second World is apparently joining the impoverished, less developed Third World.

Third World countries have had 30 or more years of market economy "development." With a few spectacular exceptions in Asia, notably Japan, Taiwan, Hong Kong, South Korea and Singapore, they have generally not fared well. Third World debt has become a threat to world banking. Greedy, nondemocratic elites often preside over hungry masses. Terror, corruption, and waste, along with massive population growth, have led to declining hopes and living conditions. Even if postmodern values are rejected, as in Iran, the ascent from poverty seems hopeless.

What is the market economy that seems so central to First and Second World ideology? For some, it may represent the laissez-faire markets of the past and the models of classical economics. The Second and Third Worlds already have markets of this type. For the leading ideologists, however, the market economy means a world market whose limits are largely those of what the United Nations now labels *transnational corporations* (TNCs). It is this market that Western governments and international organizations try to promote and it is the TNC world that the countries of the former Soviet Union and Eastern Europe wish to join; that is, they want investments from the large multinational corporations.

Underlying the new capitalist thinking is a fundamental individualist belief in democracy. As Schiller (1976) has noted, "market ideology claims that individuals will make better choices than their governmental representatives; therefore dispense with governmental responsibility whenever possible" (p. 16). However, the outcome has not been an anarchist utopia. Instead, the deregulation policies in the United States and elsewhere "can be understood as the structural reorganization of the world economy, under TNC direction, assisted by the new information technologies" (p. 16). Schiller claimed that "nothing remains in the way—at least, not in the short run—of rampaging capital" (p. 17) and concluded that if this new order is not broken, the current trends of unemployment, the increasing numbers of information have-nots, the decline of the welfare state, and the revival of ultraright politics will continue.

This simple democratic appeal of market ideology has been conducive to TNC market expansion. These corporations have certainly been a source of innovation and dynamism but their goal is obviously not social welfare. Although they may best be considered a neutral rather than benign or malevolent social force, their self-interest is likely to conflict with social goals. Certainly their resources are not likely to be directed at such major global problems as overpopulation, ignorance, famine, poverty, cruelty, greed, drugs, and other self-destructive tendencies of the human species. The task of the TNC is the acquisition, not redistribution, of wealth.

There is a conflict in current ideology between what people (and corporations) want in the short term and long-term social needs. Market ideology assumes the former will provide the latter. Along with this view, proponents of the market economy appear to assume that it is working well and will continue to do so. They have embraced the idea of progress.

Even though the world corporate economy is usually assumed to be growing, the "trickle down" effect on national economies is highly suspect. Although First World countries are undeniably richer that the rest of the world, they too are experiencing stagnation. According to World Bank figures, very few countries achieved sustained growth from 1965 to 1990. Many low-and middle-income countries registered an annual average decline in gross national product per capita for the period. Of the 43 low income-countries, only China, Lesotho, Indonesia, and Egypt had growth rates above 4%. Middle-income economies achieving this rate were Paraguay, Thailand, Botswana, Malaysia, and Korea. Among the high-income countries, only Singapore, Hong Kong, and Japan grew at more than the 4% rate. Whether this stagnant world economy justifies an evolutionary growth view or whether impending world crises make a new chaos theory more appropriate is the subject to which I now turn.

Images of the World Market Economy

It is clearly impossible to review even a fraction of the literature on the world economy. Most people have not, of course, worked out a coherent world perspective. The now largely discredited *modernization theory* is examined first, followed by a brief look at a new perspective coming from the social sciences, known as *world systems theory*. I conclude with the enigmatic world vision of the British writer and reporter Anthony Sampson.

The modernization theory of economic growth was widely espoused in the 1950s and 1960s. It assumed that economic growth would occur in nations that underwent modernization. Thus, growth was considered natural and relatively easy. The mass media were considered to be instruments of modernization and therefore an economic asset. This simple optimistic view has been largely discarded by media researchers (e.g., Jayaweera & Amunugama, 1987; Melkote, 1991; Stevenson, 1988; Wells, 1972). Rogers (1978) questioned the applicability of the modernization paradigm to the contemporary Third World. It assumed a model that demanded the replication of the Western experience of industrialization, capital-intensive technology, and Western values while ignoring the quality of life and distribution of wealth in the Third World. Rogers noted a growing recognition of ecological limits on growth and alternate development approaches (he cited the case of China, which is perhaps less compelling now that market principles are being adopted there). He added that development was "not going very well in the countries that had closely followed the paradigm" (p. 66) and noted the dismal record of most of Latin America, Africa, and Asia.

World systems theory proposes a view of the world that focuses on order. Now an established part of social science, it has recently spawned a textbook that outlines the theory as well as the criticisms of it (Shannon, 1989). Based on a historical analysis of the spread of European commerce, the theory stresses the growth of global interdependence. The growth of the system is largely assumed and its systems terminology ignores the use of force in the domination of ever larger areas of the world during its formation. The theory is holistic and also rather abstract. With nations and their economies as its major conceptual units, it largely ignores the existence of TNCs and lesser groups and individuals (Wells & Reynolds, 1986). The view of the world that emerges is, therefore, primarily one of inevitability and progress.

A much more disturbing picture is given by Sampson (1989). His investigation of global wealth became a documentary series on British television (cosponsored by Japan's TV Asahi). Although much of Sampson's work would be considered speculative by academicians, his interviews with the rich and powerful add interest to his thesis. Money, he claimed, has become the new world religion and world finance has created a new generation of the super rich, a group unashamed of its instant fortunes. The Trumps, Boeskys, Milkens, and their like have profited by purely financial dealings, corporate takeovers and speculations, and have used the world's $400 billion (U.S. currency) per day electronic money flow to their advantage. This instant global liquidity, Sampson believed, is the cause of much of the world market's instability and unpredictability.

Sampson (1989) argued emphatically that Japan is now the world's economic power. Its strength resides largely in its interlocked corporations and their production emphasis. Low defense expenditure and high personal savings have also contributed to the financial surpluses that have made Japan the leading world banker. The other new successful Asian countries, he noted, are all assisted by extensive state intervention in their economies. It should be noted that Germany, the financial giant that Sampson overlooked, is a strong welfare state. The United States has declined because of speculation and high levels of consumer, corporate, and government debt and is now beholden to Japan for credit. The Third World and the former Eastern Bloc, meanwhile, are left out of the new world economy. Debt-ridden Latin America is not only left out, it is de-developing.

Sampson (1989) viewed the world as dominated by electronic finance "cowboys" who control the money to back TNCs and governments. He cited the Pope, John Reed of Citicorp, and Barber Conable of the World Bank on the desperate world needs that are not being met by the world market. Sampson, however, remained guardedly optimistic. He believed that governments are not down and out despite recent losses to the TNCs, and it is they who must shape an ecologically and socially sound economy.

With modernization theory and world systems theory showing increasing distance from reality, Sampson's observations are interesting. Less empirical, but also intriguing, views are being developed by cultural studies theorists: for example, Baudrillard's (1988) *consumer society* and Harvey's (1989) *casino economy*. Mainstream commentators on the world scene typically reify the state and national economies and stress the continuity of global political and economic patterns (e.g., Kennedy 1987). In the absence of other systematic theories that are reasonably in tune with economic realities, *cultural imperialism* (CI) has become the preeminent, if controversial, theoretical attempt to understand world communications.

Global Media: CI Theory and Its Critics

Much of the material that is used by cultural imperialism's proponents is concerned with the media TNCs and the flow of information and programming. There is a growing body of such information to complement more readily available information on national (often governmental) media organization. Much, but not all, comes from CI-oriented researchers. Hamelink (1977) provided a listing of corporate interests in world communication. After painting a bleak description of the corporate system, he called for "countervailing power" against intrusions of the TNCs, by governments, the United Nations, labor unions, churches, universities, and action groups. Europe, where media organization is in turmoil (Palmer & Tunstall, 1988), has produced its own corporate giants (Becker, 1985), and is influenced by U.S. media giants (Kalkkinen & Sarkkinen, 1985). Mattelart, Delcourt, and Mattelart (1984) provided information on TNCs, including Globo of Brazil, the subject of Chapter 10 in this book. Sources for data on the international flow of television programming are Guback and Varis (1982) and Varis (1984, 1986b), which show continued U.S. program dominance but also increasing regional exchanges (see also Hoskings & Mirus, 1988; Pendakur, 1985; Renaud & Litman, 1985; Schlesinger, 1986). CI theory emerged as an alternative to modernization theories of development in the late 1960s. The publication of Schiller's (1969) book was perhaps the first extended presentation of CI. Other works soon followed. Wells (1972) critiqued modernization theory and argued that the penetration of Latin America by U.S.-based media and advertising companies complemented the sales efforts of American TNCs. Together they promoted the values of "consumerism" that allegedly detracted from the "producerism" needed for grass roots economic development.

Mattelart (1976), like other CI scholars, addressed the general issue of who controls CI—the TNCs or the U.S. government. He believed that the corporations are increasingly taking on the government's functions. Nonetheless, there is an overall Americanization effect. Local elites, he claimed, are part of the CI apparatus and American organizations influence education as well as media and advertising. For Mattelart, it seems, CI is primarily an American, not a world market, phenomenon, even though a later statement somewhat modifies this view (see Mattelart, 1983; Mattelart et al., 1984). Nonetheless, as Schiller (1986) pointed out:

> Capitalism has achieved remarkable popular support with its fostering of consumerism. It has sold successfully a way of life and a set of beliefs that tie human well-being to the individual possession of an ever-expanding array of purchasable goods and services. Acquiring material goods has either superseded or been made the equivalent of love, friendship, and community. (pp. 97–98)

Schiller (1986) saw a world dominated by TNCs but also a world in crisis. The world economy cannot achieve satisfactory growth and the TNCs do not constitute a viable order: "The likelihood of achieving a stable world system—the prerequisite for the successful operation of an information-based global order under transnational corporate direction recedes measurably with each initiative in the construction of that order" (1986). The Third World masses cannot enter the global consumer market and Schiller believed that the TNCs are promoting "future massive political instability" (p. 12).

CI has analyzed the part played by advertising in international communication. Schiller (1976) noted that the growth in U.S. exports and foreign investments in the 1950s to the 1970s was coupled with the expansion of U.S. advertising. More recent studies of advertising from a "dependency" perspective similar to CI have been done by Hamelink (1986) and by James and Roncagliolo (1986). The latter describe the spread of a transnational consumer model by advertising in the Third World. They note the contradictions between the commercial aims of advertising and the United Nations development strategy that calls for drives to promote literacy, health, nutrition, personal savings, and so forth. Varis (1986a) also pointed to current problems in agriculture, mineral resources, and pollution control.

The cultural imperialism perspective was often used in the United Nations (UNESCO) debate on the new world information and communication order (NWICO) and the influencial MacBride report on it (see McPhail, 1987). Nordenstreng (1980) criticized the report for its "one world," Western, "trilateral" bias (p. 16), whereas Varis (1986a) also saw the Trilateral Commission as a united front for developed country governments and the TNC's. The latter, though, are presumably dominant because, Varis claimed, "transnational corporations and the internationalization of capital are the dominant, central features of the international order" (p. 12). These TNCs "must be taken into account as important factors in the promotion of NWICO" (Guback & Varis, 1982, p. 3).

Hamelink (1980) made similar criticisms. He found the MacBride report "totally inadequate in confronting the vast politico-economic power exercised by those (TNCs) that play a key role in international communications" (p. 47). Eighty TNCs, he claimed, "account for three quarters of world production and distribution of communication goods and services" (p. 47). They constitute the fourth largest world industry and in 1980 had a 20% share of world trade. The NWICO, he concluded, "could very well be the world order of the TNCs (the 'corporate village') with international political blessing" (p. 51). The U.S. government, which withdrew from UNESCO in part over its objections to the organization's NWICO proposals, presumably had a different interpretation. Although restrictions on the "free flow" of information and the proposal for more Third World government controls appear to be its primary objections, U.S. opposition was not without its contradictions (see Roach, 1987).

European media have also been analyzed from a CI perspective. In a case study of the award of Irish direct broadcast satellite to a private consortium, Bell and Meehan (1988) claimed that rapid TNC investment in Ireland, pressure from the U.S. government and corporations, and Irish government collusion led to the decision. They concluded rather ominously:

> We are witnessing the increasing integration of the public service systems
> of Western Europe into the international marketplace for cultural and
> informational commodities and the dismantling of their public service
> communication industries. Evidence to date suggests that this can only
> further reduce the standards of European broadcasting by homogenizing
> their products and programming and sever their political responsibilities
> to their national publics. (p. 82)

The same arguments were raised in the debate on the recent restructuring of British broadcasting. They convey a fear not only of economic change, but also of serious political and cultural repercussions.

Criticism of CI

Because the CI perspective is so often used ideologically, it may be fruitful to consider criticisms of it before considering its relevance for new theories. Boyd-Barrett (1982) claimed that CI is one of three possible paradigms. It is an offshoot of neo-Marxist (as opposed to functionalist neo-Weberian) sociology. Boyd-Barrett believed that it is more political propaganda than scientific theory. CI, he claimed, equates imperialism with dependency. He cited India as an important case that does not fit the model. Then, adding a presumably neo-Weberian element to his critique, Boyd-Barrett noted that CI ignores the "machinery of the nation state" (p. 178). Furthermore, he found little evidence for the "cultural changes attributable to mass media" (p. 180). This uncertain influence of media messages has also been noted in a friendlier critique by McAnany (1987).

Many critics do not challenge the overall CI perspective but question some of the more detailed claims of its proponents. Tracey (1988), for example, claimed that television programs neither flow in only one direction nor is the U.S. inevitably dominant. Imports such as *Dallas* are seldom as popular as domestic programs. Tracey stressed the complexity of program flows and the diversity of audiences. Rather than the emergence of a single world market culture, he saw the growth of cultural pluralism with some wealthy public broadcasters contributing to it.

Several CI scholars have claimed that U.S. programming corporations fix prices and unfairly price their products on overseas markets. Hoskings, Mirus, and Roseboom (1989) attempted to refute this claim but fell short of complete success:

> Our evidence suggests that there is not a perfectly competitive international market for television programming but rather that U.S. producers, acting like a dominant firm, are responsible for establishing the general level of foreign program prices in each national market. (p. 69)

They do, however, defend the claim of "dumping," that is, selling a product below its cost. Their data show that, for example, a half-hour program costing $230,000 in the United States will be sold for between $12,000 and $14,000 to the United Kingdom and $1,400 and $2,000 to Mexico. They explained this difference by arguing that, in the pricing mechanism, the buyers also have some power. The price arrived at through negotiation must exceed only the incremental cost of the program to the seller. This minimum cost is very low because original production costs have already been recouped in the U.S. domestic market. What Hoskings et al. really achieved, then, is a defense of the seller's motives: Domestic programs clearly cannot be produced at the price of U.S. imports.

Meyer (1988) selected propositions from the CI perspective and operationalized them for quantitative testing. As in other studies of this genre, there are massive measurement problems. Testing the proposition that media exposure leads to a taste for modern consumer goods is a case in point. Meyer used the total percentage of television imports (with no attention to the type of programs or advertising) and the consumption of luxury goods (e.g., yacht sales), which are surely not what CI scholars had in mind as indicators. His small sample of Third World countries failed to support the hypothesis, so Meyer questioned the validity of CI theory. Whether it is the CI perspective that is simplistic or his test of it is open to interpretation. Nonetheless, Meyer's work offers some useful modifications. We do not know in much detail how television programming affects viewers or who watches specific programs, although presumably advertisers have confidence that their spots have some effect on consumer tastes. Meyer pointed out that radio, perhaps the most important medium, is almost self-sufficient in the Third World.

Despite the validity of several criticisms, CI remains the most useful contemporary orientation to media and development issues. Although earlier views were open to charges of reifying national economies, widespread recognition now exists that TNCs are the primary actors (see the recent revisions of CI in Schiller, 1992). CI should no longer be seen as specifically American. With the advantage of hindsight, it may be noted that CI was developed during the American phase of world market expansion. The economic reverses in the United States, the takeover of major U.S. advertising agencies by British interests, and the rise of Asian economic power have denationalized the world market. Suspicions of evil intent may also be dispelled: Corporate salespeople are selling for profit, not to subvert cultures. Numerous other organizations should not be excluded from the analysis of world media dynamics.

Conclusion: Suggestions for New Theorizing.

A composite picture of the world today may be summarized as follows: There is an interrelated world market economy that embraces most of the developed economies but excludes poorer regions even though they wish to enter. The world market is composed of TNCs but is also influenced by finance and currency institutions, including governments. This world economy, as widely recognized by its leaders, is incapable of expanding to include the world's population or to solve pressing world problems. In sum, it is closer to being a corporate anarchy than a stable world system.

Although a more status quo view informed earlier communication theories (see Hardt, 1988), it is something approximating this view that informs the work of the cultural imperialism school. World realities and the media perspective based on a reformed CI may indicate some problem areas. Commercial media corporations cannot be expected to be altruistic. They are necessarily interested in sales, not human welfare. Their alleged hegemony must be overcome. First World governments, which surely also may have their own interests, and many Third World elites usually support TNC enterprise but may not always do so. There are some other potentially countervailing forces: international organizations (e.g., United Nations agencies), political groups and unions, religious groups, intellectuals, and military organizations. Media are often an integral part of the TNC world economy but many have at least partial autonomy and may be influenced or controlled by countervailing groups. Television is most influenced by TNC commercialism. Radio and perhaps new media (e.g., video see Ogan, 1988), and traditional "little" media are far less influenced. Last, we cannot assume that media messages affect their audiences in a simple predictable way.

The issue of cultural broadcasting surfaced in the NWICO debates and is now central to European policymaking. Eastern Europe may see a resurgence in cultural programming to complement political and national freedoms but Western European broadcasting sees itself under seige. World market forces are apparently gaining strength. There is considerable confusion in the European Union's broadcasting regulations and whether they will encourage or discourage program imports (see Chapman, 1987; Guback, 1984). U.S. corporate interests, however, are not discouraged, as indicated by the cover story headline in the trade magazine *Variety:* "Yanks brush off Euro quotas: Commercial interests win out as governments yield control of the process" (1989). Since then, efforts have continued to open the European market to U.S. programs.

Even with increases in mass entertainment imports, the powerful public service broadcasting organizations will no doubt continue to produce indigenous cultural programs. If pricing reform to prevent dumping is eventually adopted, their position will improve particularly because imports are often not very popular. Opening more channels (through satellite and cable) may eventually lead to specialization and more locally originated programming. Pan–European and regional services, Nordic Satellite TV for example (see von Feilitzen, 1988), may increase cultural diversity. Video also shows the same promise once the Hollywood catalog is exhausted.

Ansah (1988) examined the concepts of culture, mass culture and cultural homogenization. He conceded that the Third World cannot be cut off from outside cultural products but argued that its governments could and should do more to produce their own. Fox (1989) added that democracy should also be a goal of media use and reports at least some success for Latin America.

Many development needs are clearly not met by commercial TNC broadcasting. The establishment or persistence of broadcasting following a public service model may be preferable (see Wells, 1976). Other possibilities, however, also exist. Rogers (1978) called for a fundamental change in our view of communication and development. Noting that mass media have not been successful in transmitting development messages from governments to people, he urged that media be used to answer grass roots requests, provide technical information and circulate news of small-scale developmental successes. This might best be achieved by a return to little media and radio. Similarly, the developmental value of video is gaining recognition (see World Association for Christian Communication, 1989). The world explosion in media availability of all types (e.g., television and video in India; see Singhal, Doshi, Rogers, & Rahman, 1988) gives some reason for at least guarded optimism.

As Varis (1986a), a presumably hard-line pessimist, claimed:

> It is clear that the development of international cooperation in which the fruits of the scientific–technical revolution can be brought to the service of all mankind will help eradicate diseases, promote the peaceful use of space, the abolishment of underdeveloped societies, etc. (p. 7).

Although the potential for such benefits exists, this is clearly neither the agenda of the TNC world economy nor most broadcasting organizations. It is the countervailing forces that must produce the blueprints for humane media use. Recent scholarly work (Jayaweera & Amunugama, 1987; Melkote, 1991; Mody, 1991; Quebral, 1988) lends some optimism that such uses will be nurtured and practiced.

REFERENCES

Ansah, P. A. V. (1988). *Mass communication and cultural identity: Dilemmas and prospects for developing countries.* IAMCR Paper presented at the 16th Congress of the Mass Communication and Cultural Identity, Barcelona.

Baudrillard, J. (1988). Consumer society. In M. Poster (Ed.), *Selected writings.* Stanford: Stanford University Press.

Becker, J. (1985). Activities in foreign countries and new technologies of a transnational corporation: The example of Bertelsmann. *Media, Culture and Society, 7,* 313–330.

Bell, D., & Meehan, N. (1988). International telecommunications, deregulation and Ireland's domestic communications policy. *Journal of Communication, 38*(1), 70–84.

Boyd-Barrett, O. (1982). Cultural dependency and the mass media. In M. Guerevitch, T. Bennett, J. Curran, & J. Woolacott (Eds.), *Culture, society and the media* (pp. 174–195). London: Routledge.

Chapman, G. (1987, January). Towards a geography of the tube: TV flows in Western Europe. *Intermedia,* pp. 10–21.

Fox, E. (Ed). (1989). *Media and politics in Latin America.* Newbury Park, CA: Sage.

Guback, T. (1984). International circulation of U.S. theatrical films and television programming. In G. Gerbner & M. Siefert (Eds.), *World communications: A handbook* (pp.153 –163). New York: Longman.

Guback, T., & Varis, T. (with Cantor, J.G., Muraro, H., Rajas, G., & Booyaketmala, B.). (1982). *Transnational communication and the cultural industries, reports and papers on mass communication,* (Rep. No. 92). Paris: UNESCO.

Hamelink, C. J. (1977). *The corporate village: The role of transnational corporations in international communication.* Rome: IDOC International.

Hamelink, C. J. (1980). One world: Marketplace for transnational corporations. In C. J. Hamelink (Ed.), *Communication in the eighties: A reader on the McBride Report* (pp. 46–52). Rome: IDOC International.

Hamelink, C. J. (1986). Dependency and cultural choice. In U. Kivikuru & T. Varis (Eds.), *Approaches to international communication* (pp. 221–230). Helsinki: Finnish National Commission for UNESCO.

Hardt, H. (1988). Comparative media research: The world according to America. *Critical Studies in Mass Communication, 5,* 129–146.

Harvey, D. (1989). *The condition of postmodernity: An enquiry into the origins of cultural change.* Cambridge, MA: Basil Blackwell.

Hoskings, C., & Mirus, R. (1988). Reasons for the U.S. dominance of the international trade in television programmes. *Media, Culture and Society,* pp. 419–515.

Hoskings, C., Mirus, R., & Roseboom, W. (1989). U.S. television programs in the international market: Unfair pricing? *Journal of Communication, 39*(2), 55–75.

James, N. & Roncagliolo, R. (1986). Advertising, mass media and dependency. In V. Kivikuru & T. Varis (Eds.), *Approaches to international communication* (pp. 7–27). Helsinki: Finnish National Commission for UNESCO.

Jayaweera, N., & Amunugama, S. (Eds.). (1987). *Rethinking development communication*. Singapore: Asian Mass Communication Research and Information Centre.

Kalkkinen, M. L., & Sarkkinen, R. (1985). The international entertainment industry and the new media. *Nordicom Review, 1*, 7–15.

Kennedy, P. (1987). *The rise and fall of the great powers.* New York: Random House.

Mattelart, A. (1976). Cultural imperialism in the multinational's age. *Instant Research on Peace and Violence, 1*(4), 160–174.

Mattelart, A. (1983). *Transnationals and the Third World: The struggle for culture.* South Hadley, MA: Bergin and Garvey.

Mattelart, A., Delcourt, X., & Mattelart, M. (1984). *International image markets: In search of an alternative perspective* (D. Burton, Trans.). London: Comedia.

McAnany, E. G. (1987). Television: Mass communication and elite controls. In A.A. Berger (Ed.), *Television in society* (pp. 203–213). New Brunswick, NJ: Transaction Books.

McPhail, T. L. (1987). *Electronic colonialism* (Rev. 2nd ed.). Newbury Park, CA: Sage.

Melkote, S. R. (1991). *Communication for development in the Third World.* Newbury Park, CA: Sage.

Merrill, J. C., & Lowenstein, R. L. (1971). *Media messages and men: New perspectives in communication.* New York: David McKay.

Meyer, W. H. (1988). *Transnational media and Third World development.* Westport, CT: Greenwood.

Mody, B. (1991). *Designing messages for development communication.* Newbury Park, CA: Sage

Mundt, W. R. (1991). Global media philosophies. In J. C. Merrill (Ed.), *Global journalism* (pp. 11–27). New York: Longman.

Namurois, A. (1964). *Problems of structure and organization of broadcasting in the framework of radio communications.* Geneva: European Broadcasting Union.

Nordenstreng, K. (1980). The paradigm of a totality. In C. J. Hamelink (Ed.), *Communication in the eighties: A reader in the McBride Report* (pp. 8–16). Rome: IDOC International.

Ogan, C. (1988). Media imperialism and the videocasettes recorder: The case of Turkey. *Journal of Communication, 38*(2), 93–106.

Palmer, M., & Tunstall, J. (1988). Deregulation and competition in European telecommunications. *Journal of Communication, 38*(1), 60–69.

Paulu, B. (1967). *Radio and television broadcasting on the European continent.* Minneapolis: University of Minnesota Press.

Pendakur, M. (1985). Dynamics of cultural policy making: The U.S. film industry in India. *Journal of Communication, 35*(4), 52–72.

Quebral, N. C. (1988). *Development communication.* Los Banos: College of Agriculture, University of the Philippines.

Renaud, J. L., & Litman, B. (1985, September). Changing dynamics of the overseas marketplace for television programming. *Telecommunications Policy,* pp. 245–261.

Roach, C. (1987). The U.S. position on the New World information and communication order. *Journal of Communication, 37*(4), 36–51.

Rogers, E. M. (1978). The rise and fall of the dominant paradigm. *Journal of Communication, 28*(1), 64–69.

Sampson, A. (1989). *The Midas touch: Money, people and power from West to East.* London: Hodder and Stoughton.

Schiller, H. I. (1969). *Mass communications and American empire.* New York: Augustus M. Kelley.

Schiller, H. I. (1976). Advertising and international communications. In Instant Research on Peace and Violence (Eds.), *Information and the crisis economy* (pp. 175–182). New York: Oxford University Press.

Schiller, H. I. (1986). Electronic information flows: New basis for global domination. In P. Drummond, & R. Paterson (Eds.), *Television in transition* (pp. 11–20). London: British Film Institute.

Schiller, H. I. (1992). *Mass communication and American empire* (2nd ed.). Boulder, CO: Westview.

Schlesinger, P. (1986). Trading in fictions: What do we know about British television imports and exports? *European Journal of Communication, 1*(3), 263–287.

Shannon, T. R. (1989). *An introduction to the world system perspective.* Boulder, CO: Westview.

Siebert, F. S., Peterson, T., & Schramm, W. (1956). *Four theories of the press.* Urbana: University of Illinois Press.

Singhal, A., Doshi, J.R., Rogers, E.M., & Rahman, S.A. (1988) The diffusion of television in India." *Media Asia, 15,* 222–229.

Skornia, H. (1965). *Television and society.* New York: McGraw-Hill.

Stevenson, R. L. (1988). *Communication, development, and the Third World.* New York: Longman.

Tracey, M. (1988). Popular culture and the economics of global television. *InterMedia, 16*(2), 9–25.

Varis, T. (1986a). Global problems and communication. In U. Kivikuru & T. Varis (Eds.), *Approaches to international communication* (pp. 7–27). Helsinki: Finnish National Commission for UNESCO.

Varis, T. (1986b). Patterns of television program flow in international relations. In J. Becker, G. Hedebro, & L. Paldan (Eds.), *Communication and domination: Essays to honor Herbert I. Schiller* (pp. 56–65). Norwood, NJ: Ablex.

von Feilitzen, C. (1988). *Nordic satellite television—A means to strengthen cultural identity?* (pp. 283–303). Paper presented at the 16th Congress of the IAMCR, Mass Communication and Cultural Identity, Barcelona.

Wells, A. (1972). *Picture tube imperialism?* Maryknoll, NY: Orbis

Wells, A. (1976). Mass media systems, economic development, and the public–private continuum. *Southeast Asian Journal of Social Science, 4* (2), 21–30.

Wells, A., & Reynolds, L. T. (1986). The ideology of wholism: World-systems theory and the global corporation. *Humanity and Society, 10,* 243–258

World Association for Christian Communication. (1989). Video for the People. *Media Development, 36*(4).

Wright, C. R. (1959). *Mass communication: A sociological perspective.* New York: Random House.

Yanks brush off Euro quotas: Commercial interests win out as governments yield control of the process. (1989, October 11–17). *Variety.*

Chapter 2

Western Europe

Matthew J. Rusher

Western Europe is a densely populated, culturally diverse, and economically wealthy region of the world. The countries of the European Union compose the world's largest market and they are avid consumers of mass media (see Table 2.1). Broadcasting in the region can be similarly characterized: It is dense and diverse and uses a wealth of technological resources. International borders are viewed more accurately as cultural rather than a political boundaries in the region because they mark centuries-old cultural divisions. Language is the most obvious feature and also the most significant obstacle to creating a unified Western European broadcast market. Many countries in Western Europe are among the most technologically advanced in the world. For instance, Belgium, and Germany are among the world's most heavily cabled countries. Areas in Western Europe without highly developed cable networks, such as Scandinavia, often rely on satellite technology to receive international broadcasts. Western European television viewers typically receive 15 to 20 domestic as well as international channels via cable transmission, satellite transmission, or both. The technological wealth of the countries is reflected in the number of television and radio receivers in the region (see Table 2.1).

Commercialization has challenged the state monopolies on broad-

Table 2.1. Western Europe

Country	Population (In Millions)	Growth (%)	Land Area (square kilometers)	GNP/Capita (1992 U.S. Currency)	Radio Sets (In Millions)	Television Sets (In Millions)
Western Europe[a]						
Austria	8.0	0.2	83,850	22,110	4.71	2.71
Belgium	10.1	0.2	30,520	20,880	7.64	4.20
Germany	81.2	-0.1	349,470	23,030	150.00	30.50
Luxembourg	0.4	0.3	2,590	35,260	0.24	0.10
Netherlands	15.4	0.4	40,840	20,590	13.40	6.50
Switzerland	7.0	0.3	41,290	36,230	5.60	2.55
Northern Europe[a]						
Denmark	5.2	0.1	43,080	25,930	5.20	2.70
Finland	5.1	0.3	338,130	22,980	4.95	1.90
France	58.0	0.4	551,500	22,300	50.00	29.30
Iceland	0.3	1.1	103,000	23,670	0.20	0.08
Ireland	3.6	0.6	70,280	12,100	2.15	1.00
Norway	4.3	0.4	323,900	25,800	3.34	2.00
Sweden	8.8	0.3	449,960	26,780	7.45	3.75
United Kingdom	58.4	0.2	244,100	17,760	65.40	20.00
Southern Europe[a]						
Greece	10.4	0.1	131,990	7,180	4.20	2.30
Italy	57.2	0.0	301,270	20,510	45.35	17.00
Malta	0.4	0.7	320	7,300	0.09	0.13
Portugal	9.9	0.2	92,390	7,450	2.22	1.69
Spain	39.2	0.1	504,780	14,020	12.00	17.00

Note. Population (mid-1994 estimates), population growth (natural increase), and Gross national product per capita (1992) in U.S. dollar equivalents are from *1994 World Population Data Sheet*, Washington D.C., Population Reference Bureau, 1994. Radio and television set figures are from A. G. Sennitt (Ed.), *World Radio TV Handbook*, Volume 49, New York: Billboard Books, 1995. Land surface area figures are from *UN Statistical Yearbook, 1991/2*. Because of their very small size and population, the following countries in the region have been omitted: Andorra, Faroe Islands, Gibraltar, Liechtenstein, Monaco, San Marino, and the Vatican.

[a] The United Nations now uses these regional designations for statistical purposes. It includes former Soviet Bloc countries; Estonia, Latvia, and Lithuania in Northern Europe; and Albania, Bosnia-Herzegovina, Croatia, Macedonia, and Slovenia in Southern Europe. These countries are examined in Chapter 6. The countries with the largest population in each region, Germany, the United Kingdom, and Italy, are the topics of Chapters 3 to 5.

casting in Western Europe since pirate radio stations first began sending signals from shipborne transmitters to Swedish and Danish audiences in the late 1950s (Noam, 1991, p. 5). Now the face of broadcasting in Western Europe is changing more drastically than ever before, driven by corporate pressures for commercialization and, more recently, by new technologies. State control of broadcasting, the modus operandi in Western Europe since the first national radio networks were legislated into existence during the late 1920s, is giving way to private ownership.

Until the 1980s, Western European broadcasting was dominated by state monopolies. Broadcast policy was often dictated by a regulatory board composed at least partially of government appointees. Advertising in most countries was either forbidden or tightly controlled by the government. Licensing fees on radio and television receivers and other state funds were used to finance most broadcasting. Reflecting the social responsibility of the press that was prevalent in Western European tradition, broadcasting was required to be informative, educational, and reflective of cultural values. In the last 2 decades, legislation providing for commercial television broadcasting has been initiated in every Western European nation. It has also been during the last 2 decades that we have seen the deterioration of coherent national broadcasting policy in Western Europe.

This chapter includes a brief history of broadcasting in Western Europe and pays close attention to broadcasting's foundation in state ownership and dedication to public service. Some significant economic and technological developments that have dynamically affected the course of Western European broadcasting in the 1990s are then discussed. The chapter concludes with a country-by-country description of the basic structure of Western European broadcast systems.

BROADCAST HISTORY

Radio broadcasting, begun largely by amateurs in the 1920s, quickly came under state control in most Western European countries. This occurred not only because governments recognized the military potential of the new medium, but also because they wanted to take control of the growing medium out of the hands of the manufacturers of radio equipment (Noam, 1991, p. 3). State control came later in some countries, such as Belgium, where private radio licenses were simply not renewed after liberation from Nazi occupation. Radio licensees in most countries were required to comply with government guidelines concerning the content and nature of programming. These guidelines often included such ideas as neutrality, fairness, and equal access, concurrent with the concept of broadcasting in the public's interest.

Broadcasting from outside the government monopoly surfaced throughout Western Europe in the form of "pirate" radio stations. Some pirates broadcast to answer those needs of their communities that were not met by licensed broadcasters, whereas others, through advertising or sponsorship, broadcast for a commercial end. In many countries, the legitimization of commercial and noncommercial pirate stations signals the vanguard of a movement toward liberalization still being played out in Western European broadcasting. Spurred by pirate broadcasters, government monopolies on radio broadcasting in many Western European nations have dissolved. National radio broadcasting in most of Western Europe today employs formatting to segment the audience and appeal to a broader range of listening preferences. In the last 30 years, radio has been eclipsed by television as the public's primary source of entertainment and information.

From its beginnings in the early 1950s, television broadcasting in most Western European countries came under the jurisdiction of state-controlled radio monopolies. However, exceptions to the public ownership rule existed. Luxembourg has always been a haven for commercial broadcasters. Luxembourg's commercial network, RTL, has enjoyed great viewership throughout Western Europe, particularly in France where until 1982 it competed against three public television channels. Great Britain initiated a tightly controlled private television in 1955 (discussed in chap. 3) and in Finland the commercially financed MTV received weekly airtime over otherwise public channels until given its own channel in January of 1993. In each of these cases except RTL, and certainly in the case of public broadcasters throughout Western Europe, the government asserted control to assure that programming remained in the public's interest. Control of entrants into broadcasting was achieved through the licensing process as well as through state ownership of the means of delivery. In most cases, advertising was either very limited or completely restricted, which meant funding was also a government controlled resource. According to Noam (1991, p. 7), as the price tag for public broadcasting became higher and higher, alternative means of funding became more attractive.

The last 2 decades have seen a recognition by governments throughout Western Europe that in the face of mounting costs and the potential of foreign commercial satellite broadcasters to attract transnational audiences and advertisers, they must relinquish their monopoly on television and allow private companies to create domestic markets. This deregulation has abolished the state monopoly system but it has not meant an end to the principles of broadcasting in the public's interest. A considerable amount of reregulation has coincided with the liberalization of broadcasting to ensure that the public's interest is met. Most new stations are at least partially commercially financed but specifications are frequently imposed concerning the amount and placement of advertising. Quotas on domestically produced programming and in-house production are frequently imposed. In many countries, private broadcasters are required to invest a percentage of their profits in domestic broadcast production. Today, public broadcasters in many Western European nations enjoy strong viewership totals but face continued deficits. In France, for instance, the two public channels, A2 and TV3, claimed 34% of viewership totals in 1990, yet together ran a deficit to the tune of 1.5 billion francs (Silj, 1992, p. 40).

Television broadcasting in Western Europe is in a period of great change. Private broadcasting has been initiated in almost every country. Commercial support of public broadcasting has also gained limited acceptance. In France, one public broadcast station, TF1, was privatized. Efforts at privatization have met only limited success in many countries and have resulted in an increased concentration of media ownership. Satellite and cable broadcasting, which grew throughout Western Europe during the 1980s despite unsuccessful development policies in many countries, is bringing more channels to more households than ever before. With increased access comes increased attention from legislators concerning the content of this broadcasting. High production costs and the need of new channels to acquire programming on low budgets have increased the amount of low-cost American products purchased by Western European broadcasters, a development that is viewed by many nations as a threat to culture and an impediment to increased domestic television production (Silj, 1992, pp. 72–73). The European Union (EU) has therefore adopted the goal of creating a broadcasting infrastructure that will rely less on American products and will encourage domestic manufacturing. Cultural and language barriers within the EU, however, pose formidable obstacles for a unified Western European broadcasting market.

The development of satellite broadcasting in Western Europe was complicated by resistance from public broadcast monopolies, which correctly viewed the new technology as a threat to current broadcast systems. Entrants into the new field were often encumbered by regulations based on outdated technology. Another impediment to the establishment of satellite broadcasting was a lack of a unified European approach. Nonetheless, by the mid-1991, there were 15 satellites transmitting 70 different television channels in Western Europe. These transmissions are received by individual households via a parabolic antenna (satellite dish,) by cable companies for distribution, and even by terrestrial stations for rebroadcast. In 1991, an estimated 2.5 million Western European households had direct satellite reception. Two million of these were in Britain and Germany. Twenty-one million households in Western Europe were subscribing to cable, with over 80% of these located in Germany, Switzerland, and the heavily cabled Benelux countries. Some of the most widely viewed satellite channels are Superchannel, which features general entertainment programming, Eurosport, TV5, a "diplomatic" channel, and MTV Europe, the music channel (Silj, 1992, pp. 101–102). The number of households with satellite and cable reception is expected to continue to increase, as are the cable offerings.

BROADCASTING SYSTEMS BY COUNTRY

The rest of this chapter gives brief summaries of each European country, arranged by the three regions now used by the United Nations. The sources of information used were Horne (1991), Noam (1991), Ostergaard (1992), Rosen (1988), Sennitt (1995), Silj (1992), and Siune and Truetzschler (1992). Basic data for each country are given in Table 2.1.

Western Europe

Austria.   Austria is one of the more culturally homogeneous populations in Western Europe. Radio broadcasting began in 1924 in the form of a collaboration between the government and private industry. The Radio-Verkehrs Aktien Gesellschaft was absorbed by German state broadcasting when the country came under German control in 1938. After World War II, allied occupation forces controlled radio. In 1955, their radio stations were transferred to a new Austrian broadcasting service, which 2 years later became the Austrian Broadcasting Company, a more independent entity. At this time television broadcasting was initiated. A 1966 restructuring, inspired by public dissatisfaction with the partisan political stance of the Austrian Broadcasting Company, resulted in the creation of three radio and two television stations under the name Osterreichiser Rundfunk (ORF). This structure remains today.

ORF is a state owned and operated monopoly with one exception: Nine regional radio stations broadcast independently 9 hr a day. ORF is financed by licensing fees (43%), advertising (39%), and license granting and subsidies (18%). The three national radio stations feature specialized programming. Channel 0–1 features cultural programming, the second channel O-Reg is for entertainment, and Channel 0–3 broadcasts in a more popular style modeled after German and Swiss stations. The new station, Blue Danube Radio, broadcasts in English, French, and German, in part for resident aliens and diplomats. There are also now four private radio stations (Sennitt, 1995, pp. 65, 68).

ORF continues to run the only two television channels. By 1989, it was producing 41% of its own television programs, a remarkably high proportion. Thirty-three percent was purchased and 25% was repeats. Approximately one third of broadcast time was allotted to entertainment and 16% to news and culture. However, viewers spent 51% of their viewing time watching entertainment and only 8% on cultural or educational programming. The most popular shows on television are Austrian folk music shows, international crime series, and game shows.

By the end of 1990, cable reached approximately 21% of the 2.5 million television households and another 20% could receive foreign transmissions over the airwaves. The Austrian legislature has a history of allowing foreign channels on Austrian cable systems but restricting access to private Austrian broadcasters. Most cable companies are local ventures involving both private and public interests. The ORF has thus far thwarted all efforts to establish private domestic television broadcasting in Austria. Most of these efforts have been launched by publishers.

Belgium. Belgium is a bilingual country. Radio began with the French language station, Radio-Belgique, in 1923, followed in 1928 by the first Flemish (a Dutch dialect) language station. After World War II, the public broadcasting system in Belgium was given an absolute monopoly. Television began in 1953. In 1960, a law created two separate broadcasting institutions, one for Flemish-speaking Flanders (BRT) and one for French-speaking Wallonia (RTBF). The public broadcast channels, BRT 1 and BRT 2 in Flanders and RTBF 1 and RTBF 2 in Wallonia, are financed mainly by licensing fees, although in 1989 RTBF did begin collecting advertising fees. Content includes more drama and entertainment and less "serious" programming largely in response to competition with the two new private channels, as well as foreign channels delivered to Belgian viewers via cable.

The Public Service Broadcasting monopoly on radio broadcasting was broken with the legitimization of pirate broadcasters in Wallonia in 1981 and Flanders in 1982. The television monopoly was legally broken in 1987 with the establishment of two commercial stations, Radio Tele Luxembourg-Television: (RTL-TVi) in Wallonia and VTM in Flanders. Of the private channels, RTL-TVi is owned primarily by Compagnie Luxembourgeiose de Telediffusion (CLT), a Luxembourg company owned in turn by a Belgian conglomerate. It is financed by advertising revenue. Since RTL-TVi began broadcasting in 1983, it has had stiff competition from French channels that can be received in Belgium and in 1989 it had an average 25% viewer share, the same as RTBF and ahead of TF1's 20% share. In Flanders, VTM, which did not get off the ground until 1987, has enjoyed remarkable success. By December of 1989, a 40% viewership level was reached, which far exceeded expectations. This success is attributed to programming content, which consists mainly of entertainment and lots of American imports.

A major challenge to the Belgian public broadcasters, and later to the private channels, was the widespread cabling of the country. By 1989, 93% of all households in Belgium were passed by cable. A Belgian cable system would usually carry four official Belgian stations, two or three stations from The Netherlands, three or four from Germany, and three to six from France, RTL-TVi, and VTM. This competitive marketplace is considered a major factor contributing to the low percentage of domestic productions on Belgian television.

Luxembourg. Luxembourg is a tiny European country that is famous for its broadcasting. Radio Luxembourg began broadcasting popular music in 1924. Since that time, Luxembourg has maintained a private rather than a public monopoly. The Luxembourg government in 1930 granted CLR (later the CLT) a de facto monopoly. The CLT-owned broadcasting company, RTL, operates the one radio and one television station in Luxembourg. Both are financed through advertising and are aimed to reach large audiences throughout Western Europe. CLT is itself owned largely by Belgian and French interests and is financially involved in several other commercial broadcast stations, such as RTL-TVi in Belgium and M6 in France.

Programming on RTL radio is American-style popularly oriented fare. It has attracted wide audiences throughout the region but does nothing to address the needs of the population of Luxembourg. The government was likely to diversify the broadcast medium by providing for up to 40 local radio stations, four regional networks, and one public radio station in a 1991 law. By 1995, their were four television stations operated by RTL: One each in German, Dutch, and French, and another in French targeted for Belgium. There were also five independent radio stations (Sennitt, 1995, pp. 100, 395).

The Netherlands. Since the beginning of radio broadcasting in the 1920s, Dutch broadcasting has been shaped by the "four pillars" of Dutch society: Catholicism, Protestantism, socialism, and liberalism. With the advent of radio and later television, these groups were given access to the state-controlled broadcast media according to their membership totals. There are currently eight broadcasting organizations, including NOS, which is both a national broadcaster and a regulatory organization. The original four pillars represented by KRO (Catholic), NCRV (fundamentalist Protestant), VPRO (liberal Protestant), and VARA (Socialist) have lost public support and are now smaller than the two entertainment oriented organizations, TROS and VOO (Noam, 1991, pp. 165–168). There are three main revenue sources for the national channels: license fees (65%), advertising (35%), and membership dues. The dues finance the production of membership brochures for each of the organizations.

Programming time is allocated via a three-tier categorization. The largest groups get some 12 hr of television and 65 hr of radio airtime weekly. The smallest groups currently receive 7 and 39 hr, respectively. Content, which is regulated by legislation, must reflect information (25%), culture (20%), amusement (25%), and education (5%). The NOS receives 23 hr of television and 86 hr of radio broadcasting every week. In 1989, a commercial, Dutch-language station broadcast via satellite from Luxembourg (and owned by CLT) began broadcasting and within 1 year had captured one-fourth of the Dutch audience, although it reached only 84% of households. Five national radio networks are divided according to format. These include information, easy listening, pop music, classical music, and services for particular groups.

Switzerland. The first radio licenses were issued in Switzerland as early as 1911. In 1921, the first public radio station began transmission. In 1931, the Swiss Broadcasting Corporation (SBC) was founded. SBC television broadcasts went on the air in 1958. Both radio and television were public service monopolies from 1931 to 1983. In 1982, pressure from advertisers and pirate radio spurred the government to give licenses to 36 private local radio stations all over Switzerland. Local private television licenses were also granted in 1985.

The SBC is registered as a private company but this is true in name only. The federal government appoints the chairman and 10 of the 21 board members of the SBC, which receives 25% of its income from advertising and the rest from license fees. Television advertising has been limited to 30 min per day since 1989. Advertising on national radio is strictly prohibited.

Programming is a policy response to the ethnic and linguistic diversity of the population. The SBC must run one television and three radio stations for each of the three language groups in Switzerland: German, French, and Italian. Programming must develop cultural values, contribute to education, and provide entertainment in the highest tradition of public service. Because Switzerland is saturated with channels from neighboring countries, the real challenge for the SBC has been to appeal to a mass audience while still cultivating particularly Swiss news and informational programs. Partly because of cabling and partly because of mountainous terrain, Swiss viewers watch a high percentage of foreign television. In 1990, SBC television stations received just over one third of total television viewership. By 1989, 70% of Swiss households were passed by cable, one of the highest percentages in Western Europe. A typical cable network provides 12 television and up to 18 stereo radio channels.

Northern Europe

Denmark. Regulation of Danish radio began in 1907 and was formalized in 1925 when private broadcasting operations were closed and replaced by the state radio authority, the Statsradiofonien. The broadcasting industry grew under state control and in 1951 Denmark initiated the first national television network in Scandinavia. In 1959, the Statsradiofonien was replaced by a new governing body independent of the government, called Danmarks Radio (DR). Radio diversified under pressure from pirate broadcasters. Three national radio channels are currently complemented by nine regional stations, all under the control of DR. In response to competition from foreign satellite broadcasters, the government provided a license for TV2, a nonprofit public channel. This ended DR's national television monopoly.

In 1988, there were two national television networks, DR TV and TV2. DR TV and radio are financed by licensing fees, whereas TV2 is financed by advertising (66%) and licensing (34%). TV2 is directed by a board of eight governors appointed by the minister of communication. By 1995, another commercial station (TV3) had been added along with 35 independent local UHF stations (Sennitt, 1995).

As a public institution, DR is committed to broadcasting in the public interest. TV2 is not quite so restrained by public responsibility but is expected to emphasize quality, diversity, and plurality. The purpose of TV2 is to produce news programs and purchase entertainment. It is obligated to make Nordic programming 50% of its total.

Finland. By 1924, there were over 1,200 private local radio broadcasters in Finland. Soon there were 11 national broadcasting stations. This plurality gave way to legislated centralization in Helsinki under a national broadcasting company, Yleisradio (YLE). In 1934, Parliament made YLE a state-owned company. Today the government owns 90% of YLE shares. The Finnish broadcasting system consists of YLE, controlling national television channels, TV1 and TV2, and five national radio channels. In January of 1993, MTV, a commercially funded television broadcaster that from its inception in 1957 has shared time on YLE's two national channels, was given its own national channel, TV3. Radio has also been restructured. Radio 1 broadcasts culture and the arts, Radio 2 pop music and news, Radio 3 regional programs and news, Radio 4 programs for Swedish speakers, and Radio 5 programs in Swedish and Lapp. In 1995, there were "approximately 60" private stations on the air (Sennitt, 1995, p. 77).

Programming has been coordinated between YLE and MTV. MTV has enjoyed wider viewership by featuring a higher percentage (52% vs. 37%) of imported entertainment programming. YLE must meet a 15% to 50% quota of total domestic programming over a 6-month period. MTV has met with great success, especially in the news field, since moving to its own channel.

Cable penetration in Finland increased rapidly in the 1980s and reached 32% of television households by 1990. This was probably due largely to an increase in the number of satellite channel available in cable (Silj, 1992, p. 622).

France. Before World War II, private and public radio broadcasters coexisted in France, although private broadcasters were held under tight government control. After the war, private licenses were not renewed. Television first appeared in France in 1935. By 1939, 15 hr of television were broadcast weekly in Paris. At the war's end in 1945, a state monopoly of broadcasting under what would become Radiodiffusion-Television de France (RTF) was established.

Radical changes in French broadcasting, which resulted from legislation in the 1980s, were an outgrowth of the political turmoil that enveloped the national government. Ironically, the 1982 liberalization law, which allowed private broadcasters to enter the formerly statemonopolized broadcast field, was passed by the socialist government of President Mitterand. Over the next few years, the name and structure of the audiovisual regulatory body changed several times but a policy of liberalization continued. With the legitimization of pirate radio broadcasters in the early 1980s, France achieved a highly diverse radio community. By 1988, there were some 1,600 FM outlets, 11 private national radio networks, and seven public radio networks. Programming included a wide variety of formats.

There are currently two state television channels in France, called A-2 and FR-3. A-2 is financed by a combination of advertising and license fees, whereas FR-3 relies on sponsorship for 80% of its revenue, the rest coming from license fees. The stations are coordinated by a "superpresident" to ensure that their programming is complementary. Programming for the two stations is characterized by public service principles, with relatively high ratios of documentary and news programs to entertainment. Together, they draw about one third of the national television viewership.

In 1983, Canal Plus, a pay television channel, became the first private channel launched in France. Its financing came from subscribers (2.8 million by 1989) and its profits were substantial. Canal Plus features sports and both French and foreign films. Canal Plus has flourished since its inception and is expanding into neighboring countries. There are also two private nonpay television channels in France, TF1 and M6. The former, with a 40% audience share, accounted for half the television advertising revenues in 1989. Programming on TF1 is primarily general entertainment. M6, was originally a music channel but has reorganized to feature light entertainment programming. La Cinq, a commercial station set up in 1986, went off the air in 1992 because of persistant financial problems.

France, a leader in the race for satellite broadcasting, launched the TDF1 and TDF2 satellites in 1988 in concert with Germany's satellite program. The venture, however, did not launch a European digital broadcast satellite boom. The French cable plan, initiated in 1982, has also failed to live up to expectations, largely because of legislative wrangling over technology standards: By 1990 there were only about 386,000 subscribers.

Iceland. Even in Iceland, the public monopoly on broadcasting ended in the 1980s. Public broadcasting in Iceland was authorized in 1930 with the establishment of the National Broadcasting Service (Rikisutvarpid). Television was introduced in 1966. Until October of 1986, television broadcast only 6 days a week.

The Rikisutvarpid operates a single television channel, two FM radio stations, and a shortwave service. All broadcast in the national language, Icelandic. Thirty-threepercent of funding comes from advertising, the rest from licensing fees. Television relies heavily on imported programming, primarily from the United Kingdom and United States. In 1995, there were four private FM stations and a private shortwave station that broadcasts in English, German, Danish, Norwegian, and Swedish (Sennitt, 1995, p. 94).

Ireland. Broadcasting in Ireland began in 1926 with the establishment of the Irish radio service. Radio remained under direct state control until the introduction of television broadcasting in 1960 when the Broadcasting Authority Act established the state-sponsored Radio Telefis Eirann (RTE) Authority. A second television station was introduced in 1978 and a second radio station in 1979.

Before 1988, private broadcasting took the form of pirate radio stations. However, the Irish Parliament passed the Radio and Television Act of 1988, establishing a licensing process for local radio stations and providing a franchise for a private television channel, TV3.

RTE operates two national television and four national radio services. Public broadcasting is financed by both licensing fees and advertising. RTE relied on foreign programming to the tune of 53% of total programming in 1988. Programming is of the usual public service variety, with a strong emphasis on news and current affairs. RTE's radio stations are Radio 1 (with a traditional public service programming emphasis), 2 FM (with a 24-hr popular music format), the Irish-language channel Raidio na Gaeltachta, and FM 3 with classical music. By 1995, there was one national commercial station, Atlantic 252, aimed at young adults, and 49 local independent radio stations. TV3 was still not in service but BBC Scotland has a transmitter in Ireland and British television can be received in much of the Republic (Sennitt, 1995, pp. 94, 392). Cable television, to which more than one third of households subscribe, also relays the British national television channels as well as up to 10 English language cable stations.

Norway. A public monopoly on broadcasting was created by the Norwegian parliament in 1933. This monopoly took the form of, the Norsk

Rikskringkasting (NRK). From 1933 until 1981, NRK enjoyed a monopoly on broadcasting in Norway, controlling the single radio and television channels both centralized in Oslo. NRK initiated television in 1954, the third last European country to do so. NRK is state owned. It is financed by license fees and a tax on radio and television equipment. Program content is one third news and 50% of all broadcasting is Norwegian in origin. Most imports come from the United States and the United Kingdom.

In 1982, the government ended the NRK monopoly by introducing local, independent radio and television and cable distribution of satellite channels. In 1990, it was decided that a new, privately owned and commercially funded television station, TV2, should be established. Regulations concerning the new station, TV2, include a domestic program quota of 50% after 8 years. TV2 began broadcasting in September of 1992 and has far exceeded projected viewership totals. It is expected to produce its own informational programming but to import entertainment.

Satellite broadcasting may hold considerable significance in the future of Norwegian broadcasting. In December of 1988, two Norwegian television satellites were launched. Currently, Norway has 30% cable penetration and 35% of houses are connected to satellite broadcasting.

Sweden. For most of Swedish broadcasting history, the Swedish Broadcasting Corporation (Sveriges Radio AB) has held exclusive rights to broadcasting. It still controls public television, national radio, local radio, and educational broadcasting. The parent company of the SBC is headed by a board of directors, half of whom are government appointed. The budget for the SBC is determined by parliament, which collects license fees. Advertising is not allowed on public radio or television.

There are now four SBC radio channels in Sweden: The First Program is news and spoken word and the Second Program is "serious music" and minority language broadcasting. The Third Program specializes in light music and entertainment for people up to 35 or 40 years of age and the Fourth Program is geared for older people (Sennitt, 1995, p. 128) There are two national television channels. Swedish television is deeply rooted in public service. Public television is widely considered heavy-handed, with a paucity of entertainment programs, which gave rise to both widespread use of VCRs and the popularity of satellite television.

Commercially financed television stations were introduced in 1987 by satellites and cable and they grew rapidly as cable penetration reached one third of Swedish households by 1990. The noncommercial grip was broken and by 1995 there were four commercial radio networks, several city stations, and TV4, an over-the-air commercial network (Sennitt, 1995).

Southern Europe

Greece. The Greek National Radio Foundation (EIR) was established after World War II while Greece was in the midst of a civil war. In 1953, a law was passed giving EIR monopoly status. Regular television broadcasting did not begin until after 1970, due partly because of the influence of movie theater owners (Noam, 1991, p. 268). With the advent of television, the EIR became the ERT (Greek Radio & Television.) ERT is a public company whose only shareholder is the state. Public broadcasting in Greece has often been dominated by partisan forces vying for control in the tumultuous Greek political scene (Noam, 1991, pp. 270–271). The ERT's lack of credibility has led to increased privatization of television in the late 1980s.

ERT runs two national television channels based in Athens (ET-1 and ET-2) and a third in Salonica (ET-3). It also controls four national radio stations, ERA 1, 2, 3, and 4, as well as 25 regional stations. Forty percent of ERT's income is from mandatory fees paid by users of the state-owned power company, regardless of whether they own a radio or television set. Forty-two percent comes from advertising and 18% from the state budget. Advertising on radio and television is limited to 10 min in 1 hr and 8% of total daily airtime. At least 50% of ERT programming must be of European origin.

There are now 13 private FM radio stations in the Athens area, as Greece, like most of the rest of Europe, diversifies its media (Sennitt, 1995, p. 92). Since autumn of 1988, satellite transmissions have been available throughout Greece via over-the-air retransmission by ERT. Although both satellite and cable are available, Greeks have not become heavy users.

Portugal. [Television penetration in Portugal is the lowest in all of Western Europe.] The earliest radio broadcasting in Portugal can be dated back to 1914. The Emissora Nacional de Radiodifusao was a state-operated corporation that controlled the three national and five regional radio stations after 1933. In 1955, Radio-Televisao Portuguesa (RTP) was established as the national television broadcaster. RTP was a private firm controlled by the government. Regular television broadcasting began in 1957. After years of political turmoil ended with the ratification of a new constitution in 1976, many changes have occurred in Portuguese broadcasting.

In 1978, a second television channel (RTP 2) was inaugurated by RTP, which is now owned by the state. RTP 1 covers 95% of the country, and RTP covers 75%. In 1989, the two stations were broadcasting about 200 hr per week. Programming on the RTP stations is typically sports and soap operas, mainly of Brazilian origin. More films have been shown recently as well. Advertising accounted for only 4.1% of air time on RTP 1 and 1.1% on RTP 2 in 1989.

An explosion of pirate radio stations forced the government to pass laws legalizing hundreds of local and regional radio stations. In addition to the three government FM channels and regional services (now operated by Radiodifusao Portuguesa), there are numerous private stations and three main FM networks based in Lisbon (Sennitt, 1995, p. 107). [Although radio has thrived in recent years, cable and satellite have made no impact.]

Spain. In 1923, the Spanish government created a state monopoly in radio but allowed entrance into the field by private broadcasters. By the outbreak of the Spanish Civil War in 1934, there were 68 radio stations in Spain. A single television channel began broadcasting in 1956, a second in 1965. Unlike radio, television broadcasting was operated as a state monopoly under the RTVE (Television Espanola). By the 1980s, several radio networks had emerged, including the private SER system, which included 54 AM stations. Many networks were politically affiliated. In 1978, local governing authorities were set up in each of the 17 regions throughout Spain. These CCAAs (Communidades Autonomas) included the provision for a local television station in each region.

In 1988, the public monopoly on television ended with the passage of the private television law. Three commercial channels were established, joining the two national (RTVE) stations and the regional (CCAA) television network. The three private channels are Antenna 3 and Tele 5, both financed through advertising, and Canal Plus, a pay channel.

Radio in Spain includes both publicly and privately owned networks, as well as a national radio network, run by Radio Nacional de Espana (RNE). In addition to RNE, which owns one AM and four FM networks, radio networks include one owned by the Catholic Church with over 80 owned or affiliated stations, Antenna 3 (which is primarily owned by press interests), and SER, the oldest private network in Spain, with one AM and one FM network totaling about 150 stations. In addition to these national networks, there are regional stations affiliated with the CCAA radio and television corporations.

There are no licensing fees in Spain. However, public broadcasters receive funds from the state and CCAA budgets. All regional broadcasters receive funding from CCAA budgets. Each of the three private channels is partly owned by media conglomerates, which hope to exploit whatever advances, technological or otherwise, result from media conglomeration.

Low funding has pushed light entertainment, films, series, sports, and whatever else will draw an audience into peak viewership periods on Spanish television. The only exception is Canal Plus, which broadcasts films and sports to pay subscribers. Each of the new private channels must offer at least 40% domestically produced programming.

Radio programming reflects one of two patterns. AM stations provide information programs, talk shows, contests, and audience participation, whereas FM radio usually features a popular music format.

Spain, like most of Western Europe, is rapidly entering a period of increased broadcast diversity. Although late in developing, satellite and cable are expanding. As domestic production increases, it is possible that Spain could take a leadership role in program production throughout the Spanish-speaking world, especially Latin America.

CONCLUSION

Beginning with the introduction of radio technology in the early 20th century, broadcasting in most Western European countries was placed firmly under state control. In the 1950s, television came under the state apparatus already in place. Today, as then, this apparatus usually consists of a governing body chosen by, but often not completely run by, the central government.

Broadcasting in Western Europe is now in a period of great change. The state-run monopolies, facing challenges from satellite and cable-delivered international broadcasting conglomerates, are giving way to commercially funded broadcast markets. Governments throughout Western Europe are hurrying to provide franchises to domestic commercial broadcasters to ensure that their market, as well as their cultural autonomy, is not swallowed by international broadcasting conglomerates.

The issue in most countries is not simply one of profit, but also the promulgation of culture. Each country in Western Europe seeks to preserve its own culture and language and sees the foreign produced programming on the international channels as a threat to its cultural integrity. For this reason, much emphasis is placed on domestic production and ownership of programming on many of these new channels. The high cost of television production coupled with the profitability of the establishment of mass markets does not bode well for the many culturally diverse Western European countries. Broadcasting trends in Western Europe appear to be heading more and more toward transnational, audience-oriented broadcasting and away from nationally oriented broadcasting.

REFERENCES

Horn, P. L. (Ed.). (1991). *Handbook of French popular culture*. Westport, CT: Greenwood.

Noam, E. (1991). *Television in Europe*. New York: Oxford University Press.

Ostergaard, B. S. (Ed.). (1992). *The media in Western Europe*. London: Sage.

Rosen, P. T. (Ed.). (1988). *International handbook of broadcasting systems*. Westport, CT: Greenwood.

Sennitt, A. G. (Ed.). (1995). *World radio TV handbook (Vol 49)*. New York: Billboard Books.

Silj, A. (Ed.). (1992). *The new television in Europe*. London: John Libbey.

Siune, K., & Truetzschler, W. (Eds.). (1992). *Dynamics of media politics: Broadcast and electronic media in Western Europe*. London: Sage.

Chapter 3

United Kingdom

Alan Wells

The United Kingdom is the official name for the three countries of the island of Great Britain—England, Scotland, and Wales—some offshore islands, and the Ulster provinces of Northern Island. It is commonly called Britain and I follow this usage in this chapter.

Britain has been an important force in the world of broadcasting and still has an influence that is far greater than would be expected from the size of its economy and population (even in Europe, it ranks much lower than Germany in both categories). This is because Britain, together with the United States, was the leading pioneer of radio broadcasting in the 1920s and 1930s and of television in the 1930s and the post-World War period. In these early years of broadcasting, Britain ruled an empire that covered about one quarter of the world's surface, if the affiliated Commonwealth countries (Canada, Australia, New Zealand, and South Africa) are included. To reach this global population, the domestic British Broadcasting Corporation (BBC) operated the World Service, which was broadcast to a world-wide radio audience. It quickly established a reputation for reliable news. (The French and Germans set up similar radio networks for their global empires.)

Domestic broadcasting operated on what became known as the *public service model*. It was run on a noncommercial basis: paid for by money from a license fee levied on the owners of radio and later television receivers) Ideally, broadcasts would be in the public interest and insulated from the government's influence) This BBC model was adopted throughout the empire and was widely imitated elsewhere, for example, in much of Europe and Japan. In the mid-1950s, the British government chartered the ITA (Independent Television Authority) to subcontract time on what was then a second television channel. In television, as in radio, the BBC has reduced its seriousness (some would say dullness) in response to this commercial competition. Because its revenues are still assured, however, it has not had to revert entirely to the American style of inoffensive mass programming.

Perhaps because of its pioneer start and the global dominance of the English language, Britain remains a broadcast leader. Its thriving theater provides talent for television, and its television programs win numerous international awards. Although the British film industry also has provided talent to television its current near extinction has induced many of its creative people to migrate to Hollywood. Nonetheless, the country is second only to the United States in program exports.

The BBC is often thought to be the defining factor in British broadcasting. This is a misleading simplification. Although radio remained noncommercial until the 1970s, Independent (commercial) Television (ITV), when it began in the 1950s, rapidly gained a commanding audience share by aiming its programming more at the audience's actual tastes rather than those assumed by the BBC) Commercial radio followed television and with recent expansion now challenges the BBC's popularity. According to newspaper reports, in 1993 commercial radio gained more than a 40% share of the audience nationwide for the first time. In London, where commercial radio is most developed, its share is almost 60%.

Unlike the BBC, ITV has not been a model for other countries. Its system may be too complex to imitate. Under a governing board, now called the Independent Television Commission (ITC) the country is divided into regional franchises, a nationwide morning franchise, and a London weekend-only license. All of these franchises combine to program a second commercial service that broadcasts throughout Britain (excluding Wales, which has a separate service) on Channel 4) Cable television and a direct broadcast satellite service) (BSky B, led by international media tycoon

Rupert Murdoch are growing slowly but may soon be a significant factor in the country's media mix.

The 1990s appear to be years of significant change in British broadcasting. Prime Minister Margaret Thatcher had a stormy relationship with broadcasters throughout the 1980s, and after her retirement in 1991, her ruling Conservative Party has made good on her resolve to shake up the media. I focus first on the changes at the venerable BBC, then the recent turmoil in ITV, and lastly on the growing potential of satellite and cable.

THE BBC

The British Broadcasting Company began as an industrial cartel under government auspices to provide national radio services (Burns, 1977; Pocock, 1988). After a short and unsuccessful period of radio broadcasting operated by this cartel, the British Broadcasting Corporation was set up as a government-licensed public (i.e., nonprofit) corporation. It was established for both technical and ideological reasons (see Wright, 1959: 34-38). Given the compactness of the country and its proximity to population centers on the continent, only three broadcasting channels were made available. The ideological commitment of the BBC was to raise the cultural standards of the mass audience.

For this purpose, the three channels—designated as the light program, home service, and the third program—were allocated to meet ascending levels of cultural taste. Programming ranged from light entertainment to serious music, drama, and debates (carried by the third program). The idea was to slowly upgrade all three stations while weaning more and more of the mass audience away from the light program offerings to the serious channels. This aristocratic domination continued until the 1960s, when transistor radios and the mushrooming of commercial stations (the English-language Radio Luxembourg and offshore pirate stations, which were outlawed in 1967) lured the young away with popular music offerings. In reaction, the BBC modified its serious, cultural-uplift image, devoting a new channel to "pop" music.

The BBC was headed by a board of governors appointed by the government. Its degree of autonomy from the government, particularly on political issues, was somewhat ambiguous from the outset, even though its financing from receiver licenses was relatively well insulated.

Public service was the guiding philosophy of the BBC's founding director general, John Reith (see Milner, 1983). Reith's view was that broadcasting should provide to diverse audiences what they need (for their own good), not necessarily what they want. His missionary aim was to educate and elevate the mass audience that radio made possible. Audience needs were, of course, to be determined by the upper middle-class directors of the BBC (Burns, 1977). Over the years, these leaders have been strong willed and often controversial (Miall, 1994), and "out-side" publics have had very little influence on the "Beeb" (as the BBC is commonly known). Even its highly regarded news programming appears to be shaped by its own corporate, rather than public, ideologies (Schlesinger, 1979). The BBC's elitist ideal, nonetheless, contrasts with the ethos of the British popular press, which has consistently appealed to the most vulgar interests of its readers.

With the advent of commercial television and its growth in the 1960s, the public service ideal of the BBC was diluted and, perhaps, replaced by what Burns (1977) called "professionalism." The current broadcasting system has less ambitious aims than Reith's BBC of the 1930s. Formal educational programming for schools is still carried (approximately 25 hr per week on BBC 2, 12 hr 30 min on commercial Channel 4, and 6 hr on BBC Radio 5), but the remainder of the broadcast schedule is predominantly entertainment and general information. Despite a strong documentary tradition, social uplift is no longer a conspicuous goal. As I argue later, continuing commercial pressures threaten the existing practices in broadcasting. Similarly, the newly unleashed technologies of cable and satellite are accelerating the trend to consumer entertainment rather than public service priorities.

The BBC operates five nationwide radio channels, 105 local radio stations in England, 20 local stations run by Radio Scotland, Radio Nan Gaidheal on the Island of Lewis, Radio Cymru in Wales, and Radio Foyle and Radio Ulster in Northern Ireland (*World Radio and TV Handbook*, 1995, pp. 133–136). This is a dramatic increase from the 37 local BBC stations reported on the air 5 years ago (Foreign and Commonwealth Office [FCO], 1990). 1FM is a rock and pop station that usually attracts the largest number of listeners, especially teens and young adults. Radio 2 carries light music (easy listening) and information and Radio 3 is devoted to classical music and serious cultural programming. Radio 4 bills itself as a spoken word, current affairs, and music station. It is the most general and middle of the road of the BBC stations. Radio 5 formerly specialized in sport and education but switched its format to all news and sports in March of 1994. This positioned it as a close competitor for the new nationwide commercial franchise (Talk Radio UK) awarded in the middle of the year.

BBC 1 is a general television channel that competes with commercial television for the mass audience. Even though it often produces good quality programs, it reaches its largest audiences with two low-brow soap operas: *Neighbours* (an Australian import) and *EastEnders*. In the summer of 1993, the former had an audience of a little under 10 million people and the latter had over 13 million. Another soap, called *Eldorado*, however, was canceled in 1993 because it could only attract audiences of about 5 million (reported in *The Sunday Times*, 4 July, 1993).

The second nationwide channel, BBC 2, is directed to more specialized, mainly elite, audiences. Like PBS in the United States, it is the most public-service oriented channel in Britain, but it attracts at best about 3 million, mainly upper middle-class viewers. It generally airs narrowly appealing programs, the early morning Open University and documentaries, but also carries some sports programming for potentially larger audiences. Because it is run by the same organization, it does not have to compete with BBC 1 for a maximum audience: The two are programmed to give the viewers a choice of very different types of programs.

BBC programming is entirely noncommercial by law and is paid for by an annual license fee of 80 pounds sterling (in 1992) for a color television and about 26 pounds for a black and white set. There is no longer a fee for radio receiver ownership. The BBC also operates the World Service and Foreign Languages Services (radio) funded by, and in cooperation with, the government (Central Office of Information [COI], 1982). It also ran television services for Europe and news and information for Asia and Africa (FCO, 1992). After a 1994 reorganization, it began a consolidated television World Service to compete with the American Cable News Network (CNN).

In the public sector, the BBC faces an uncertain future in both funding and mission. The current activist Director General, John Birt, has "down sized" the BBC by cutting about 7,000 jobs, 2,000 alone in the year ending in April of 1993, about 9% of that year's workforce (*The Times,* July 29, 1993). He has also instituted what he calls *producer's choice,* the external contracting for program production. As staffing and internal production capacity have been reduced, morale has dropped. To many people in Britain, the BBC's place is assured in the society: They believe that it is an Institution. Others see much more cause for alarm.

A speech at an industry conference by a respected veteran BBC writer, Dennis Potter, set off a national debate on the future of public broadcasting. Potter was highly critical of Birt's leadership and "reforms." In a review article on the affair, ominously titled "Could the Sun Ever Set On the BBC?", the *New York Times* (October 3, 1993) described some of the underlying causes of concern. The BBC's charter must be renewed by the government in 1996 and the government at present appears to be hostile and willing to play on the public's resentment of the license fee that finances the corporation. Even though Mrs. Thatcher's disdain for the BBC was defused by her retirement as Prime Minister, the current regime still makes veiled threats. Government spokesman Peter Brooke was quoted by the *New York Times* as follows:

> If the BBC had not made and does not continue to make changes, the future of the license fee in the short term, and of the BBC itself in the longer term, might need to be considered from a very different perspective.... We might now or in the future find ourselves contemplating, rather sadly, the demise of a dinosaur. (Oct. 3, 1993.)

Birt's changes, then, must prevail.

COMMERCIAL BROADCASTING

The Radio Authority and the Independent Television Commission (formed by the reorganization of the Independent Broadcasting Authority in 1991) oversee commercial broadcasting. In 1990, the government proposed three new nationwide radio channels and another nationwide commercial television channel (planned for 1994, but not yet in place) and claimed that there will "be opportunities to launch hundreds of private local radio and television channels" (COI, 1990 p. 1). There were 49 independent local radio stations on the air by 1988 (COI, 1988), 79 by 1991 (FCO, 1992), and a large expansion to 234 stations in 1995 (*World Radio TV Handbook*, 1995, pp. 141–142). The three promised national radio channels are also in operation. Classic FM, which plays mainly light classical music, and British tycoon (Virgin Airlines and, until its recent sale, Virgin Records) Richard Branson's Virgin 1215, an AM-only pop station, were the first to broadcast. The third nationwide station franchise was awarded and the station (called Talk Radio UK) was on the air in late 1994. All three broadcast from more than 20 transmitters to cover the entire country (*World Radio TV Handbook*, 1995, p. 140).

The ITC owns and operates the nationwide television Channel 4 (except in Wales) and controls the premier commercial television Channel 3. The latter is leased to 14 regional companies, a nationwide early morning service, and a London weekend-only franchise. The companies produce and purchase programs for their own regions, engage in extensive networking with one another (under ITC auspices), and jointly support a single news producer, Independent Television News (INT).

The ITV channels have a broad variety of programming and attract a larger audience than the BBC. Top-rated programs on Channel 3 are the long running soap operas *Coronation Street* (over 16 million viewers in June, according to the *Sunday Times*, July 4, 1993) and *Emmerdale*, and *The Bill*. Channel 4 appeals to minority and artistic tastes but it also carries some American programs, such as *NFL Football, The Cosby Show*, and *Oprah Winfrey*. Its audience is much smaller than ITV or BBC 1 and in the summer seldom exceeds 5 million. The nightly ITN news is carried at 10:00 p.m. to avoid competition with the BBC's 9:00 p.m. (BBC 1) and 10:30 p.m. (BBC 2) news.

Independent broadcasting has been reshuffled by the round of franchise bidding required by the 1990 Broadcasting Act (see Reville, 1991) and by subsequent merger activity. An excellent account of the recent license round is given by Davidson (1993), who covered the battle for the *Sunday Times* newspaper. In 1987, the government extended ITV contracts to the end of 1992 while it formulated the rules for the new franchise round. After much business lobbying, the 1990 Broadcasting Act retained the government's original "competitive tender proposal"

(Davidson, 1993, p. 294) but also added financial and programming standards and an ambiguous "exceptional circumstances" provision. The bidding was to be judged by the newly established ITC. Bids were received in May of 1991 and the results were announced in October.

[There were 40 bids for the 16 licenses that would take effect on January 1, 1993. Four licenses changed hands] The morning franchise was captured by Sunrise with a bid of over 34.6 million pounds from the incumbent franchise holder, named TV-am, which bid only 14.1 million. Thames TV, a major producer and exporter of high-quality drama and entertainment programs, bid 32.8 million pounds but lost its London weekday license to newcomer Carlton TV, which bid 43.2 million. In the South and Southeast region, incumbent TVS's bid (59.8 million) was significantly higher than its rivals' bid but it was judged to have failed the quality standard. Meridian, with its bid of 36.5 million pounds, was awarded the region's franchise. A similar fate struck TSW (16.1 million pounds), which lost the South West region to Westcountry TV (7.8 million). TSW launched a legal appeal but ultimately lost in the country's highest court, the Parliament's House of Lords.

Of the successful incumbents, three were unopposed and paid only token sums for their licenses (Border TV with 52,000 pounds, Scottish TV and Central TV each with a token bid of only 2,000 pounds). Four were high bidders: Anglia (17.8 million), Tyne Tees (15 million), HTV (Wales and the West, 20.5 million), and Yorkshire (37.7 million). The remaining five incumbents won on lower bids than their challengers, all of which were disqualified for failing to meet the quality threshold. Channel TV prevailed with a bid of only 1,000 pounds, Ulster with 1 million, and Grampian with 700,000. Luckiest in the auction, perhaps, were two of the major market incumbents, London's weekend franchise, LWT (7.6 million pounds), and Granada (9 million), which beat competing bids of 35.4 and 35.3 million pounds, respectively (Davidson, 1993, p. 297).

Since 1991, the government has changed its rules to allow ownership of licenses to any two major ITV regions by a single company. In the 1991 bidding, Carlton was a partner (with ITN, the American NBC and *The Telegraph* newspaper) in a failed bid for the Breakfast franchise, won by a consortium of LWT, STV, Disney, and GMEN. Incumbents Granada, Border, Mersey, Yorkshire, Tyne Tees, and TSW were all involved in bids outside their regions. Although newspapers are currently barred from controlling an ITV franchise, several were minority partners in the bidding.

The new rules permitted some consolidation in the 1st year of the new licenses. Carlton, initially a minority partner, bought control of Central, and Yorkshire acquired Tyne Tees. Yorkshire (with 1993 losses of 8 million pounds) and LWT (with profits of 40 million) then failed in an attempted merger. Early in 1994, LWT was resisting a hostile takeover bid from Granada (*Sunday Telegraph*, Jan. 9, 1994). This merger offer of 700 million pounds was apparently supported by London financiers and it inflated the stock of both companies. It was strongly opposed by LWT's chief executive, Greg Dyke. He argued that Granada was not a suitable partner and that the government was likely to relax cross-media ownership rules in the near future: "Why sell now? Even without the Granada bid the share price would not fall back to the level it was when the bid was made. We could see other competitors from publishing or U.S. companies entering the market." *The Observer*'s (Jan. 9, 1994) business editor, however, advised LWT shareholders either to accept the offer or to sell their stock while the price was high.

According to the *Daily Telegraph*, (Jan. 8, 1994) "Advertisers have formally lobbied the Office of Fair Trading and the Independent Television Commission to express their concerns about the concentration of television advertising sales as a result of the proposed industry mergers." The concern stemmed from the proposed merger of Granada and LWT and the "agreed deal" between Carlton and Central. Granada's and LWT's sales houses, which also handle sales for Scottish, Grampian, Border, and Yorkshire Tyne Tees TV franchises, would together control over 40% of ITV advertising. So, while the bankers and traders favor mergers, the advertisers appear cautious.

It seems likely that the ownership restrictions on publishers and foreigners will soon be lifted and that several will enter the ITV market. Rupert Murdoch, the global media tycoon with a British newspaper empire, already owns 50% of the BSky B satellite service, Associated Newspapers is in cable television and has a 20% stake in West Country TV, and Conrad Black of the *Telegraph* newspaper group has a share of the London region's Carlton TV. The owner of the *Financial Times* holds 15% of Yorkshire Tyne Tees and 17.5% of BSkyB and has bought

Thames TV (now only a giant production company) for 99 million pounds. (The production studios of the other major franchise loser, TVS, were bought by the American Pat Robertson, presumably for use in his global religious broadcasting operations.) LWT's Greg Dyke thinks that in the near future "we will see three or four very large independent production companies formed as suppliers of programmes, and the separation of programme production and broadcasting will be a major change within the industry" (*The Observer*, Jan. 9, 1994). Carlton, it should be noted, made no pretense to in-house production competence in its bid for the country's most lucrative franchise. Dyke lauds the French for their cultural protectionism in the recent GATT round and hopes that the government will insist on a 51% domestic program quota. This, he thinks, will pressure American media interests to invest in European television and he has a company to sell them.

CABLE AND SATELLITE

Cable and satellite services have expanded rather slowly in Britain but they may soon have a greater impact on over-the-air broadcasting in the country. Direct broadcast satellite service began in Britain in 1989 with Rupert Murdoch's four Sky channels beamed from the Luxembourg Astra satellite. The rival British Satellite Broadcasting (BSB) service, with a monopoly on the five channels allocated to Britain on the Marco Polo satellite, was slower in providing direct broadcast satellite services starting in 1990 with a cable-only service (British Film Institute, 1990). Public acceptance was slow, with Sky claiming to have gained (a probably inflated) 500,000 subscribers in its 1st year, but the current availability of channels may well produce rapid growth in the near future.

Programs for 13 satellite channels were listed in newspapers by early 1991: Sky Movies, Sky One, Sky News, Eurosport (Sky), Screensport (W.H. Smith and ESPN), MTV (Maxwell, Viacom), Lifestyle (W.H. Smith and others), and the Children's Channel (D.C. Thompson, Central, Thames TV and British Telecom) were broadcast from the Astra satellite. The Marco Polo satellite relayed BSB's The Movie Channel, Sports Channel, and The Power Station, along with terrestrial programming. The Superchannel, owned by Beta TV and Virgin, was relayed on Eutelsat and Ted Turner's CNN for cable subscribers used Intelsat (*Weekend Guardian*, Feb. 2 and 3, 1991).

After a short period of competition, BSB and Sky merged to form BSkyB, which gave the new consortium a near monopoly of satellite services (such concentration was predicted by Collins, 1989). BSkyB has since experienced some modest growth. According to *The Wall Street Journal* (Feb. 4, 1994), for the last half of 1993 profits "soared to 81.8 million pounds from 12.48 million a year earlier. The venture said the number of its subscribers rose 40% during the half year to 3.225 million, or 15% of British homes." Subscriptions were reported to range from 7 to 20 pounds sterling per month.

By the beginning of 1994, four of the satellite channels (Screensport, the Sports Channel, Lifestyle, and The Power Station) were no longer in service. They had been replaced by Sky Movies Gold, UK Gold (movies, *Lassie, EastEnders* reruns), Sky Sports, and country music video channel, CMT. Seven other channels were now in service, primarily U.S. satellite subsidiaries: Nickelodeon, Family Channel, Discovery, Bravo, The Cartoon Network, and TNT. UK Living, the other new channel, carries predominantly recycled British programs but also U.S. imports, including *The Young and the Restless, Divorce Court,* and *Dr. Ruth*. The two general entertainment channels are quite dissimilar. The Superchannel had a magazine format aimed primarily at Continental Europe but now appears to have moved more into news, rebroadcasting both NBC and ITN. It also relays NBC sports and *The Tonight Show With Jay Leno.* Sky One consists primarily of imported adventure, soaps, and sitcoms from the United States (*The Daily Telegraph,* Jan. 8, 1994).

All satellite services are clearly market oriented and provide little that is new to British television. They generally give "more of the same" on single format channels: more news, sports, or music.

The development of cable television in Britain has lagged behind the United States and several European countries, despite the early development of wired radio and television services. Government restrictions and opposition to program origination no doubt discouraged cable penetration (Hollins, 1984; Negrine, 1985). New attitudes appear to promote cable growth, particularly to relay the available satellite programming. It is doubtful, however, that cable subscribers will continue to support two all-news services (Pearce, 1988) and three sports channels.[Currently, cable systems "carry up to 30 television channels, including the terrestrial broadcasts, satellite television, channels delivered by videotape and local services. Some also provide their own telephone services, home shopping and other interactive services"](FCO, 1990, p. 9).

Estimates of cable penetration vary: The Central Office of Information lists 1.37 million homes in cabled areas, of which 257,000 were subscribers in March of 1988 (COI, 1988, p. 4).[By of June 1990, 1.5 million homes were within reach of cable and more than 300,000 were subscribers] When all 135 cable franchises issued by mid-1990 are in service, 14.5 million homes will be within reach.[FCO (1990) projects that by 1996 two thirds of British homes will have access to cable service.] Hollins (1984), on the other hand, predicted that cable would have a 60% penetration by 1990: It has evidently grown much more slowly.

CONCLUSION

The 1990s appear to be years of significant change in British broadcasting. In the public sector, the BBC faces an uncertain future, both in funding and mission. The current Director General has down sized the BBC and instituted external contracting for program production. Independent broadcasting has been reshuffled by franchise bidding and subsequent merger activity. Nonetheless, radio broadcasting has grown rapidly in the first half of the decade in both the commercial and public sectors. Cable and satellite services, meanwhile, have expanded rather slowly.

The recent development of British broadcasting may point to an increased number of channels and perhaps a net gain in high-quality programming along with volumes of inferior fare (Dunkley, 1985). Although Britain has long imported programs, primarily from the United States, the number of such programs has been limited by broadcast policy, but also, it seems, by popular tastes. Recent broadcast ratings have been dominated by domestically produced programs. In 1989, for example, only two foreign programs appeared on the British top 20 lists: the Australian soap opera *Neighbours*, and the movie *Crocodile Dundee*. American programming, the lifeblood of Sky One, is carried by over-the-air channels but with little rating success.

Nonetheless, if Britain moves rapidly from four to more than 30 television channels, domestic production will probably not suffice. As we have already seen, the turmoil in both the BBC and ITV is likely to repress domestic programming and there is probably insufficient recyclable stores of old British video and film to meet program demands. Thus, the vast U.S. back catalog, mediocre as it may be, may find a growing British audience. An alternative would be the development of a European media market to match the E.U.'s economic integration. However, as Chapter 2 reported, overcoming the cultural and linguistic problems in European media production has scarcely begun.

REFERENCES

British Film Institute. (1990). *Film and television handbook: 1991.* London: BFI.

Burns, T. (1977). *The BBC: Public institution and private world.* London: Macmillan.

Central Office of Information. (1982). *Fiftieth anniversary of the BBC external services* (No. 178/82). London: COI.

Central Office of Information. (1988). *Television and radio in Britain* (No. 69/88). London: COI.

Central Office of Information. (1990). *Reform of broadcasting in Britain: Legislative proposals* (No. 341/90). London: COI.

Collins, R. (1989). The prognosis for satellite TV in the UK. *Space Policy*, 5, 47–58.

Could the sun ever set on the BBC? (1993, October 3). *New York Times.*

The Daily Telegraph. (1994, January 1–7). Television and Radio, Seven-Day Programme Guide.

Davidson, A. (1993). *Under the hammer.* London: Mandarin Paperbacks.

Dunkley, C. (1985). *Television today and tomorrow: Wall-to-wall Dallas?* Harmondsworth, England: Penguin.

Foreign and Commonwealth Office. (1990). *Television and radio in Britain.* London: FCO.

Foreign and Commonwealth Office. (1992). *Broadcasting in Britain: Recent developments.* London: FCO.

Hollins, T. (1984). *Beyond broadcasting: Into the cable age.* London: Broadcasting Research Unit, BFI.

Miall, L. (1994). *Inside the BBC: British broadcasting characters.* London: Weidenfeld and Nicolson.

Milner, R. (1983). *Reith: The BBC years.* Edinburgh: Mainstream.

Negrine, R. M. (1985). *Cable TV and the future of broadcasting.* London: Croom Helm.

Pearce, K. (1988). Rupert, Ted go head-to-head in UK: Sky News vs. CNN. *Channels, 8,* 20.

Pocock, R. F. (1988). *The early British radio industry.* Manchester: Manchester University Press.

Reville, N. (1991). *Broadcasting: The new law.* London: Butterworths.

Schlesinger, P. (1979). *Putting "reality" together: BBC news.* Beverly Hills, CA: Sage.

Sennitt, A. G. (Ed.). (1995). *World Radio TV Handbook* (Vol. 49). (1995). New York: Billboard Books.

Chapter 4

Germany

Ernest A. Hakanen

No matter where you go in Germany, you will find two levels of German culture. You will be in the Germany that we imagine when we hear German spoken or think of the strong work ethic of the German people. This is *deutch*, which originally meant, "common things and common language," the national culture. Historically, this culture developed out of a need to differentiate factions of central Europe and to develop a stronger, competitive economy. On the other hand, you will not be able to ignore the strong cultural differences that exist between the German regions (e.g., in food, dialect, clothing, and values). This is what Germans call *Kulturhoheit der Lander*, the culture of the state or region. The traditions of the former small kingdoms and city states are still proudly protected, practiced, and maintained.

These two levels of culture have served as the foundation of German broadcasting. The first goal of each cultural region, called a *land*, is to broadcast programming that serves its own local cultural interests. Broadcasting has traditionally been legislated, programmed, and financed by each land. On the other hand, the second goal of each land is to share its programming with all of Germany's *lander* (plural form of land) to strengthen national (deutch) identity.

Germany is the largest national broadcast market in Europe with over

30 million households within its borders (one third more than in the United Kingdom, France, or Italy) and 150 million German-language speakers on the continent (Kleinwachter, 1993). These populations are served by both regional and national public (both commercial and license-supported) systems and newer private (commercial-only) systems within Germany, and by international services and joint ventures outside the country.

Germany, like the rest of the global village, is also being influenced by the global culture. Despite legislative promises to protect the structure and stature of the public land broadcasting service and the national services; the influence of new technologies (including cable and satellite) and the fairly recent addition of a private, commercial system are quickly changing the look of the German broadcasting system. To understand the direction in which German broadcasting is heading, one must first start at the roots of German broadcasting philosophy.

In 1815, the Germanic Confederation began under an agreement between 39 sovereign states and four free cities. Formerly kept separate by the Napoleonic Confederation, the states agreed to defend not only the whole of Germany, but also one another. Consequently, the regional cultures came together in the name of all things deutch (here referring to language boundaries and not national boundaries). This is a very important distinction even today, especially in the discussion of cultural versus national sovereignty. The Germanic Confederation lasted until 1848 when it was dissolved in the turmoil of a revolutionary movement that spread across Europe.

The German states were again united in 1871 to create the Second German Empire which was dominated by the strongest state, Prussia. Chancellor Otto von Bismarck's conservative policies transformed the alliance into a strong economic force. Regional identities, loyalties, and prerogatives were assured under the new rule. This retention of regional Germanic culture and society is the foundation of the legal and cultural concept called Kulturhoheit der Lander (Peck, 1983).

EARLY BROADCASTING: REGIONAL PROGRAMMING DUTIES

The first radio stations in Germany were established and programmed by large commercial interests. However, they were controlled at both federal and local levels in a variety of ways. First, because of the need for transmission rights the stations were regulated under the Reich Post Ministry (RPM), which held a monopoly in telegraphy. Reich decrees gave the RPM authority over transmission as well as radio receiver authorization and manufacturing. The RPM supported the construction of transmitters through the collection of license fees paid on the purchase of each receiver and from a flat fee paid by the manufacturers and dealers. By 1923, organized by the RPM, 10 regionally representative radio stations collectively formed one German system called the Bezirkssender (Peck, 1983). The stations were required to reflect their regional public's interest. This was assured by requiring the broadcasters to transfer a portion of their shares of ownership to the appropriate land government.

As political tension increased during the 1920s, another federal government body gained some control of radio, this time at the programming level. In 1926, the Reich Ministry of the Interior (RMI) became the official news programmer in Germany. The news was gathered by a "private" wire service, the Wireless Service for Book and Press A.G. (DRADAG), which represented the interests of the RMI. (RMI began with 51% of shares in the company, but eventually acquired total control). Editors at every radio station had to have DRADAG approval on all official news and political content (Peck, 1983).

During this period, although there could have been a heavy degree of centralization in the structure of German broadcasting, regional programmers were left relatively free to serve their public's nonnews interests. The political content of early German radio remained fairly neutral under heavy external demands, many coalition governments, and the leadership of Hans Bredow, the father of German broadcasting. DRADAG–RMI control was also weakened by demands to increase its board memberships to include a wider range of viewpoints. These gestures are the first signs of modern German broadcasting's heavy reliance and demands on operating boards made up of socially representative groups.

The Depression: Mixed Economy

The hyperinflationary period of the early 1920s, after Germany's humiliating defeat in World War I, made new types of financial support for radio necessary. To protect the economic welfare of the stations, a mixed economy solution was adopted in 1926. Both private and public means of support were used. An umbrella organization, the Reich Broadcasting Corporation (RRG), was created as a supervisory and coordinating body. The RRG was supported by the holding and sales of shares in the regional stations, profits from sponsored programs, and new listener license fees. The complicated formula included the following arrangement:

> Each station turned over 25% of its shares to the appropriate state government, and 17% to the RRG. The RRG stock were preferred shares with multiple voting rights and constituted a controlling majority. In turn each station turned over 25% of its shares to the appropriate state run, 51% of shares in the RRG were transferred directly to the RPM.... In this way the RPM acquired control not only of the RRG, but through the RRG a controlling interest in all of the regional stations.... In spite of the official character of the state bodies involved, the negotiated agreement was based on private (civil) law and the RRG was established as a private company. (Peck, 1983, p. 253)

The RRG used profits to support the radio infrastructure as follows: Fourty-five percent was used for expansion and improvement, another 45% was used for promotion, and 10% was placed in reserve. As a matter of fact, the reserve became so great (mainly because of the expanded listenership who were now paying a license fee) that large, even embarrassing, dividends and salaries were being earned by managers during the Great Depression.

Nazi Control and the Postwar Occupation

With the ascent of Nazi power, Eric Scholz became broadcast officer in 1932 and enforced the following reforms, which were a great step toward tighter central control:

1. The RRG and the regional stations became publicly owned corporations, all of the shares outstanding in private hands being transferred to the state (51% to the Reich and 49% to the Lander).
2. "State Commissioners," equipped with wide-ranging powers, were

appointed to the Reich government (i.e., by the RMI) and dispatched to all regional stations, thus effecting de facto centralized control.

3. Control of the RRG was henceforth vested in two Reich Broadcasting Commissioners, one appointed by the RPM and responsible for administration (i.e., financial and technical affairs), and one appointed by the RMI and responsible for programming. The DRADAG was dissolved and replaced by the "Wireless Service" (Drahtloser Dienst) as an organization within the RRG and directly subordinate to the RMI commissioner. (Peck, 1983, p. 253)

Joseph Goebbels, minister of the Reich Ministry for Public Enlightenment and Propaganda (RMVP), gained complete control of radio in March 1933. RPM and RMI surrendered to the government, and the Wireless Service was incorporated into the Press division of the RMVP. The Ministry of Posts (PTT) retained control over the technical facilities and the collection of license fees under the consultation of the RMVP. Most local programming had to be approved by the federal government.

Goebbels "bureaucratized" the control of broadcasting through the newly formed Reichs Propagandaleitung (RPL). The RPL was based on a complicated pyramid structure. Goebbels directed five *Amtsleitungen* (division leaders). Each Amtsleiter was in charge of radio in his or her region and was also in charge of five area representatives, each of whom was the head of five main sections. In each of the sections there were five county leaders, and so on. At the bottom of the RPL pyramid were 14,000 people (Bramsted, 1965) who closely monitored public opinion, enabling broadcasters to narrowcast and refine their propagandistic purpose.

After the war, the Western Allies almost immediately put West German citizens in key broadcasting positions. There was no attempt by the allies to impose their own systems in West Germany; instead, they encouraged a strong public, regional Lander system. The British, in the north, gave decision-making authority to the Land governments. In the American zone, various political, economic, educational, and cultural groups were given the right to choose representatives to run the broadcast operations.

The Allies did not invent the concept of Kulturhoheit der Lander but they certainly put it back at the center of broadcasting. Although this seems to have worked well for Germany, the Allies were consciously developing a broadcast system that was easily monitored by the individual occupying forces and decentralized enough to prevent any problems with coordination of propaganda between the lander.

In East Germany, the Soviets swiftly set up radio operations and by 1952 both radio and television programming was under direct state control. The structure largely replicated the Soviet broadcast model. At the height of the East German system, there were two television channels and five radio channels. Because of geography and proximity, most East Germans also received signals from the West. The communist government permitted the reception of these signals by allowing the manufacture and purchase of duel-system television sets (both the PAL system for Western programs and the SECAM system used by the Soviet Bloc and France).

MODERN BROADCASTING

The following description of contemporary German broadcast system starts with the public system and then discusses the more recently developed private stations. Nine regional autonomous, nonprofit public land corporations on the air since 1952 and five "new" lander added to the broadcasting system in 1992 from the former East Germany serve the broadcasting needs of their particular regions and Germany as a whole (see Table 4.1). Together, the companies comprise a national system called the *Arbeitersgemeinschaft der offentlichrechtlichen Rundfunkanstalten der Bundesrepublik Deutschland* (ARD).

Each ARD corporation produces at least three regional radio programs designed to suit various listener information or entertainment needs. The individual corporations produce television shows for their own audiences, broadcast generally in the afternoons. The most unique characteristic of the ARD corporations is their production and coproduction of programs for the ARD national news and programming cooperative. Regional productions are usually shown in the early evening (5:30 p.m.–8:00 p.m.) with no more than 20 min of commercials. Regionally produced and coproduced programs are shown nationally during prime time without commercial interruption.

ARD programming consists of contributions by the individual cor-

Table 4.1
The ARD

Public Broadcasting Corporation Name	Service Area (Lander)
Bayerischer Rundfunk	Bavaria
Hessischer Rundfunk	Hesse
Nordeutscher Rundfunk	Hamburg, Lower Saxony, Schleswig-Holstein, Mechlenburg-Vorpommern
Radio Bremen	Bremen
Suddeutscher Rundfunk	Part of Baden-Wurttemburg
Sender Freies Berlin	Berlin
Saarlandischer Rundfunk	Saar
Sudwestfunk	Rhineland-Palantinate and part of Baden-Wurttemburg
Westdeutscher Rundfunk	Northrhine-Westphalia
Mitteldeutcher Rundfunk	Saxony, Saxony-Anhalt and Thuringia
Ostdeutcher Rundfunk	Brandenburg

porations that are proportional to the station's audience size. Westdeutscher Rundfunk, the largest corporation, contributes 16.1% of total programming, whereas Radio Breman and Saarlandischer Rundfunk, the smallest, contribute 3% together. About 41% of the programs are coproduced for the ARD's "first television program," *Duetsches Fernsehen* (Hellack, 1992). Each of the corporations also produces television programs for its own regional or cooperative interregional "third program," an educational channel. The ARD also has a satellite service called 1 Plus.

The function of the ARD is to represent the common interests of the corporations, handle joint program matters, and deal with legal, technical, and general administrative questions. The individual corporations are not obligated to air the ARD signal and may preempt programs at any time, which happens often for political reasons. For example, Breman, a conservative state, has canceled some of the cooperative's more liberal programs and substituted its own programs.

Although there are some slight differences in the management structures of the individual *land* corporations, each administers its own budget independently from the state budget. State supervision, to which every public utility is subject under law, is restricted to purely legal supervision in the case of the public broadcasting corporations. The state's legislative powers extend to the right to decide financial, organizational, and procedural rules of the system; jurisdiction over selection and admission of licensees; and the right to enact laws regulating state control of broadcasting. Individual state courts also have the power to litigate. The *land* governments exercise only an indirect influence over broadcasting through political parties and their membership in the broadcasting councils or boards and the administrative committees. This follows the traditional thinking that broadcasting is a representative voice in the overall cultural system.

The individual corporations are run by elected representatives, appointed officials, or both. Broadcasting boards are the largest supervisory body in any of the broadcasting corporations (membership varies between 18–49). Members of the board are elected by either the *land* parliaments or public organizations, such as political parties and churches. The board generally holds budget rights and appoints a director general and the majority of a board of administrators. The director general represents the corporation in and out of court in matters dealing with the corporation's programming policies. The board of administrators, usually consisting of seven or nine members, manages the broadcasting corporation and approves all major contracts submitted by the director general (Porter & Hasselbach, 1991).

The ARD networks are complemented by another, more centrally controlled network called Zwietes Deutsches Fernsehen (ZDF). ZDF was formed after a long struggle that began with a 1957 challenge to the public corporation television monopoly. A federal radio bill, which attempted to transfer control from the *lander* to the federal government, was rejected by the German parliament, the *Bundesrat*. Again in 1961, the Federal Constitutional Court thwarted a similar attempt at a second television channel. The court confirmed that radio and television were a "cultural phenomenon" and thus within the control of the *lander* (Akalin, 1984).

The *lander* jealously guarded their rights. However, the stage was set for alternative broadcasting systems in the Federal Republic of Germany. The ARD corporations themselves took advantage of the situation and set up a centralized but independent second television system in Mainz. The new oganization, named ZDF, was given a public, nonprofit constitution modeled on the existing ARD corporations, with a broadcasting board (66 members) delegated by the federal states and an appointed director general. Since its first broadcast in 1964, the ZDF has attempted to provide contrasting programs by coordinating its programming schedule monthly with the 11 ARD corporations.

The federal government runs and finances two radio stations. The first, Deutschlandfunk, broadcasts cultural information (e.g., programs about tourist sites or dancing events) to the whole of Germany and it can be heard throughout most of Europe. The second, Deutche Welle, is Germany's international voice, broadcasting in 34 languages daily. With an operating budget of over DM 400 million, Deutche Welle targets "parts of the world in which freedom of the press is suppressed or restricted" (Hellack, 1992, p. 15). Currently, the Near and Middle East, Southeastern Europe, and Latin America are important targets for Deutche Welle. By mid-1994, Deutche Welle television went on the air and is currently distributing a news program in various languages worldwide.

Financial support for public broadcasting comes from the Radio and Television Receivers License Fee, collected monthly by a fee collection center operated jointly by the corporations and levied by state treaty which requires the approval of all federal states. Currently, 34.9 million radio licenses and 31.2 million television licenses have been issued (Hellack, 1992). The licenses cost DM (Deutsch Mark) 8.25 for radio and DM 15.55 for television.

Each license fee is then distributed as follows: Two percent is paid directly to the lander for administrative costs; DM 1.00 goes to subsidize the development of the new members of the system, DM .75 goes to support international broadcasting, and DM .75 goes to a forthcoming joint venture with France, ARTE. The remaining monies are distributed to the public networks. The ARD receives 70% (the ZDF receives the remaining 30%), which is divided among its members according to the size of their audiences, although the smallest stations may receive extra compensation to help them produce competitive programs.

Advertising also provides revenues for the individual public corporations. The corporations operate subsidiaries in the form of limited liability companies that acquire commercial advertising. There are few restrictions on radio advertising; therefore, most radio stations, especially the smaller ones, have relied heavily on advertising. ARD television receives about 30% of its revenues from advertising, whereas the ZDF receives 40%. ZDF tends to run national ads and ARD broadcasts mostly local ads.

Private Broadcasting

In the early 1980s, various political groups fought for the introduction of private broadcasting to West Germany. Several political parties, namely the Christian Democrats, Federal Democrats, and Christian Socialists, favored the privatization of broadcasting, arguing that a greater number of political viewpoints could be fostered by adding channels. The Greens and the Social Democrats had been strongly opposed to the introduction of private broadcasting based on the argument that it may harm public broadcasting as a system and cultural force.

This same dichotomy was familiar to most of Europe: "The New Right was questioning the very idea of public culture, and the New Left was calling the national broadcasters elitists, statist, unaccountable, divisive, and exclusive" (Rowland & Tracey, 1990, p. 8). Embracing the rhetoric of the information age, the right argued for the distribution of new technologies (digital broadcast satellite [DBS] and cable) as a cure for the scarcity argument. The political left armed itself with media imperialism arguments mainly the threat of the flow and import of foreign programs into vulnerable cultures (e.g., Sepstrup, 1989; Tunstall, 1977; Varis, 1984) or poststructural arguments of the inevitable commodification of audiences (Rowland & Tracey, 1990).

In Germany, states that were strongly Christian Democrat, Federal Democrat, and Christian Socialist soon began to court the idea of privatization. The Social Democrats were under political pressure and soon began to change their stance in return for guarantees that the public system would be preserved. On November 4, 1986, the Federal Constitutional Court passed the "Fourth Broadcast" decision allowing for a private system. The decision required that private broadcasters set up broadcast boards (Browne, 1989). The ruling also set guarantees for the survival of the public media, even at the possible expense of the private system.

In March of 1987, the State Treaty on the Reorganization of Broadcasting, as written by the Social Democrats, was signed. It guaranteed the further existence of the public system, assured that states would tolerate each other's private broadcasting, established advertising standards, created balanced distribution of satellite channels, assured income for the public corporations by regularly raising fees, and guaranteed precise accounting for collected fees. Responding to the treaty, individual lander began to structure their broadcast laws accordingly. Each state holds licensing power over commercial broadcasting and has guaranteed the continuation of public broadcasting without its having to increase advertising time.

The first private, commercial radio stations were licensed in Bavaria and Rhineland-Palatinate. Today, there are over 180 private radio broadcasters. Private television is growing more slowly. Startup costs are higher and spectrum allocation are more difficult in television. With the development of cable television, these barriers will fall much more easily. There are five major private television broadcasters (terrestrial and DBS) that call Germany home: RTL Plus, RTL 2, SAT 1, Tele 5, and Pro 7.

Cable Television

Cable television was slow in coming to Germany. Traditional telecommunications law, which is under federal jurisdiction, is separate from broadcasting law, which is under land jurisdiction. This made the emergence of cable more politically than economically problematic. The federal government declared the first attempt at private cable, Senne TV, illegal in 1970 and land-based cable, Bremen Cable Company, in 1974. In 1977, despite protests from the lander, the Bundespost (the PTT) began wiring 11 cities that were considered poor reception areas. During the early 1980s, the PTT laid wire to just over 3 million homes (less than 12% of all households). In March of 1984, the PTT created Landescentrale Fur Neven Medien to regulate the cable industry and grant licenses to cable operators ("Germany's pilot", 1985).

Each state began to permit private services via cable. The first to do so included Bavaria, Lower Saxony, Schleswig-Holstein, Saarland, and Rheinland Palatinate. All are Christian Democratic states. Northrhine-Westphalia, Bremen, and Hesse abstained from the new technology. By the end of 1985, all *lander* permitted cable ("German TV," 1985). Cable now passes over 16 million homes in the former West Germany, with some 60% connected by 55 newly established, regional, mixed public and private cable service companies. Cable penetration is still low in the former East Germany at 8% (Hellack, 1992).

A cable service typically delivers about 20 channels, including the local and national public channels (5 channels), RTL Plus, RTL 2, and SAT 1 (private German DBS channels), Tele 5 and Pro 7 (private German), 3SAT (ZDF DBS in cooperation with the Swiss and Austrians), 1 Plus (ARD DBS), MTV Europe, Cable News Network, and two other news channels called Vox and n-tv, as well as various Euro sports channels.

The integration of DBS into Germany's system started on a rocky road. In the early 1980s, West Germany opposed Luxembourg's DBS service, the RTL. In certain cases, the PTT was known to jam broadcasts other than those of the three public channels ("Broadcasting in Europe," 1980). The Lander have revised laws to allow for the free flow of foreign broadcast signals, and the RTL is currently received by most Germans either through DBS ground technology or cable. The Bundespost's SAT 2, successfully launched in 1989, became Germany's first domestic DBS provider. The limited number of transponders (the number of channels on a satellite) was controversial, as ARD and ZDF received transponders for their satellite programs. This limited the number of transponders available for private interests. RTL (two networks) and SAT 1 received three other channels.

Future Trends

After the fall of the Berlin Wall, Germans, particularly from the East, refused to refer to a "unification" or "reunification" of Germany. *Die wende* was evoked, meaning a turn or gradual change. It suggests that the peoples, the "confederation," had never been separated. This kind of self-awareness confirms that although cultural institutions are changing, there is a great amount of conscious control of the direction of the changes.

Political pressures, changing economies, shifting audience desires, and new technologies have created a broadcasting system that looks very different from the original public television system. The result is a dual system that includes public and private systems. Beyond systemic changes, what programming and market changes are there? More specifically, how well is the public system's service-focused programming faring in the face of the entertainment-driven programming of the private, commercial broadcasters? What are the trends in foreign program use? How is the market holding up? That is, how close is the market to full saturation (a state in which the market can no longer support another competitor without damage to the existing players)?

One indicator of how well the public system's programming is faring in the new environment is market share. The ARD's audience share declined from 33% in 1989 to 20.4% in 1992. The ZDF's share has declined from 32.5% to 20.5% in the same time period. RTL Plus had obtained 18.1%, whereas SAT 1 was garnering 14% by 1992 (Hellack, 1992). These figures show a weakening but still relatively strong public system. However, greater cable penetration and increased numbers of channels will probably lead to greater declines in the public system's popularity. This is evidenced in the audience-share figures for cabled areas. In those areas, ZDF holds 15.5%, ARD 15.6%, RTL Plus 19.2%, and SAT 1 15% (Siek, 1993). These figures also illustrate the part that cable plays in the distribution of channels. The figures for the major private players are not significantly changed, but the figures for the public channels have changed to reflect audience lost to other providers.

What are the trends concerning foreign programming? Germany's public television system has maintained a high percentage of indigenous programs compared to imported programs. Germany's ratio of indigenous to imported programming is outstanding compared to other European countries. In addition, the trend is toward even fewer foreign imports and more in-house production. In the past, only about 20% of ARD programming and 14% of ZDF programming were imported. Most of this programming came from the United States (75% for the ARD and 50% for ZDF). The average for all imported programs for public, commercial systems in West Europe has been about 28%, with more than half coming from the United States (Sepstrup, 1989).

The fact that Germany is not a large market for foreign television is probably the result of many factors. The lander philosophy itself has created a greater sense of broadcasting as a cultural institution. That is not to say that other European countries do not have strong cultures but that Germany's emphasis on multiple and related cultures, instead of one culture, fostered a strong base from which to work. In this way, the system was also already diversified and less vulnerable to outside influence.

Economics is another strong and more recent factor in Germany's aversion to imported programming. Expenditures on advertising are rising faster in Germany (28.4%) than in any other country in Europe (all are at less than 6%; Siek, 1993, p. 3). The public stations are producing more in-house programs and commissioned work with the new revenues from advertising. (ZDF is benefiting from an increase in ad monies, whereas ARD is suffering a loss even in this time of growth.) This trend refutes the argument that public systems import more programs as they attempt to compete with private systems that use popular imported programs and as their share of advertising expenditures dwindles. The public broadcasters, along with the private ones, are also building markets for German-language television programming outside of Germany, especially in Austria and Switzerland.

Of course, the private commercial television systems have used foreign programs to a greater extent than has the public system. Although figures for Germany are not available, a look at Western Europe can give us some idea of private broadcasters' use of imported programs. Western Europe previously imported 57% of its programs, 82% of which came from the United States (Sepstrup, 1989, p. 47). Private satellite channels used less imported programs (42%; Sepstrup, 1989). Of course, these figures would also be true for Germany, as it receives the bulk of these satellite services. The use of foreign programs by private broadcasters was probably due mostly to economic factors. Imported programs cost one sixth less than in-house productions (Siek, 1993). Obviously, foreign programs were ready for viewing. It takes time in a fledgling system, no matter how wealthy, to produce new programs.

However, there is much evidence that Germany's private broadcasters are producing their own programs at a faster pace than broadcasters in any other country. RTL Plus and SAT 1 have dramatically increased their budgets for in-house productions. For example, RTL spent DM 200 million in 1990, DM 330 in 1991, and DM 540 million in 1992 on in-house productions. At the same time, spending for imports declined from DM 470 million to DM 120 million (Siek, 1993, p. 3)

How many stations can the system support? Analysts believe that the market can support many more television channels. Although advertising expenditures are up for television, they account for only 34.4% of total ad monies (compared to 51.3% in Italy and 42.1% in the United States; Schiphorst, 1993, p. 4). As more television stations come into the market and begin to define their audience, and as competition forces airtime prices down, television should become an even more important media choice for advertisers.

These factors are evidence of a healthy growth in the system. However, most of all, they show that the cultural integrity of a broadcasting system is in the philosophy that drives the choices within the overall system. Cultural integrity is not exclusive to public systems. In the case of Germany, it shows that public systems do not have a monopoly on the maintenance of cultural integrity.

The German system is changing rapidly. The introduction of new technologies, political struggles, and the global market have been recognized in a new private broadcasting system, growing cable system, increased DBS use, and restructuring of broadcast laws to account for these changes and to maintain the traditional public broadcasting system. Above all, it seems that there is continued interest in maintaining a system that accurately represents the cultures that make up and unite Germany.

REFERENCES

Akalin, R. (1984). *Broadcasting laws*. Cologne: InterNationes.

Bramsted, E. K. (1965). *Goebbels and national socialist propaganda*. East Lansing: Michigan State University Press.

Broadcasting in Europe heading toward independence; Government losing grip. (1980, January 28). *Television and Radio Age*, p. A35.

Browne, D. R. (1989). *Comparing broadcast systems: The experience of six industrial nations*. Ames: Iowa State University Press.

German TV is busting loose. (1985, February 13). *Variety*, p. 80.

Germany's pilot projects test whether cable can pave way for private TV. (1985, February 13). *Variety*, p. 62.

Hellack, G. (1992). *Press, radio and television in the Federal Republic of Germany*. Bonn: InterNationes.

Klieinwachter, W. (1990). Green light for unification of the German broadcasting systems. *Media Law and Practice, 11*, 140.

Peck, R. E. (1983). Policy and control—A case study: German broadcasting 1923–1933. *Media, Culture and Society, 5*, 349–372.

Porter, V. & Hasselbach, S. (1991). *Pluralism, politics and the marketplace: The regulation of German broadcasting*. London: Routledge.

Rowland, W. D., & Tracey, M. (1990). Worldwide challenges to public service broadcasting. *Journal of Communication, 40*(2), 8–23.

Schiphorst, B. (1993). New German channels offer ad opportunities. *European Media Business and Finance, 2*(22), 4.

Sepstrup, P. (1989). Implications of current developments in West European broadcasting. *Media, Culture and Society, 11*, 29–54.

Siek, R. (1993). German programming dominates TV market. *European Media Business and Finance, 2*(21), 3–4.

Tunstall, J. (1977). *The media are American.* New York: Columbia University Press.

Varis, T. (1984). The international flow of television programs. *Journal of Communication, 34* (1), 110–150.

Chapter 5

Italy

Osabuohien P. Amienyi
Julio Soler-Burguillos

Modern Italy is in fact one of the youngest countries in Western Europe. It is often believed that the origin of Italy dates back to the Roman Empire but the country as it exists today was only born in the 19th century. The Kingdom of Italy was declared in 1861 following the nationalist movement led by Giuseppe Mazzini, the revolution led by Giuseppe Garibaldi, and the subsequent wars against both the Austrians and the French. However, Venice was not annexed until 1866 and Rome, where the Pope resisted becoming part of a secular Italy, was not acquired until 1870. (The church still retains sovereignty for Vatican City.)

Italy occupies a land area that is smaller than Spain, France, or Germany (see Table 2.1 in chap. 2). It is slightly larger than the state of Florida in the United States. This area comprises a peninsula that extends from southern Europe to the Mediterranean Sea and a number of adjacent islands (including Sicily and Sardinia). The Alps form a natural boundary to Italy's north where it is also bordered by France, Switzerland, Austria, and Slovenia. The geography of the country varies from the central Apenini mountain range to the plains in the south. Like Spain, Italy has an extensive coastline that greatly facilitates communications and trade. The country is divided into 20 regions. Five of these regions (mainly in southern part of the country) enjoy a special economic status and a great deal of autonomy (Evans, 1991).

The climate is temperate in the north and Mediterranean in the south, with mild winters and long, dry summers. Average temperatures range from 45.3F in January to 78.3F in July in the capital city of Rome. The major cities in Italy are Rome (with a population of 2.7 million), Milan (with 1.4 million), and Naples (with 1.2 million). Almost all the inhabitants of Italy are Christians. More than 90% are Roman Catholic. There is freedom of expression for other religious denominations and for non-Christian religions.

By 1914, Italy had developed into a major democratic nation but World War I overwhelmed its resources. The hopelessness and chaos that followed gave rise to Fascism and the totalitarian dictatorship of Mussolini. In 1922, King Victor Emmanuel III asked the National Fascist Party of Benito Mussolini to form a national government in order to end the general strike that was paralyzing the country. Mussolini established the principle of state supremacy in every important aspect of national life, including the communication media. It was within this context that he allied his country with Hitler's Germany during World War II and Italy was almost totally destroyed by the Allied forces (Emery, 1969).

At the end of World War II, the monarchy was rejected in a public referendum and Italy was reconstructed as a democratic republic with aid provided through the Marshall Plan. Today, Italy operates as a parliamentary democracy. Accordingly, the country's legislative power is vested in a bicameral parliament elected by universal suffrage every 5 years on the basis of strict proportional representation. The president is the constitutional head of state and is elected for a 7-year term by an electoral college made up of members of both chambers of parliament (Evans, 1991).

There are four main political parties in the country: the Christian Democrats, Social Democrats, Socialists, and Communists. Since 1945, the Christian Democrats have governed the country but the party has never had the absolute majority required to govern without coalitions with other parties. This difficulty has been primarily the result of the philosophy of direct proportional representation in parliament prescribed by the Italian constitution. This idealistic prescription has created a situation of bureaucratic inefficiency in every public institution that has led to the increased influence of local Mafia, who are seen as a solution to the political inadequacies in the most depressed areas of the country.

Italy's population of over 57 million people and its high per capita wealth make it the major economic country in Southern Europe (see Table 2.1). Economically, Italy is one of the most industrialized nations in the world. It is a member of the G-7 and one of the original founders of what is now called the European Union. In the 1980s, Italy replaced the United Kingdom as the world's fifth-most powerful economy. According to World Bank estimates, the gross national product (GNP) for Italy in 1991 was US $1,072,198 million. Between 1980 and 1991, the GNP increased at an average annual rate of 2.4% (Andrews, 1993). Fragmented national industries have struggled against international competitors. This has made Italy a weak power in terms of capital (Evans, 1991). As Glover (1992) noted, with the exception of the government bond market, Italy's financial markets are small and thin and are struggling to catch up with markets in other advanced economies. It is predicted that Italy will experience little or no growth in gross domestic product in the next few years ("Business outlook abroad," 1993).

Italy has faced a number of challenges in recent years. The vast economic differences between the northern and southern parts of the country have been a main area of concern. The north is heavily industrialized, whereas much of the south is greatly impoverished. Another problem has been of maintaining national cohesion in an atmosphere of linguistic pluralism. Inhabitants of every region of Italy speak different dialects of the Italian language. This is why Italians say that "Italy doesn't really exist; only the national soccer team, and Ferrari, unite Italians" (Godbout, 1993, p. 4).

Perhaps the greatest challenge yet has been dealing with the political corruption that has been institutionalized in the country. Although Italy is an advanced nation, its political and administrative institutions are basically still inept. The government is not taken seriously because politicians are generally distrusted by the people. Because of this distrust, the power of the underworld has increased in the depressed rural areas of southern Italy where Mafia bosses are perceived to be more efficient than government officials. Thus, one of the main problems facing Italy today is how to eliminate both corruption and the growing power of local Mafia.

These are the challenges that paved the way for the election of the famous and polemical media tycoon Silvio Berlusconi as prime minister of Italy in March of 1994. With the election, many Italians hoped that Berlusconi and his coalition of conservative parties (which included two neo-Fascist parties) would purify the country's political system. The general belief was that a Berlusconi government could transform Italy into a country with limitless originality where technology and industrialization would protect past traditions and where social inequities would effectively redressed. These high hopes were dashed, as so often happens in Italian politics, when Berlusconi's coalition collapsed. New elections have not assured stability. This is the chaotic atmosphere under which broadcasting presently exists in Italy.

THE DEVELOPMENT OF RADIO

Radio broadcasting began in Italy during the Mussolini dictatorship. On December 14, 1924, Mussolini gave the Ministry of Posts and Telegraphs permission to grant a broadcasting license to a limited liability company Unione Radiofonica Italiana (URI). The lincense gave URI the exclusive right to broadcast throughout Italy for 6 years. It also specified that the company establish its main station in Rome and regional stations in Naples, Palermo, Milan, and any other city that needed one.

From the very beginning, URI was under the tight control of the Mussolini government. The programs aired by its broadcasting stations were stipulated by the government, which required that each station employ a state official who could censor any programs that were perceived as violating Fascist policies. A daily program schedule was decreed that specified that the time from 1:00 p.m. to 2:00 p.m. and 7:00 p.m. to 8:00 p.m. be set aside for broadcasting government messages. In the event of an emergency, which of course was determined by the government, URI's facilities were commandeered for official releases any time, day or night. Mussolini established a special agency that worked with the military and was empowered to interrupt or suspend broadcasting operations at any time if such action was deemed in the interest of national security. In 1925, Mussolini issued a decree that secured the government's control over broadcasting throughout Italy and its colonies (e.g., the island of Sardinia).

By the end of 1926, 27,000 radio receivers had been sold or registered

in Italy. The interest in radio was growing and Mussolini began to realize the power the medium could have in foreign affairs and in the expansion of Italy's colonial empire. Seeking ways to expand radio for political
purposes, he formed a commission of loyal, Fascist representatives from
various sectors of the society to study broadcasting. The recommenda-
tions of the study were implemented in 1927 and a new broadcasting
organization was established to replace URI.

The new establishment was named Ente Italiano Audizioni
Radiofoniche (EAIR). Like URI, EAIR was granted a monopoly over
broadcasting in Italy and was guaranteed the same sources of revenue
as its predecessor: license fees on receivers, taxes on sales of radio parts,
and special contributions by municipalities. However, it was allowed an
additional source of revenue, advertising, that could not exceed 10 % of
the total broadcast time. EAIR's programming was strictly censored.
The government reserved the power to interrupt, limit, or even take over
the station if the Council of Ministers believed that such action was mil-
itarily necessary or in the interest of public safety. Vigilanza committees
were formed to oversee broadcasting in Rome, Milan, Naples, Turin,
Genoa, Bolzano, Florence, Bari, Palermo in Sicily, and Trieste. These
committee evaluated, and sometimes restrained, local radio programming and kept government officials in Rome informed about programming practices, especially those deviating from the party line.

During the depression of the early 1930s, Italy embarked on a policy of self-sufficiency. Mussolini used every possible means to increase
domestic production, accumulate raw materials, and make Italy less
reliant on other countries. He expanded radio services, increased the
transmission power of stations, and began broadcasting messages of
self-reliance, mainly to farming and industrial regions of the country.
In 1933, he established the Ente Radio–Rurale (Rural Radio Agency)
to encourage sales of receivers and increase radio listening in rural
areas. Increasingly, Mussolini began to exercise dictatorial powers over
broadcasting. To this end, he established a Ministry of Press and
Propaganda to control all broadcasting.

During the war, Mussolini continued to maintain his control over
broadcasting until 1943, when he was renounced by the Fascist Grand
Council and was forced to resign as prime minister. Thereafter, he was
abducted and taken to Germany. He later returned to northern Italy and

established a Fascist Republic. From this base, he ordered the nationalization of EAIR and moved its headquarters from Rome to Turin. As a countermeasure, Umberto, King Victor Emmanuel III's son who had assumed the royal authority, renamed the radio system in Rome Radio Audizioni Italia (RAI) to avoid confusion with EAIR, which Mussolini and the Fascists still controlled. RAI was operated initially by a temporary commission until its normal functions were restored. In April of 1954, television was added to its operations and RAI's name was officially changed to *RAI–Radiotelevisione Italiana.* RAI remains publicly owned but it is nevertheless free from state control. In April of 1975, a law was passed that guaranteed the political independence of RAI (Emery, 1969).

Since 1950, RAI has operated three national radio networks: Radio Uno, Radio Due, and Radio Tre. Radio Uno AM transmissions provide a wide range of general programs 22.5 hr per day. The programs include classical and popular music, plays, news, literary and scientific discussions, documentaries, and school and religious broadcasts. These programs are also relayed via several shortwave stations. In addition, Radio Uno provides a separate music program on FM, called Stereo RAI (*Europa World Yearbook* 1994, 1993).

The second network, Radio Due, is the principal recreational channel designed to reach a larger and less sophisticated audience than that for Radio Uno. Its programs are also varied but the main focus is entertainment. The bulk of its schedule is made up of news, popular music, quiz shows, and other light entertainment. Like Radio Uno, the network is transmitted mainly on AM for 22.5 hr per day and its programs are relayed via shortwave. It, too, provides a separate music program on FM that also includes news and weather reports.

Radio Tre is designed for the more sophisticated audience. Its programming consists mainly of classical music and historical, literary, and scientific discussions geared mainly to the listener with cultivated tastes in music, drama, literature, or with an interest in in-depth news analysis or scholarly and critical lectures in science, philosophy, and current affairs. The duration of its broadcasts is 23 hr per day (*Europa World Yearbook* 1994, 1993).

RAI also operates a foreign and overseas service called Radio Roma. This service broadcasts in 27 languages to Africa, the United States, Australia, Europe, Japan, the Near East, and South Asia (*Europa World Yearbook* 1994, 1993).

In 1976, Italy abolished the principle of state monopoly over broadcasting. Since then, over 1,000 private radio stations have been established in the country. A number of these FM networks are funded by advertising. Other stations are operated by religious groups, professional associations, and foreign governments. For example, the U.S. military operates the Southern European Broadcasting Service, which has 10 stations scattered throughout Italy. The Seventh-Day Adventist Church runs the Adventist World Radio with one medium wave and 10 shortwave stations. The International Broadcasting Association owns Nexus, which runs Globe Radio (an FM service for Milan) and the Italian Radio Relay Service on shortwave. These stations are funded by the various organizations sponsoring them. RAI continues to be the dominant broadcaster in Italy with a 52.5% audience share (World Radio TV Handbook, 1993).

THE DEVELOPMENT OF TELEVISION

The first experiments in television broadcasting were carried out by RAI in 1949. The experiments followed a study by a special commission appointed by the prime minister to research the problems related to the establishment of television. In 1950, the plan for a national television network was published. Roughly a year later, the technical standards for the new establishment were approved and RAI began executing the first stage of the national television plan (Emery, 1969).

By December of 1953, three television stations were operating in Turin, Milan, and Rome and broadcasting 35 hr per week to more than 50% of the population. These stations formed the nucleus for RAI's first national television network. Inaugurated in 1954, this initial network broadcasts mainly on VHF. It had over 30 main channels, almost 600 auxiliary transmitters, and could reach more than 97% of the population (Emery, 1969).

Television has undergone rapid expansion during the past 3 decades. RAI inaugurated a second national network in 1961 that broadcasts mainly on UHF. It has more than 30 main channels linked together in a extensive chain with 50 repeaters and relays. In 1976, a law was passed that abolished RAI's monopoly on broadcasting. Soon after, 600 private stations operated throughout Italy. RAI established a third network in 1979 in the hopes of curbing the local television explosion. In the early 1980s, four nationwide commercial networks, established by local business owners (including Silvio Berlusconi), were in operation. When two of these failed they were purchased by Berlusconi (*Europa World Yearbook* 1994, 1993).

In 1990, a new broadcasting act finally ended the explosion of broadcasting in Italy. By then, there were three national public television networks—RAI UNO, DUE, and TRE—which were complemented by 12 national private networks, 5 of which were owned by Berlusconi. In addition, there were 840 small and medium-sized private stations mostly in local service. Another network included nine main stations and 122 low-power television stations, operated by the autonomous province of Tyrol, called Rundfunk Anstalt Sudtirol (RAS) (World Radio TV Handbook,1993).

RAI remains a public-share capital company but the government holds the majority of its shares. RAI derives 52% of its income from licensing fees, 32% from advertising, and 16% from other commercial activities. Entertainment appears to be the dominant form of programming on RAI's three television networks. In 1989, entertainment constituted 46%, followed by information (27%), cultural programming (17%), and educational broadcasting (5%). Cultural and information content make up 73.5% of RAI radio programming (Noam, 1991).

RAI and Berlusconi's company, Fininvest, together control 90% of Italy's domestic television market. RAI broadcasts a significantly greater amount of locally produced programs than Fininvest, which imports much of its programming. In 1988, RAI produced 74% of its content locally. Fininvest devotes 76% of its programming total to popular entertainment. Advertising takes up another 14%, whereas the remaining 10% is made up of all other types of programs (Noam, 1991).

The growth of cable television in Italy was effectively halted by the local television wars. To this day, Italy does not have a cable television service. However, one of RAI's channels is carried by the Olympus satellite.

SILVIO BERLUSCONI AND ITALIAN BROADCASTING

No one has affected Italian broadcasting as much as the ambitious son of a former Milan bank director, Silvio Berlusconi. During the past 2 decades, Berlusconi has acquired a vast amount of broadcasting power not only in Italy, but also throughout Western Europe. In less than 10 years, his media empire grew from a single local television station in Milan into one of the largest media holding companies in the world: Fininvest.

Berlusconi exerts media power not only because he owns numerous television stations in several European countries, but also because he tightly controls his station's programming content through a centralized production and distribution center, making him the subject of much controversy. Audiences who watch his programs say that his is not a "serious" kind of television. Yet, his peculiar programming style of producing low-cost materials remains one of the most profitable and emulated on the European continent. This section of the chapter focuses on Berlusconi's operating style. It analyzes the processes through which his media empire has developed.

Berlusconi "entered the world of entertainment as a part-time performer on a tourist ship" (Noam, 1991, p. 146) when he was 16 years old. Even though he began his educational career with the study of law, he ended up with a doctoral degree in advertising. When he was 25 years old, he obtained financial support from a bank that dealt previously with his father and he formed a construction company in Milan. In just under 15 years, his construction business became the largest in northern Italy. In about the same period, he established himself as a dominant force in Italian private television.

The centerpiece of Berlusconi's media empire is the holding company Fininvest. At the beginning of the 1990s, Fininvest's holdings included a Milan conservative newspaper *Il Giornale*, the Publitalia advertising agency, two thirds of Italy's private television stations, 25% ownership in the French private television channel La Cinq, 20% ownership in the German television channel Tele-5 (Tele-funf), and a 25% ownership in Spain's private television channel Tele-5 (Tele-cinco; Noam, 1991). In addition, Berlusconi entered into a 3-year contract with Gosteleradio, the Russian broadcasting company, in which he would provide the commercials used on Russian television. He proposed establishing private broadcasting stations in Poland, Hungary, and Czechoslovakia. He sought part ownership of England's Channel 5 but the British parliament has opposed his entry into the British television market (Dawtrey, 1992).

In 1979, Berlusconi began direct investments in private television stations throughout Europe. That year, he created his television empire out of a basic station in Milan, Milano-2. Durnett (1990) noted that the key to Berlusconi's broadcast expansion was the concept of *integration*. Durnett explained that as the number of television stations owned by Berlusconi increased, he began producing his own programs. He built a huge production studio in Milan that supplied programming to all of his stations throughout Italy. This centralization of programming source allowed him to maintain total control over his stations.

Berlusconi's media expansion was aided by an Italian Supreme Court ruling in 1976 that allowed "the establishment of private stations" in Italy, even though the public corporation, RAI, had a monopoly in national broadcasting (Dunnett, 1990, p. 154). This ruling facilitated Berlusconi's quest for media power by allowing him to purchase local stations and to create new ones in areas where they did not exist. Prior to this ruling, the only way a private broadcaster could reach the national audience was through affiliation with local stations, as in the American model (Dunnett, 1990).

Prior to the legalization of private television in Italy, the public enterprise RAI was allowed to use advertising to supplement its allocated revenues from licensing fees. However, as Paulu (1967) explained, RAI advertising adhered to very strict rules. They were required to be "honest, true, loyal, clear, and complete" and could deal "only with commercial goods, with no references to politics, religion, or controversial issues" (Paulu, 1967, p. 104). With the legalization of private stations, more outlandish advertising could be broadcast.

Generally, until the 1980s European governments were opposed to the establishment of private television channels. The governments were afraid the private television may lead to the rebirth of Fascism on the continent. Furthermore, the governments believed that private television would minimize the perceived role of broadcasting in the ongoing reconstruction of Europe. The belief was that by controlling all audiovisual media, European governments could air development-oriented programming to the society. In the 1980s, however, the global economic recession forced many European governments to allow private investments in broadcasting, albeit under continuing government supervision. It was in this environment that Berlusconi created Canale-5 in Milan in 1980.

Canale-5 was formed from the acquisition of other stations and the expansion of Milano-2 into a national network.

Noam (1991) believed that Berlusconi's success was based on his investment-making acumen. According to Noam, Berlusconi "put more money than others into stars and technology, and he paid independent antenna installers more to ensure that the signals from his channels would be technically [superior to others]" (p. 156). Berlusconi's greatest ambition was to establish his own rules by taking advantage of the lack of solid private television regulations in Italy. Instead of obtaining a license from the government to broadcast through the national antenna network he installed his own network. Following his success with Canale 5, he began to consider private television a very profitable business. In 1982, he decided to invest heavily in television.

Presently, Berlusconi owns or controls seven national television networks that are connected to local affiliates all over the Italian peninsula. The networks are Canale Cincue, Italia Uno, Rete 4, Rete-Europe, Italia 7, Junior TV, and Capodistra Sport (Noam, 1991, p. 156). These networks all depend on the parent corporation, Fininvest, for program distribution. Rete 4 and Italia Uno were initially owned by other private enterprises but were bought by Berlusconi in 1982. Rete 4 was acquired from the Italian publishing group Mondadori that sold the network when operational incompetence put it in a weak position to compete against Canale 5. Italia Uno was bought from another Italian magnate, Edilio Rusconi, who thought the private television business would never achieve success in Italy. With these assets, Berlusconi has become the "czar" of Italian television, controlling most of the private television channels in the country (Noam, 1991).

Berlusconi also created his own advertising agency to sell advertising for all of his broadcasting stations. This company, Publitalia, operates almost as a monopoly in Italy. Berlusconi's influence has grown enormously as he has integrated all of his companies in a single line. Noam (1991) wrote that "by 1986 his domestic production budget accounted for 60 percent of all Italian films and features" (p. 157). .

Berlusconi's private stations filled a programming gap the Italian public system could not satisfy. Prior to Berlusconi, the audience had grown tired of a television system that was based soley on educational programs. He capitalized on the audience's frustration by offering what the average public demanded. Instead of following a policy of "competence by quality," he offered the commercial strategy of "competence by quantity." He realized that the programming fare that the average Italian viewer demanded was light entertainment and varieties. This was what he provided.

Initially, he implemented his programming strategy by filling his schedule with cheap American programs. Later, he began to develop a special interest in producing light entertainment programs that would provide his networks with content that was closer to Italian culture. In 1986, "Italia Uno carried 92 percent light entertainment" (Dunnett, 1990, p. 154). His productions were quite successful because he demonstrated a special talent for producing numerous episodes at a very low cost. He minimized his production costs by producing programs meant for different countries on the same set and with just a few cast changes. In essence, he offered audiences exactly what they wanted with little quality and low investment. This became his trademark and his personal style.

The policy of offering the audience the kind of programming it wanted not only led Berlusconi to commercial success, but also modified Italian viewing patterns. Noam (1991) wrote that after Berlusconi's networks were established

> the total television viewing increased: the prime-time adult audience in 1979 was 16 million; by 1983 it had grown to 18.6 million. And audiences watched longer. During the RAI monopoly days, the average Italian household watched three hours of television a day; by 1984 viewing time had increased to five hours and ten minutes. (p. 160)

THE FUTURE OF BROADCASTING IN ITALY

As Italy moves toward the next century, its broadcasting will likely be controlled more and more by conglomerates headed by two or three significant persons. Berlusconi's Finivest will probably remain a successful media holding company in both Italy and Europe.

The election of Silvio Berlusconi as prime minister may have seemed like a great opportunity for Fininvest to widen its sphere of influence. It may become easier for the holding company to expand into more European markets and provide an avenue for marketing Berlusconi's broadcasting philosophy. Some suspect that if he regains power, Berlusconi could draft new legislation for broadcasting to his personal advantage. If ongoing investigations absolve Berlusconi of corrupt practices in influencing Europeans to control the growing power of multinational empires, Fininvest could become the most powerful media empire in the world and Berlusconi could become the most important media magnate in the world. The question for Italian voters, perhaps, is how much media and political mixing will they tolerate?

REFERENCES

Andrews, J. (1993). The economic imperative. *Economist, 327,* 19–21.

Business outlook abroad: Italy. (1993). *Business America, 114,* 23–26.

Clark, J. (1993). Two-headed monopoly wearing down Italo TV biz. *Variety,* 39, 42.

Dawtrey, A. (1992). U.K.'s Channel 5 lures high stakes gamblers. *Variety, 346,* 39, 46.

Dunnett, P. (1990). *The world television industry.* New York: Routledge.

Emery, W. (1969). *National and international systems of broadcasting.* East Lansing: Michigan State University Press.

Europa World Yearbook 1994. (1993). London: Europa Publications Limited.

Evans, D. A. (1991). *The cultural and political environment of international business.* Jefferson, NC: McFarland.

Glover, J. (1992). Italy faces the music. *International Management, 47,* 51–58.

Godbout, T. (1993). Employment change and sectoral distribution in 10 countries, 1970–90. *Monthly Labor Review, 116,* 3–20.

Noam, E. (1991). *Television in Europe.* Oxford: Oxford University Press.

Paulu, B. (1967). *Broadcasting on the European continent.* Minneapolis: University of Minnesota Press.

Young, D. (1993a). Clean hands shake Italo TV. *Variety,* 37, 41.

Young, D. (1993). Pending Penta divorce: Who gets the name. *Variety,* pp. 25, 31.

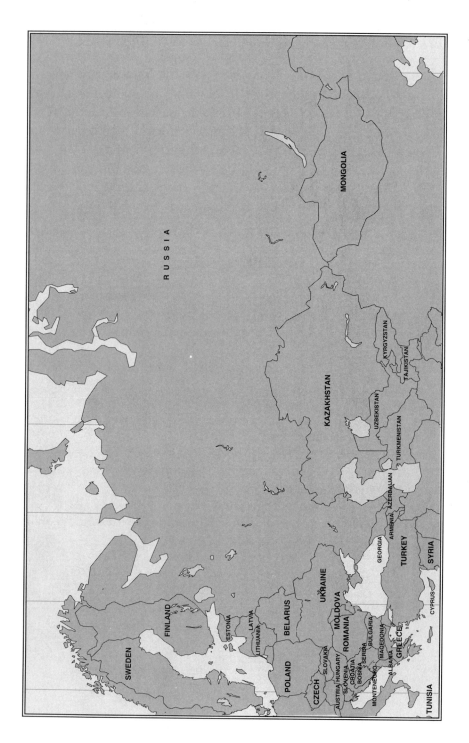

Chapter 6

The Former Soviet Union and Eastern Europe

Janis E. Overlock

THE FORMER SOVIET UNION

The former Soviet Union, which covered one sixth of the earth's surface, was slow to realize the potential of broadcasting. Although Alexander Popov, a 19th-century Russian scientist, demonstrated the first crude radio receiver in 1895, widespread use of radio did not come until the early 1950s. The first experimental voice broadcast was made in Russia in 1920 and the first broadcasting station opened in 1922. Even after radio became fully functioning and accessible to most of the Soviet Union, the Soviets did not fully utilize the broadcasting possibilities, using the radio instead as a public address system for the printed word (Hopkins, 1974).

One of the main obstacles to radio was the huge initial investment needed to reach the entire territory of the country, with the population too dispersed in the provinces to make radio economically feasible. To circumvent these obstacles, the Soviets utilized both radio receivers and diffusion networks by which broadcasts were carried over telephone lines to loudspeakers. The loudspeaker network typified Soviet broadcasting

Table 6.1
The Former Soviet union and Eastern Europe

Country	Population (In Millions)	Growth (%)	Land Area (square kilometers)	GNP/Capita (1992 U.S. Currency)	Radio Sets (In Millions)	Television Sets (In Millions)
Eastern Europe						
Belarus	10.3	0.1	20,7600	2,910	—	—
Bulgaria	8.4	-0.2	110,912	1,330	3.92	3.13
Czech Republic	10.3	0.0	79,228	2,440	9.10	—
Hungary	10.3	-0.3	93,032	3,010	5.25	4.26
Moldova	4.4	0.6	33,700	1,260	—	—
Poland	38.6	0.3	321,677	1,960	16.30	10.00
Ukraine	51.5	-0.2	603,700	1,670	—	—
Romania	22.7	-0.1	237,500	1,090	4.50	4.00
Russia	147.8	-0.2	17,075,400	2,680	—	—
Slovakia	5.3	0.4	48,666	1,920	2.90	—
Northern Europe						
Estonia	1.5	-0.4	45,100	2,750	—	—
Latvia	2.5	-0.1	64,500	1,930	2.00	1.20
Lithuania	3.7	0.3	65,200	1,310	1.42	1.40

Region / Country						
Southern Europe						
Albania	3.4	1.8	28,748	—	0.55	0.3
Bosnia–Herzegovina	4.6	0.7	51,127	—	—	—
Croatia	4.8	-0.1	56,540	—	2.0	0.75
Macedonia	2.1	0.8	25,719	—	—	—
Slovenia	2.0	0.1	20,254	6,330	—	—
Yugoslavia[a]	10.5	0.4	69,775	—	2.69	1.64
South Central Asia						
Kazakhstan	4.5	1.2	2,717,300	1,680	—	—
Kyrgyzstan	17.1	2.1	198,500	810	—	—
Tajikistan	5.9	2.9	143,100	480	—	—
Turkmenistan	4.1	2.6	488,100	1,270	—	—
Uzbekistan	22.1	2.7	447,400	860	—	—
Western Asia						
Armenia	3.7	1.4	29,800	780	—	—
Azerbaijan	7.4	1.9	86,600	870	—	—
Georgia	5.5	0.8	69,700	850	—	—

Note. Population (mid 1994 estimates), population growth (natural increase), and Gross national product per capita (1992) in U.S. dollar equivalents are from *1994 World Population Data Sheet*, Washington D.C., Population Reference Bureau, 1994. Radio and television set figures are from A. G. Sennitt (Ed.), *World Radio TV Handbook*, Volume 49, New York: Billboard Books, 1995. Land surface area figures are from *UN Statistical Yearbook, 1991/2*.

aOn April 27, 1992, Serbia and Montenegro formed a new state, the Federal Republic of Yugoslavia.

until the mid-1950s (Hopkins, 1974). However, as the Cold War between the United States and the Soviet Union escalated, radio receivers began to be perceived by the Soviet authorities as tools of propaganda and warranted more investment. By the end of the 1960s, nearly 100% of the population of the Soviet Union had access to radio and the number of transmitters surged from 100 in 1950 to over 430 in 1968 (Hopkins, 1974; see Table 6.1).

Television also had a lag time much behind Western development. The first experimental television transmission was made in the Soviet Union in April of 1931. "Regular" television broadcasting began in March of 1939 in Moscow when 100 very small screen sets received a slow-motion 30-minute program. By 1941, 400 television sets had been produced and construction of television stations in major Soviet cities began, although the construction was postponed due to World War II (Hopkins, 1974). By the end of the war, the number of television sets in the Soviet Union dropped to 200 and by the end of 1950 had only reached 15,000 sets.

Television, like radio initially, was seen as too costly a venture for the government. In the early 1960s, however, such attitudes began to change and the authorities began to consider the possibilities of television as an "educational" device. The national network utilized cables, relay transmitters, and artificial earth satellites to reach distant points and a major programming center in Moscow. By 1965, cables and relay transmitters linked most of the Soviet Union west of the Urals to Central Soviet Television. Even so, it was not until the 1970s that 39 cities, including Moscow, Kiev, and Leningrad, finally got color broadcasts (Hopkins, 1974).

By the time the former Soviet Union broke apart in the early 1990s, the broadcasting network was well established, centered primarily in Moscow. Russia took over the facilities of Central Soviet Television, which was better funded and had better technical equipment than any of the other Soviet Union republics (RFE/RL Research Staff, 1993). In most of the countries, the broadcasting outlets remained primarily under state control due to the heavy burden of operating costs (only the government could afford it in many cases) as well as the various governments' reluctance to release their hold over the media.

The development of the media varied by country and by region. In the

Central Asian republics, repressive Communist regimes and ethnic conflicts stymied the growth of free media, whereas in the Baltics the countries tried to assimilate as quickly as possible into the new democratic order taking steps to unfetter the media (RFE/RL Research Staff, 1993).

One of the main problems of the media in the countries of the former Soviet Union is a basic lack of understanding of the role of the media in a democracy. After years of Soviet domination, many of the governments as well as journalists view the media as a propaganda tool for the government. Even though many of the countries of the former Soviet Union have adopted media laws proclaiming the freedom of the press, this proclamation does not often reflect reality (RFE/RL Research Staff, 1993).

THE BALTICS

Estonia

As of the mid-1990s, there was no specific law on broadcasting in the restored 1938 pre-Soviet constitution (Webster, 1993). There is an absence of censorship, although journalism standards continue to be low with a proliferation of plagiarism and deliberate misrepresentation of facts (RFE/RL, Research Staff, 1993).

Eesti Raadio, Estonian Radio, broadcasts four programs, three of which are in Estonian and one in Russian. The main channel, Channel One, airs news, cultural programs, and music 20.5 hr per day. Channel Two broadcasts commercial programs targeted at teenagers 24 hr per day. Channel Three airs classical music, live concerts, as well as transmissions from Voice of America and others approximately 6.5 hr per day. The fourth channel, broadcasting 16 to 18 hr, caters to the Russian-speaking audience (Webster, 1993). Estonia also has about 16 local radio stations, of which eight are private, (Webster, 1993). The state-run radio is perceived to be much more innovative than the state-run television (RFE/RL, Research Staff, 1993).

Privately owned stations, such as Radio Kuku, broadcasting pop music, news, and weather have attracted the best talent from the former state radio. Radio Kuku has inspired many competitors, four of which are in the capital city of Tallinn (RFE/RL Research Staff, 1993).

The state-owned Eesti Television, Estonian Television, broadcasts on one channel for 48 hr per week in Estonian and Russian. In addition, there are approximately eight television channels throughout the country with four privately owned television stations and more scheduled to open in the 1990s (Webster, 1993).

Latvia

In 1992, the parliament passed a law on radio and television, specifying the creation of separate administrative bodies for radio and television, as well as assigning frequencies. Up until the mid-1990s, however, Latvian radio and television continued to be run by a public authority council, financed by the state budget, with 23 public representatives. The council is responsible for the granting of broadcast frequencies, policy decisions, and the program content in terms of retransmission of foreign programs (Webster, 1993).

Latvian State Radio, Latvijas Radio, broadcasts three programs: The first and second are on the air 133 hr per week covering news, music, and special features. The first program targets the Latvian speaking audience and the second targets the Russian. The third program, airing classical music and literary programs, broadcasts approximately 95 hr per week (Webster, 1993). Since its inception, the Latvia Radio and Television Council has granted frequencies to more than 20 enterprises for radio broadcasts (Webster, 1993).

The first program of Latvian State Television may not be broadcast in anything but the Latvian language, broadcasting 55 hr per week and covering 97% of the population. The second channel, geared toward the Russian-speaking audience, broadcasts 41 hr per week, covering 96% of the population. Additionally, two channels are open to commercial enterprises on a rented-time basis. Twenty-five enterprises and municipal offices have been granted broadcasting time and licenses (Webster, 1993).

As of the mid-1990s, however, evening television viewers had the choice of three concurrent programs, all in Latvian (an ethnic group which represents only 52% of the population, the largest "minority" are

Russians at 34%), offering uninteresting fare (RFE/RL Research Staff, 1993). As of 1995, there were 2 million radio sets and 1.2 million television sets in Latvia (Sennitt, 1995).

Lithuania

The Lithuanian parliament was considering a new law on radio and television in the early 1990s that would have reorganized public broadcasting, established a licensing proecedure for new radio and television stations, and guaranteed the press freedoms of journalists. Even so, political parties continued to try to influence the electronic media, making the rent of transmitters and relay lines very expensive. This made it difficult for new ventures to compete with the established state television and radio. In addition, the state television and radio organizations were alledgedly "low balling" their advertising rates, provoking protests of unfair competition by other broadcasters (Webster, 1993).

As of the mid-1990s, there were two national channels used by state radio. Radio Vilnius broadcasts in Lithuanian, Russian, Polish, English, Yiddish, Belarussian, and Ukrainian. In addition, a commercial radio station, M-1, broadcasts primarily music throughout the country, and three independent radio stations operated in the capital city of Vilnius. Regional stations are also operated by municipalities (Webster, 1993).

Lithuanian state television broadcasts programs created by independent producers over one channel. Three regional stations, funded mostly by local municipalities, broadcast 6 hr a week on the national channel as well. The programming of the regional stations includes regional news and local development, films, and video concerts (Webster, 1993). Two independent channels were also in operation in the early 1990s. Baltijos Televizija, a joint stock company formed by an American–Lithuanian businessman, rents a channel and broadcasts some locally produced programs on weekends (RFE/RL Research Staff, 1993). Tele-3 is a private station with its own channel, broadcasting imported programs from Eurosport, MTV, Film Net and Discovery, as well as from Russian television (Webster, 1993).

EASTERN EUROPE

Belarus

In Belarus, a government council of ministers supervises the media under two bodies: the Center for Information Security and a commission to control pornography, violence, and cruelty in the mass media (Webster, 1993). As of mid-1993, 205 television and radio stations were registered with the Ministry of Information, of which 16 were founded by the government, 104 by nonstate small enterprises and joint stock companies, 27 by public organizations, 17 by private persons, and 19 by legislative bodies. Of all the nonstate television and radio stations, only half were working as of the mid-1990s (Webster, 1993). All Belarusian television and radio stations work on transmitters belonging to the Ministry of Communication, so no stations are completely independent from the state.

The Belarusian State Television and Radio Company runs 16 state-owned stations. Belarusian Radio broadcasts on three channels. It broadcasts two Western-style programs, the *Radiofakt* news program and the *Belaruskaya Maladzezhnaya* talk show. The latter is the only venue in which opposition leaders can present their views (RFE/RL Research Staff, 1993). State television broadcasts only 4 hr per day of original programming and 14 to 16 hours daily of films and materials produced by other television companies (Webster, 1993). As of the mid-1990s, there was little news or analysis on the state television and what little there was was often claimed to be outdated and biased (RFE/RL Research Staff, 1993).

Commercial television companies have been denied broadcasting rights since January 1, 1993 when the prime minister ordered an investigation of broadcasting organizations to determine compliance with technical requirements. Consequently, there were no independent television stations in Belarus as of the mid-1990s (Webster, 1993). The real motive behind the suspension of licenses for independent television stations appears to be due to political rather than technical considerations. The independent stations were providing a forum for people who were denied access to the official media (RFE/RL Research Staff, 1993).

Moldova

The National Radio and Television of Moldova was created in 1990 by the Supreme Soviet of Moldova, and it is subsidized by the state budget. The parliament appoints the general director who is assisted by a consulting board of 11 to 13 specialists (Webster, 1993). Moldova lacks legislation governing nonstate broadcasting media and had no formal licensing procedures as of the mid-1990s (RFE/RL Research Staff, 1993).

The National Radio broadcasts 37 hr per day on two programs, RN-1 and RN-2 (Webster, 1993). The first nonstate local radio station was set up in the early 1990s in the capital city of Chisinau but its broadcasting radius was very short and its equipment outdated (RFE/RL Research Sraff, 1993).

The National Television broadcasts approximately 15 hr per day in Romanian, Russian, Ukrainian, Bulgarian, Turkish, and Idish. The television program is accessible to 4.5 million viewers in its home country, 2 million in the Ukraine, and 2.5 million in Romania (Webster, 1993).

Ukraine

In 1992, the Ukrainian parliament adopted the Law on Information and the Law on the Printed Mass Media, which banned censorship and guaranteed the right to receive and disseminate information. In spite of these assurances, these freedoms remained fragile in the mid-1990s as much of the former Soviet structure remains in place, a structure which has little regard for a free media (RFE/RL Research Staff, 1993).

Ukrainian Television and Radio is a state-owned organization. It broadcasts radio programs in Russian and Ukrainian for its domestic audience as well as external broadcasts for the rest of the former Soviet Union, Europe, Australia, and North America. The state radio company broadcasts on four radio channels for 94.3 hr per day with programs encompassing information, entertainment, and culture (Webster, 1993).

Nationwide television programming is monopolized by the state. Ukrainian Television broadcasts over two national television frequencies. The first features music programs, entertainment, news, and documentary films for 17 hr per day. The second channel broadcasts commercial programming and rebroadcasts programs from the Russian Television Company (Webster, 1993).

In addition, there are over 200 local commercial television stations, with some cities having between two to five local commercial television stations in the same market. As of the mid-1990s, there were about 1,000 companies that were granted permission to produce television programs (Webster, 1993). However, most of the independent and commercial television stations restricted their programming to Western B movies or retransmitting programs pirated from foreign stations transmitting by satellite (RFE/RL Research Staff, 1993).

Russia

Even after the breakup of the Soviet Union, Russia remained the largest country on earth and one wielding great power throughout the region. Although it had only been a middle-level economy by world standards and has experienced recent years of drastic economic decline, it is still a military super power. The media played a significant role in the downfall of Communism and the disintegration of the Soviet empire through their promotion of glasnost but they have been less successful in building up a democratic system in the Russian Federation. Even so, the media have reportedly made greater progress toward reform than any other institutions in Russia (RFE/RL Research Staff, 1993).

A media law passed in 1990 ended the Communist Party's monopoly on regulating ownership and controlling media outlets. The registration of broadcast media became a formal procedure, safe from the veto of the Communist government or is institutions (McNair, 1994). However, these newly won freedoms were put in jeopardy after the attempted coup to overthrow the government in August of 1991. The supporters of President Yeltsin used various strategies to consolidate their control over broadcasting, including the proposition of "regulatory bodies" to oversee the work of broadcasters. By 1991, however, another law, similar to the 1990 one, was enacted, guaranteeing press freedoms and editorial independence (McNair, 1994).

Russia inherited the facilities of Central Soviet Television as well as many other broadcasting outlets from the Soviets, thus allowing for a greater diversity with better technological equipment, than anywhere else in the former Soviet Union (RFE/RL Research Staff, 1993). By the mid-1990s, there were four major state-owned broadcasting organizations: All Russia State Television and Radio Broadcasting Company Ostankino, the Moscow state television and broadcasting company Moskva, and the state television and radio broadcasting company Petersburg Channel. In addition, two Moscow-based satellite channels, Ostankino and Russian television cover the entire former Soviet Union (Webster, 1993).

The Russian Television and Radio Company was founded in late 1990 by the Supreme Soviet and the Congress of People's Deputies. It was granted an all-Russia television Channel 2, Channel 4, and a number of educational channels. It also has two radio services, Radio of Russia (broadcasting up to 20 hr a day) and Voice of Russia, the world service in Russian for 24 hr a day (Webster, 1993).

The private Ostankino Radio and Television company, started in December of 1991, provides political, economic, and cultural coverage as well as international news. Ostankino transmits on Radio One for 22 hr to 93% of the population, on Yunost to 25% of the population 24 hr a day, on Orfey for 18 hr a day, and on Mayak reaching 96% of the population (Webster, 1993).

Other private radio stations have also prospered in the Russian market. Since the 1991 media law allowed the foundation of private stations, 200 independent television and radio stations registered. One of the most successful in Moscow and Saint Petersburg is Europa Plus, a 51% French-owned concern with substantial foreign investment and modern equipment. Europa Plus broadcasts Western music with 1- to 2-min news segments (Webster, 1993).

Ostankino has also carved a niche in the television market. It broadcasts on Channel One for 19.5 hr per day throughout the entire former Soviet Union to an audience of nearly 300 million people. Its Channel Four broadcasts 6 hr a day and reaches 28% of the population. Throughout Russia there were about 30 state-run television centers and about 180 independent companies in the mid-1990s. (Webster, 1993).

SOUTH CENTRAL ASIA

Kazakhstan

The Ministry of Posts and Telecommunications owns and operates the transmitters in Kazakstan, charging public and private broadcasters for air time. The State Committee for Radio and Television, Teleradio Company of Kazakhstan, is responsible for programming on the public broadcasting channels (Webster, 1993). Even so, both the independent and state-owned media enjoy a great deal of freedom of expression (RFE/RL Research Staff, 1993).

The state-run radio utilizes a lower band than is traditionally used for FM broadcasting throughout most of the rest of the world, which causes some difficulties for new radio stations trying to enter the market. Kazakhstan's first commercial FM station, Radio Max, began with assistance from American companies (Webster, 1993).

The Kazakh State Television and Radio Broadcasting broadcasts on two television frequencies. In addition, there are four privately programmed television channels in the capital city of Alma-Ata. Asia TV broadcasts mostly Turkish films and musical dramas. A/O KTK TV, a commercial venture, broadcasts mainly foreign films and two news programs. TAN + TV targets the Turkish audience and TVIN TV broadcasts music videos and news inserts (Webster, 1993).

Kyrgyzstan

Kyrgyzstan, the first post-Soviet republic to separate state and party structures, is considered to be nearest to a Western-style democracy in Central Asia. Although the broadcast programming is limited due to financial constraints, the rural people in this mountainous country rely on its coverage, which is considered to be lively and independent (RFE/RL Research Staff, 1993; Webster, 1993).

Five channels transmit radio programs and the national station broadcasts approximately 12 hr a day. Private broadcasting outlets are located only in and around the capital city of Bishkek. Kyrgyz television, the state-owned television outlet, broadcasts on only one channel for 3 hr a day. Due to the high fees charged by the Ministry of Posts and Telecommunications, the amount of programming the state television can broadcast is limited. As of the mid-1990s, there were no independent television stations in Kyrgyzstan (Webster, 1993).

Tajikistan

Like much of the rest of the former Soviet Union, Tajik broadcasting is still state controlled. Radio broadcasts on three channels in Tajik, Uzbek, and Russian languages and relays three channels from Russia. No information on state television programming are available but "various main and relay transmitters throughout the country relay programmes of OK-1 from Moscow, as well as TRT from Turkey and IBIB from Iran" (Sennitt, 1995, p. 422).

Turkmenistan

Turkmenistan, still controlled by a conservative Communist government, has failed to develop any form of an independent media since the collapse of the Soviet Union (RFE/RL Research Staff, 1993). The government-funded national Television and Radio Company of Turkmenistan is the only broadcasting agency in the country. It provides about 7.5 hr of color television and 16 hr of radio broadcasting daily (Webster, 1993).

Uzbekistan

Although the current media law of 1991 clearly stipulates there is to be no censorship in Uzbekistan, in practice almost all media are subject to review by censors. In addition, press freedom, political activities, and freedom of expression are limited as well (Webster, 1993). Uzbekistan State Television and Radio, Uzteleradio, monopolizes all radio and television broadcasting. There are four television channels including a central channel from Moscow. Radio broadcasts are transmitted on four channels on both AM and FM frequencies (Webster, 1993).

WESTERN ASIA

Armenia

Armenia was one of the first among the Soviet Republics to institute privatization programs but the Nagorno–Karabah war as well as political instability has undermined economic and democratic reforms (Webster, 1993). As a result, opposition political parties have only limited access to the broadcast media in spite of a 1991 law guaranteeing the freedom of the press (RFE/RL Research Staff, 1993). Radio and television are still state owned and controlled. Due to energy shortages they were only able to broadcast about 3 hr a day in the mid-1990s. The television programs are broadcast in Armenian and Russian and radio broadcasts in Armenian, Russian, and Kurdish (Webster, 1993).

Azerbaijan

Political instability has continued through the mid-1990s, due, in no small part, to the fighting in the Armenian enclave of Nagorno–Karabakh. The country has been slow to adopt market-oriented economic reforms, thus further stalling the development of the media there (Webster, 1993). In July of 1992, the Azerbaijan's People's Assembly passed a media law guaranteeing free flow of information. Even so, there have been reports of physical violence against journalists (RFE/RL Research Staff, 1993).

Both television and radio are state owned and operated. Baku television broadcasts in Azerbaijani and Russian. Radio Baku broadcasts in Azerbaijani, Russian, Arabic, Persian, and Turkish (Webster, 1993).

Georgia

In the mid-1990s, the media remained under assault in the newly formed republic of Georgia. The democratically elected leadership, so weak in its control over the country, refused any sort of media access to members of the opposition and supporters of the deposed president, who left office in 1992 (RFE/RL Research Staff, 1993). Reports of systematic censorship and harassment of reporters continued through the mid-1990s (Webster, 1993).

Little information is available about the state of the media in Georgia. Both radio and television remain under state control. Tbilisi Television broadcasts in Georgian and Russian. Tbilisi Radio broadcasts in Georgian, Russian, Armenian, Azerbaijani, Abkhazian, and Ossetian (Webster, 1993).

EASTERN EUROPE

The broadcasting scene in Eastern Europe in the early 1990s could be described as kaleidoscopic. Until 1989, the region had been dominated by the Soviet Union and governed by satellite communist governments. The Soviet model, one of censorship and propaganda, typified the media systems throughout the region. In 1989, however, Communism collapsed leaving political mayhem throughout the region. The Communists' rigid hold on existing media outlets lessened and new ones developed rapidly. The growth of these outlets outpaced laws and legislation to guide the development of broadcasting, a trend that has continued through the 1990s. Providing an overview of the broadcast media systems is therefore an unwieldy task, as governments and press freedoms have not yet stabilized. Information about the media systems in each of these countries is sketchy and unreliable at best.

Broadcast Media Under Communism

The dilemma of broadcasting in Central and Eastern Europe is rooted in the 4 decades of Soviet domination. After the Allied victory of World War II, the Soviet Union forcefully maintained its sphere of influence throughout the region. The broadcasting media were an important tool for the communist regimes. By controlling the news and media outlets, they were able to disseminate their propaganda and restrict the flow of ideas into the region. On the other hand, Soviet domination of the region also provided advanced technological broadcasting equipment in many countries, such as Bulgaria and Romania, that had been historically underdeveloped. The introduction of television broadcasting in many of these countries coincided with their becoming Soviet satellite states.

Vestiges of the Soviet's use of broadcasting outlets remain. Although Communism as a political system has been largely abandoned, the mindset of the politicians regarding control of broadcast media lingers. In most of the Central and Eastern European countries, the governments remain in control of broadcast media outlets. Although many countries have fledgling media laws before their parliaments, the governing parties are reluctant to relinquish control over such powerful tools of persuasion. Members of the opposition do not press the issue for they, too, hope to control the airwaves once they achieve power. The laws determining media ownership and frequency distribution are likewise caught in the gridlock of politics.

In the early 1990s, however, there was a great influx of technology into the region; the use of satellite antennas, VCRs, and cable was more commonplace. Broadcasts from other countries were no longer jammed as they had been under the Communist regimes and greater media freedoms existed than in previous decades.

Albania

Located on the outskirts of Central and Eastern Europe, Albanians considered themselves truer Communists than the Soviets and were allied with China. When Communism collapsed and democracy was finally established in 1992, the costs of Albania's isolation became apparent. One of the most impoverished countries in Eastern Europe, it is also one of the most technologically backward.

During Communist domination, news directors at media outlets would censor the news, a common occurrence throughout theregion. In Albania, however, there was a special news directory that dictated guidelines to the editors as to what could be aired or published. Noncompliance with the guidelines could result in the execution of the news editors.

Both radio and television remain under the control of the Central Committee of the Albanian Party of Labour. Radio was introduced in November of 1938, coinciding with the Albanian Independence Day. Although television was broadcast in experimental form in 1960, it was not until 1971 that regular programs aired. Color television was introduced very late, in 1981. Only since 1986 has television coverage reached all areas of Albania (Xhixho, 1992). The national radio station, Radio Tirana, broadcasts from the capital city of Albania with four branches in other parts of the country: (a) Radio Gjirokastra in the south, which includes some programming in Greek for the Greek minority; (b) Radio Korce, covering the southeastern part of the country; (c) Radio Rukesi in the northeast; and (d) Radio Shkodra in the north (Xhixho, 1992).

Only one television channel services Albania, RTV, airing from 5:30 p.m. to 11:00 p.m. daily with a 3-hr program on Sunday mornings. In the 1990s, extended negotiations have been underway for expanded broadcasting utilizing foreign television programming.

Although the broadcast media remain under state control, the arrival of democracy in 1992 spurred an improvement in professional standards, an expansion of programming, and plans to start satellite broadcasting. The Albanian media are still inhibited by party influence, lack of tolerance, and economic limitations—problems that may only be resolved as democracy takes hold (RFE/RL Research Staff, 1993).

Bulgaria

Bulgaria was the Soviet Union's staunchest ally in the Eastern Bloc, never challenging Soviet domination, deviating from Soviet directives, or questioning the Soviet's political, economic, cultural, domestic, or foreign policy (Rothschild, 1989). In return, the Soviet Union lavished extensive and sustained capital assistance to the technologically under-developed country. The fall of Communism unleashed a political power struggle in which the broadcast media became a pawn. In the early 1990s, each new governing majority dismissed the incumbent media directors and elected people who supported its own policies (Bruno, 1992).

Bulgarian Radio broadcasting began in 1929 with the first Bulgarian radio station, Rodno Radio. In 1935, all radio was subsumed by a state-owned monopoly. Bulgarian television began in November of 1959. The first broadcast was a report from the working people's celebration of the 42nd anniversary of the Russian Revolution (Horlamus, 1976).

In 1992, the first private radio stations were licensed. Applicants received permission to broadcast locally, although many aspired to a national media market. Of the more than 100 applicants who received license to operate local radio stations, one third were functioning as of July of 1993. The radio stations air Western music but only a few can afford extensive newscasts and special programming on major political, social, and economic issues (RFE/RL Research Staff, 1993) The best-funded stations are in the capital city of Sofia.

Two television stations operate in Bulgaria's native language. Channel One reaches about 85% of the nation, whereas Channel Two covers only about 65%. In addition, there is a Russian station that reaches about 35% of the region and a French channel that can be seen in the capital city of Sofia and surrounding regions. Curiously, considering world market media tastes, the Bulgarians appear to be more serious television viewers. The most popular programs are those alerting viewers to new laws, weekly business reports, economics, and current affairs, as well as talk shows on political, economic, and social problems (Reid, 1992).

In 1993, the Bulgarian government was in the process of forming a 10-person commission to study the viability of independent radio and television stations. The speed of these reforms, however, was slowed by political power plays. Bulgarian National Radio, Bulgarian National Television, and the Bulgarian Telegraph Agency continue to wield most of the broadcasting power in the country. After the demise of communism, these organizations voluntarily shifted to a "freer" style for the press, providing the journalists with a greater amount of independence. However, Bulgarian politicians remained hesitant to entirely release control of these broadcasting outlets in the 1990s.

Czech Republic and Slovakia

On January 1, 1993, Czechoslovakia split along territorial and ethnic lines into two separate countries: the Czech Republic and Slovakia. Most information on broadcasting systems predates the division. In 1923, regular radio broadcasting began and in 1953 television broadcasting began. In 1958, both television and radio were concentrated under the Radio Ministry but 1 year later television had its own ministry. Four radio stations broadcast nationwide, two were general interest and two aired mostly music. In addition, there were 10 regional stations.

When Vaclav Havel came to power after the fall of Communism, there was no central broadcasting authority to grant new licenses or to assign or open new frequencies. In the absence of a determined authority, Czech Radio, a government agency, permitted a French–Czech joint venture, Radio 2, to lease a frequency in 1990. In 1991, Europe 2 became the first commercial radio service in Czechoslovakia (Fletcher & Herzmann, 1992).

To fill the void of a broadcasting law, the Federal Commission on Independent Broadcasting was formed in 1990 to function until the new law was ratified. When the law passed, the Czech Republic became the first country of the former Eastern Bloc to establish an independent broadcasting council to franchise and regulate the industry. Radio and television are no longer state owned but are public broadcasting corporations ("A Report on Freedom," 1993). Using their authority, the Federal Commission on Independent Broadcasting allowed a station playing underground rock to operate independently as Radio One (Fletcher & Herzmann, 1992).

Television broadcasting was under the authority of Czechoslovakia Televize, which produced programs in Czech and Slovak languages on its three channels. Channel One reached 80% of the country and broadcast in the Czech. Channel Two was split into Czech and Slovak versions, broadcasting to the appropriate regions of the country. A third station, OK3, originally used by the Soviet armed forces, was opened for retransmitting free programs from the United States and European sources. OK3 was projected to become a private channel in the early 1990s (Noam, 1991), but

Czech television has retained the right to broadcast on the channel until the end of 1995 and its future remains unclear (Webster, 1993). Czechoslovakia's first commercial broadcast venture was Masseba 10, which aired economic and managerial programming to support emerging private enterprise.

Since the split in January of 1993, Slovak radio and television have continued to be under government control, which is particularly inhibiting to free speech. The government of Prime Minister Vladimir Meciar espouses that the media should present a "truthful picture of Slovakia" and could incur harsh penalties if this tenant is ignored. This chilling of the media has created a new propaganda model for the press in Slovakia (RFL/RE Research Staff, 1993).

Hungary

Among the former Eastern Bloc countries, Hungary has the longest tradition of media reform. Although the printed press was being rapidly privatized and was attracting considerable foreign direct investment, broadcast media development was kept at a much slower pace in the 1990s. The government still controls the electronic media outlets, although broadcast media laws determining profit-making ability, subscription fees, regulating agencies, and frequency distribution have been discussed.

Hungarian radio broadcasts began on December 1, 1925. The broadcast system operated throughout World War II but the German army destroyed most of it as it retreated. Once the Communist Party took control in the postwar years, it nationalized broadcasting. Television broadcasts began on May 1, 1955 (Horlamus, 1976).

The state system, Magyar Radio, operates three national systems: Kossuth Radio, Petofi Radio, and Bartok Radio, and two commercial stations, Radio Danubius and Radio Calypso. The programming differs at each station. Kossuth Radio emphasizes politics; Petofi Radio plays popular entertainment and literature, and Bartok Radio caters to a more "intellectual" listener with symphonic music and educational programs as well as minority language programs in Serbo–Croatian, Slovak, Slovene, Romanian, and German. Radio Danubius, the state commercial channel, began broadcasting in 1986 for German tourists. Now broadcasting in Hungarian, the programming showcases light music and information (Orcutt, 1992).

Radio Calypso, a joint venture between Magyar Radio and a British company called Multi-Media Organization, was launched in 1989. It plays nostalgic music, keeping news and information to a minimum (Orcutt, 1992). Radio Bridge, launched in 1990, is the only privately owned station in Hungary. A moratorium on frequency allocation instituted by the Communists in 1989 remains in effect, barring any other private radio or television stations (RFE/RL Research Staff, 1993).

Hungarian Television (Magyar Televizio), which has been operating as an independent legal entity since 1974, broadcasts on two channels with regional stations in Szeged, Pecs, and Budapest. Magyar TV1 "broadcasts news programs, shows, and reruns 66 hr per week to nearly 100% of the population. Magyar TV2" reaches 98% of the households and broadcasts 34 hr per week. Magyar Televizio views its purpose as promoting the moral and spiritual advancement of the nation, serving the tastes of viewers including minorities, and promoting the knowledge of Hungarian history and culture (Webster, 1993). By the mid-1990s, there were no independent television stations in the country, although a "media war" in Hungary has erupted over the state's monopoly on broadcasting.

Poland

Poland has often been at the crossroads of history, torn between Russia or the Soviet Union and Germany. Poles have clung to their religious heritage for strength and national unity. This tenacity of purpose spawned the Solidarity movement and continues to influence modern-day broadcasting as well. The history of Polish broadcasting dates from 1926 when the Polski Radio Company began regular national broadcasts. The first public television broadcast occurred in December of 1951.

Poland now has three television channels, Telewizji Polskiej on each of its two channels, one providing general entertainment including news, films, and serials, and the other channel focusing on cultural programming. The cultural channel also has its own satellite channel reaching other ethnic Poles in other European countries. In addition, the third channel broadcasts 12 regional services from Poland's largest cities. These are also run by Telewizji Polskiej (Webster, 1993). Cable was scheduled to be provided to 10 Polish cities in the 1990s under a cooperative agreement with an American firm, Chase Enterprises, and four Polish state entities (Noam, 1991). At the end of 1993, there were approximately 25 private television and 110 private radio stations, as well as numerous pirate television and radio stations. There are four state radio networks which have a large degree of autonomy as well as competition from the private stations (RFE/RL Research Staff, 1992).

In the early 1990s, a new media law was introduced that applied to all radio and television stations. The law protects Polish productions against Western imports, limits the amount of advertising, and restricts programs unsuitable for children. Although this law may seem appropriate to Westerners, it contains a twist reminiscent of earlier times. Polish authorities can censor certain subject areas, for example, topics concerning the "Patria" fatherland and "Religio"Religion. Poland allows no programs damaging to the state or offensive to Christian values to be aired. The interpreter and enforcer of this law is a nine-member radio and television council that is empowered to license new radio and television stations (Jakubowicz, 1993).

Romania

Of all the Eastern Bloc countries, Romania's recent history has been most directly influenced by the broadcast media. The Romanians watched the unraveling of communism in the other Eastern Bloc states in 1989 and were inspired to overturn their own communist government in December of that same year. Perhaps unwittingly, the state broadcaster Radio Televiziunea Romania (RTR) played a key role in the revolution.

Regular public broadcasting began in November of 1928 and television was introduced in 1956. A state monopoly was in charge of programming and the Ministry of Posts and Telecommunication handled transmission. The new leftist government in Romania has tried to keep the national television stations in particular under strict control. An ambiguously worded Law on the Broadcasting Media, adopted in 1992, established a National Audiovisual Council to supervise the electronic media services. This council, packed with government loyalists, grants licenses and allocates broadcasting frequencies. As a result, Romanian television has been charged with being merely a mouthpiece of the government (RFE/RL Research Staff, 1992). Nevertheless, the amount of airtime has increased dramatically since 1989. The state broadcaster RTR (renamed RTRL for libera, or free) expanded its broadcasting from 2 hr per day on one channel at the time of the revolution to 18 hr per day on two channels (Noam, 1991).

The state-controlled radio network has more freedom than the television network and provides more objective and balanced coverage of current events. Radio Bucharest has had to raise its standards to remain competitive with the smaller independent stations as well as Romanian-language services of Western radio stations. Prior to 1989, there were four separate radio channels. In the early 1990s, however, several pirate radio ventures sprung up.

MASS MEDIA IN THE FORMER YUGOSLAVIA

In 1918, the republics of Croatia, Slovenia, Macedonia, Bosnia-Herzegovina, Montenegro, and Serbia all unified into a common state named the Kingdom of Serbs, Croats and Slovenes, later to be renamed the Kingdom of Yugoslavia in 1929. The kingdom disintegrated during World War II in April of 1941 when the armies of Germany, Italy, Hungary, and Bulgaria occupied the territory. The leader of the Communist party, Josip Broz Tito, led a national liberation struggle in the summer of 1941, which paved the way for the establishment of the communist-governed country of Yugoslavia (Lekovic & Bjelica, 1976) until its collapse in 1989. Like the former

Soviet Union, the actual confederation of the republics was not based on ethnicity, rather on economic and political strong-arm considerations. After 1990, when the formal structure of the Yugoslavian state was torn down, deep ethnic rivalries erupted and many of the former republics of Yugoslavia, now countries, were engaged in a bitter war.

In many of these newly created countries, the media played a significant part in escalating the conflict, intensifying differences between the ethnic groups and ideological orientations. As such, most media in the Yugoslav republics became instruments of militant nationalist propaganda in the early to mid-1990s (RFE/RL Research Staff, 1994). Although some of the new countries made significant inroads toward a freer media system, the media in others such as Bosnia and Herzegovina were at a standstill due to the war. In almost all of the former Yugoslavia, the civil war provoked the introduction of internal control over the media. Government authorization was required for content, transmission, and financing as of the mid-1990s (Radojkovic, 1994).

The first public radio station in Yugoslavia was in Zagreb (Radio Zagreb), which began broadcasts in 1926. The second was in Ljubljana in 1927 and the third began in Belgrade in 1929 (Lekovic & Bjelica, 1976). Television broadcasting began in Zagreb in 1956, with television studios also being established in Belgrade and Ljubljana within 2 years. By 1975, television studios were operating in all republican and provincial centers. Color television programming was launched in 1971 in Ljubljana and Belgrade (Lekovic & Bjelica, 1976).

Under the authority of the former government, eight semiindependent units operated, one for each of the six republics and two autonomous provinces. There were eight major broadcasting networks, 214 local radio and roughly 20 local television stations, financed by communal budgets. There was one central state radio station, Radio Yugoslavia, financed from the federal budget (Radojkovic, 1994). Even though privatization was allowed by the last operating federal budget, response was minimal. The State remains the only agency capable of adding money to the insufficient subscription revenue and the operating costs. When the former republics of

Yugoslavia broke away, the first symbolic act was to nationalize the broadcasting institutions, renaming them from cities (e.g. TV Belgrade, TV Zagreb, etc.) to national names (e.g., TV Srbije, Hrvatska TV, TV Slovenje, etc.; Radojkovic, 1994).

Bosnia–Herzegovina

All aspects of mass media in Bosnia–Herzegovina were affected by the war in the early to mid-1990s. Radio Televizija (RTV) Bosnia-Herzegovina is the national broadcast company that broadcasts two television programs and four radio programs. The radio transmissions have been only sporadic throughout the war. Due to the unrest in the country, there was no pending legislation on media issues or press law as of the mid-1990s. (Webster, 1993, p. 13).

Croatia

Hrvatska Radiotelevizija (HRT) is a public company owned by the Republic of Croatia that operates three radio and three television frequencies. The state radio network, Croatian Radio, broadcasts 180 hr of programming per day on three networks. In addition, there are six regional Croatian Radio centers and numerous local radio stations (Webster, 1993). The local private radio stations broadcast mainly music and entertainment, whereas news, commentary, and political analysis remains in the domain of the state-run radio network.

HRT produces and transmits a daily total of 38 hr of TV programs. Croatian Television (HTV) operates two channels. Although transmitters and equipment were the target of Serbian forces, the Croatian media continued to operate under difficult conditions. There are five private and local TV stations: TV Marijan in Split, OTV-Youth TV in Zagreb, and one each in Osijek, Cakovec, and Opuzen (Webster, 1993). Croatian Television, a state-run organization espousing the views of the government, opposed the influx of cable and satellite television although foreign programs, such as

CNN, Sky News, RAT UNO (Italy), and Austria I and 2, were accessible to television viewers in the 1990s. (RFE/RL Research Staff, 1993; Webster, 1993). As of 1995, there were 2 million radio sets and 750,000 television sets in Croatia.

Macedonia

The Macedonia Radiotelevision (MRT), a public organization established in 1991, covers 95% of the territory of the country. Both television and radio broadcast in the national language of Macedonian as well as Albanian, Turkish, Romanesh, and Vlach, with plans to broadcast in the Serbian language as well (Webster, 1993). Although the infrastructure supporting the broadcast media is statefunded, there appears to be no evidence of state censorship and information flows freely (RFE/RL Research Staff, 1993).

The MRT operates three radio networks on FM and medium wave, National Radio, Kanal 2000, and Radio Kultura, providing about 70 broadcasting hr per day. In addition, there are approximately 25 small and private stations throughout the country providing music and popular programs but most are poorly equipped. The most important of the local radio stations is NOMA, which competes with state radio for news and current affairs coverage (RFE/RL Research Staff, 1993; Webster, 1993).

Three television networks belong to the MRT. The daily broadcast schedule consists of 15 to 17 hr on the first channel, 10 to 12 hr on the second channel (providing mostly information programs), and 12 to 14 hours on the third channel which covers only half of Macedonia. The MRT produces roughly 50 % of its own programs. There are also about 15 small and private stations in Macedonia but, like the private radio stations, they are poorly equipped.

Slovenia

The public institution of broadcasting, Radiotelevizia Slovenija, is governed by a board of directors selected by parliament. The state-run radio and television system continues to be run by the old Communist bureaucracy that only allows broadcasts reflecting government views (Webster, 1993). A common complaint in Slovenia is that there is an unequal allocation of radio and television airtime to political parties, especially discriminating against the opposition parties (RFE/RL Research Staff, 1993).

Radio Slovenija has three nationwide programs: (a) the first broadcasts news, music, and current events; (b) the second broadcasts traffic information in Slovenian, German, English, and Italian; and (c) the third broadcasts cultural, artistic, and educational programs. In the capital city, Llubljana, there are two local radio stations as well as over 20 other regional stations throughout the nation. The regional stations are usually part of a community structure or organization (Webster, 1993).

Slovenia has one national television station and one small private television station, "Kanal A Ljubljana," a joint stock company financed through private investment and advertising. Fourteen local cable television systems and programs operate throughout the country, as well as an Italian television channel for the Italian minority living along the coast (Webster, 1993).

SUMMARY

Even though many of the borders of Eastern Europe were sketched out in peace agreements after World War I and II, it is a mistake to consider these countries as a homogeneous Eastern Bloc. In spite of their common heritage of Communist domination, these countries are ethnically distinct and culturally divergent not only from one another, but also from region to region within their own territories. Furthermore, capitalism and democracy have much greater relevance and chance of survival in countries with some past association with such ideas (e.g., the Czech Republic, Hungary, the Baltic countries) than those that have historically been isolated and economically backward (Albania, Romania, and most of the Soviet Union countries). These differences are reflected in the attitudes toward the development and control of broadcast media outlets.

After decades of Communist control of the media, it is difficult for many of the governments to loosen their grip and allow free media to emerge. Many of these countries are so unstable that their governments rely on the broadcast media as a cohesive force against political cleavages, ethnic rivalries, and economic tensions. The last decade of the 20th century will certainly prove to be crucial to these countries if broadcast diversity evolves in tandem with greater political and economic freedoms in the region.

REFERENCES

Bruno, S. (Ed.). (1992). *Bulgarian communications: 1992 update.* Washington, DC: Center for Strategic and International Studies.

Fletcher, J. E. & Herzmann, J. (1992). Commercial radio in Prague. In A. L. Hester, L. Reybold, & K. Conger (Eds.), *The post-Communist press in Eastern and Central Europe: New studies* (pp. 37–50). Atlanta: The University of Georgia Press. pp. 37–50.

Hopkins, M. (1974). Media, party, and society in Russia. In A. Wells (Ed.), *Mass communications: A world view* (pp. 42–73). Pacific Palisades, CA: Mayfield Publishing Company.

Horlamus, S. (Ed.). (1976). *Mass media in C.M.E.A. countries.* Debrecen: Interpress.

Jakubowicz, K. (1993). Freedom vs. equality. *East European Constitutional Review, 2*(3), 42–48.

Lekovic, Z., & Bjelica, M. (1976). *Communication policies in Yugoslavia.* Paris: United Nations Educational, Scientific and Cultural Organization.

McNair, B. (1994). Media in post-Soviet Russia: An overview. *European Journal of Communication, 9*; 115–135.

Noam, E. (1991). *Television in Europe.* New York: Oxford University Press.

Orcutt, A. (1992). Radio in Hungary: A slow transition. In A. L. Hester, L. Reybold, & K. Conger (Eds.), *The post-Communist press in Eastern and Central Europe: New studies.* (Pp. 51–70). Atlanta: The University of Georgia Press.

Radojkovic, M. (1994). Mass media between state monopoly and individual freedom: Media restructuring and restriction in former Yugoslavia. *European Journal of Communication, 9,* 137–148.

RFE/RL Research Staff. (1992). The media in Eastern Europe. *RFE/RL Research Report 1,* 26–58.

RFE/RL Research Staff. (1993). The media in the countries of the Former

Soviet Union. *RFE/RL Research Staff* 2, 5–15, 27.

RFE/RL Research Staff. (1994). The former Yugoslavia: The media and violence. *RFE/RL Research Report, 3, 5,* 40–47.

Reid, J. E. (1992). A media system on the verge of change: TV in Bulgaria. In A. L. Hester, L. Reybold, & K. Conger (Eds.), *The post-communist press in Eastern and Central Europe: New studies.* Atlanta: The University of Georgia Press.

Rothschild, J. (1989). *Return to diversity.* New York: Oxford University Press.

Sennitt, A. G. (Ed.). (1995). *World radio TV handbook* (Vol 49). New York: Billboard Books.

Webster, D. (1993). *A report on freedom of the media in Eastern Europe and in the countries of the former Soviet Union: A work in progress.* City: Transatlantic Dialogue on European Broadcasting.

Xhixho, A. (1992). Albania's radio and television. In A. L. Hester, L. Reybold, & K. Conger (Eds.), *The post-Communist press in Eastern and Central Europe: New studies.* Atlanta: The University of Georgia Press.

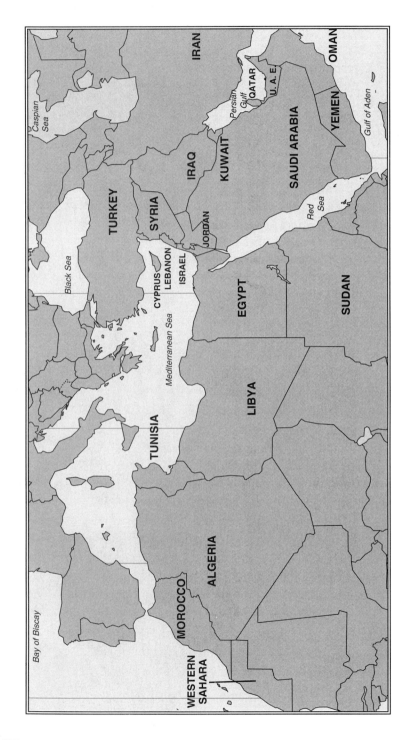

Chapter 7

The Middle East and North Africa

Hussein Y. Amin

This chapter describes radio and television broadcasting in the Middle East focusing on the Arab World, which includes North Africa. It is important to note that the term "Middle East" is subject to different geographical interpretations and includes Turkey, Iran, Israel and Cyprus. The term "Arab World," which is also used in this chapter, describes those countries in the Middle East and North Africa that are bound together by strong religious, linguistic, ethnic, cultural, and psychological ties. Therefore, the countries discussed in this chapter include Algeria, Bahrain, Cyprus, Egypt, Iran, Iraq, Israel, Jordan, Kuwait, Lebanon, Libya, Morocco, Oman, Palestine, Qatar, Saudi Arabia, Syria, Sudan, Tunisia, Turkey, United Arab Emirates (UAE) and Yemen (see Table 7.1).

The Arab World occupies a large geographical area that is estimated at approximately 13,738,000 square kilometers equivalent to 10.8 % of the Earth's surface. It extends from the shores of the Atlantic Ocean in the West to the Persian Gulf in the East. The population was estimated in early 1990 at around 200 million (Labib, Kandil, & Abu Bakr, 1983).

The function of the media in the Arab World can be defined as conveying news and information of general interest, interpreting and com-

Table 7.1
The Middle East and North Africa

Country	Population (in Millions)	Growth (%)	Land Area (square kilometers)	GNP/Capita (1992 U.S. Currency)	Radio Sets (in Millions)	Television Sets (in Millions)
Northern Africa[b]						
Algeria	27.9	2.5	2,381,741	1,830	3.50	2.00
Egypt	58.9	2.3	1,001,449	630	16.45	5.00
Libya	5.1	3.4	1,759,540	—	1.00	0.50
Morocco	28.6	2.3	446,550	1,040	5.10	1.21
Sudan	28.2	3.1	2,505,813	—	5.76	0.25
Tunisia	8.7	1.9	163,610	1,740	1.70	0.65
Western Sahara	0.2	2.8	266,000	—	—	—
Western Asia[b]						
Bahrain	0.6	2.4	678	7,150	0.32	0.27
Cyprus	0.7	1.1	9,251	9,820	0.20	0.23
Iran	61.2	3.6	1,648,000	2,190	13.00	7.00

	Population	Population growth	Land surface area	GNP per capita	Radio sets	TV sets
Iraq	*19.9*	*3.7*	*438,317*	*—*	*3.70*	*1.00*
Israel	*5.4*	*1.5*	*20,770*	*13,230*	*2.25*	*1.50*
Jordan	*4.2*	*3.3*	*97,740*	*1,120*	*0.98*	*0.25*
Kuwait	*1.3*	*3.3*	*17,818*	*—*	*1.00*	*0.80*
Lebanon	*3.6*	*2.0*	*10,400*	*—*	*2.25*	*1.10*
Oman	*1.9*	*4.9*	*212,457*	*6,490*	*0.90*	*1.50*
Qatar	*0.5*	*1.0*	*11,000*	*16,240*	*0.18*	*0.25*
Saudi Arabia	*18.0*	*3.2*	*2,149,690*	*7,940*	*3.80*	*4.70*
Syria	*14.0*	*3.7*	*185,180*	*1,170*	*3.00*	*0.70*
Turkey	*61.8*	*2.2*	*779,452*	*1,950*	*8.80*	*10.53*
United Arab Emirates	*1.7*	*1.9*	*83,600*	*22,220*	*0.49*	*0.17*
Yemen	*12.9*	*3.4*	*527,968*	*520*	*0.67*	*0.10*

Note. Population (mid 1994 estimates), population growth (natural increase), and Gross national product per capita (1992) in U.S. dollar equivalents are from *1994 World Population Data Sheet*, Washington D.C., Population Reference Bureau, 1994. Radio and television set figures are from A. G. Sennit (Ed.), *World Radio TV Handbook*, Volume 49, New York: Billboard Books,1995. Land surface area figures are from *UN Statistical Yearbook, 1991/2*

ᵇ These are the new categories used by the United Nations. The former Soviet Republics Armenia, Azerbaijan and Georgia are also classified as Western Asia. They are discussed in Chapter 6. Iran is now officially classified as South Central Asia, but is included in this chapter because of its close geographical and cultural ties with these countries.

menting on events as well as providing opinion and perspectives, reinforcing social norms and cultural awareness through the dissemination of information about the culture and the society, providing specialized data for commercial promotion and services, and entertaining (Rugh, 1979).

Radio and television broadcasting in the Arab World are absolute monopolies and under direct government supervision. Most Arab states' governments own, operate, and control the broadcast institutions. The main reason for centralizing broadcasting in the Arab States is the desire of the states to preserve their national unity as well as centralization in government and administration. Other reasons include the high cost of establishing a radio or television system in terms of technology and resources, Arab governments' utilization of the broadcast media as a political and a propaganda tool and their interest in keeping them out of hostile hands, and the relatively high illiteracy rates in the Arab World. Because radio and television bypass illiteracy, it is used as an arm of the government to control the public (Amin & Boyd, 1993). Most Arab radio and television systems are subsidized by governments and partially financed by advertising revenues.

DEVELOPMENT OF RADIO IN THE ARAB WORLD

Radio broadcasting started in many of the Arab states on a commercial basis, funded by individuals or corporations as in Algeria in 1925, Egypt in 1926, and Tunisia in 1935. All of these stations were profit-oriented operations based on the selling of broadcast program products, radio sets, and broadcast commercial messages (Labib et al., 1983).

Government radio stations were established in these countries after the elimination of those private stations. Many Arab states started their systems by giving the task to a foreign company. Egypt, for instance, authorized the British Marconi Company to operate the government system (1934–1948). Tunisia authorized the French broadcasting authority to establish radio broadcasting (1939). Radio made its entry to the rest of the Arab states at various times during the next 30 years: Morocco in 1928, Iraq in 1936, Lebanon in 1938, Libya in 1939, the Sudan in 1940, Syria in 1941, Somalia in 1943, Northern Yemen in 1947, Jordan in 1948, Saudi Arabia in 1949, Kuwait in 1951, Southern

Yemen in 1954, Mauritania in 1956, the occupied territories in 1964, Oman in 1970, and the United Arab Emirates (UAE) in 1971 (Labib et al., 1983).

Nearly all of these radio broadcast stations are nonprofit government services. However, during the last decade, the Arab states have witnessed a move toward commercial radio broadcasting operations, such as Radio Mediterranee Internationale in Morocco in 1982, and Arab Radio and Television (ART) and the Middle East Broadcasting Center (MBC) in 1993, both of which are Saudi-owned radio and television networks which operated from outside Saudi Arabia. In addition, Dubai has commercial radio stations that derive their income from advertisements and exist alongside the governments' owned and operated noncommercial stations.

DEVELOPMENT OF TELEVISION IN THE ARAB WORLD

Television is pervasive in nearly all of Arab society; the only countries where television is not used by large numbers of citizens are Yemen and the Sudan, as these countries are less developed economically. Television broadcasting began in the Arab world in the 1950s. It was introduced in Morocco in 1954 and in Algeria, Iraq, and Lebanon in 1956. It progressed to the other Arab states during the 1960s and 1970s, being introduced in Egypt and Syria in 1960, Kuwait in 1961, Sudan in 1962, Democratic Yemen in 1964, and Saudi Arabia in 1965. Tunisia's system followed in 1966 and after the Middle East War in 1967 Jordan established its television system. Libya started its own system in 1968. Qatar developed its system in 1970, followed closely by Bahrain in 1973, Oman in 1974, and Yemen in 1975. In the UAE, Abu Dhabi was the first to develop a television system in 1969, with Dubai following in 1972 (Labib et al., 1983, p. 15). With the exception of some experiments in North Africa and Lebanon, Arab television in general is a government-operated activity. Historically, governments have set the media agenda and have viewed television as an effective means of promoting their political, religious, cultural and economic agenda.

Both the desire of Arab governments to support the development of a strong television industry and the popularity of television in the Arab world are related to political, cultural, and social factors. Arab households are closely knit and selfcontained, especially in the conservative Gulf States where most entertaining is done in the home. Saudi Arabia, the most conservative of the Gulf states, saw the visual medium as an acceptable alternative to public cinemas (still not permitted in the kingdom), reasoning that they would of necessity show both Western films and television programs as well as material from other Arab countries, mostly from Egypt. Also, state -or quasi-state-controlled television is a means of filtering what receivers see. At least this was the case before videocassette recorders became popular in the Arab world (Amin & Boyd, 1993).

ARAB RADIO AND TELEVISION SYSTEMS

Regardless of the fact that most Arab radio and television broadcast systems are under the direct control of Arab governments and have similar organizational structure and characteristics, there are some significant differences among them in the political rules by which they play. Arab radio and television systems can be divided into two groups. The first group operates under the mobilization type of broadcasting system, as in Algeria, Egypt, Iraq, Syria, Libya, South Yemen, and the Sudan. These countries have treated radio and television in a very similar manner and have exercised complete control over the broadcast media. They have also strongly pushed the use of radio and telvision as instruments of political communications with the exception of Egypt, which is the most influential state in terms of television development, program appeals, and exports (Rugh, 1979).

Egypt's theater tradition and long-established film and radio industry have provided the talent to a strong television industry that not only has enabled Egypt to produce most of its own television programming, but also has provided television products and talents that Arab countries lack in creating an indigenous television production industry (Amin & Boyd, 1993).

The second major group includes all other Arab states except Morocco and Lebanon. This group can be labeled as having the governmental type of broadcasting system. These states have governmental control over radio and television broadcasting but they are more relaxed than the previous group in that they do not push or use their broadcast media to gain total government support (Rugh, 1979, p. 114).

The Mobilization System

It is important to understand that the development of radio and television in the mobilization system began when revolutionary regimes came to power. These regimes gave great attention to electronic media, promoting the expansion of a government-owned media empire inside the state which could be used as a political tool to mobilize the public and to deliver the official line.

Egypt. Egypt has the most powerful and the most extensive as well as influential radio broadcasting system in the Arab world. Radio broadcasting started in Egypt in the early 1920s but the official radio service did not begin broadcasting until May 31, 1934. After the Egyptian revolution in 1952, broadcasting came under complete government control and radio became the voice of the Egyptian revolution.

Nasser, Egypt's first president, understood the power of the medium and was able to capitalize on the oral Arab culture and the power and the emotionalism of the Arabic language. Therefore, he devoted a great deal of the Egyptian administrative energy and extensive economic resources to develop Egyptian radio broadcasting. Programming was expanded to include the general program, the national European program, the Sudan program, the foreign language and the beamed services programs, the Voice of the Arabs program, the Alexandria local service, the Palestine broadcast, the People's program, the second program, the Middle East program, the Holy Koran broadcast, and the youth broadcast. Most of these radio services and programs were somehow politicized and promoted the image of the President.

Nasser's successor, Anwar Sadat, made sure that the government maintained control over the broadcast media after an incident in 1971 when Vice President Aly Sabry attempted a coup by trying to obtain control of the radio and television building. After the failure of this coup, the Egyptian head of state paid much more attention to the radio and television broadcast (Napoli & Amin, 1994, p. 7).

In 1971, the Egyptian Radio and Television Union (ERTU) was formed with the objective to exercise complete and full control over all broadcast material for either radio or television in Egypt. On April 1, 1981, the broadcasting network concept was introduced in Egypt. Egyptian radio is now composed of seven networks: (a) the main network, (b) the regional network, (c) the educational network, (d) the religious network, (e) the commercial network, (f) the Arab network, and (g) the beamed international service network (El Halwani, 1984).

Egyptian television began broadcasting on July 21, 1960, a date chosen to mark the 8th anniversary of the 1952 revolution. The choice of dates reflected Nasser's high level of interest in establishing television in Egypt. The broadcast began with a verse from the Holy Koran and a speech from Nasser on the celebration. From the very beginning, the most important source of programming on Egyptian television was films, as Egypt had already established the most advanced and sophisticated film industry in the region. American and British programs were also used by Egyptian television until the 1967 war. After the war, the amount of foreign programs broadcast over Egyptian television decreased substantially due to the withdrawal of the diplomatic relations between Egypt and both the United States and Britain. Programs from the Soviet Union were substituted. This situation continued until the 1973 war. At the conclusion of the war, Egyptian television tended to reflect the changing international political orientation of the country toward the Western countries (El Halwani, 1984).

In 1975, the government decided to convert the television system to color. The conversion to color did not occur until 1977. The next major shift in television broadcasting did not occur until the late 1980s and early 1990s. Until that point, Egyptian television services were composed of two national networks covering almost all parts of the state. In 1990, the Egyptian government under President Hosni Mubarak started to decentralize and liberalize the system by establishing five local television channels covering different parts of the state, in addition to a teletext service information channel (Amin, 1990). At the same time, the Egyptian government began privatization of the medium by introducing the first cable system in Egypt. Cable News Egypt was introduced in June of

1990 as a joint venture between the ERTU and other investors and carried services like MTV music television and the Cable News Network (CNN) (Foote & Amin, 1993).

Syria. The development of radio started in 1946 when the Syrian broadcast organization was founded. However, the advancement of the system occurred differently than it had in Egypt. Syria's radio broadcasting was greatly influenced by the country's union with Egypt from 1958 to 1961. Syria's radio employees learned from the Egyptians the philosophy of radio propaganda. Syria's main radio services continue to be the main program and voice of the people (Boyd, 1993).

Television in Syria started in 1960 as a result of its brief unification with Egypt. In addition to the main station in Damascus, other stations were introduced during the 1960s in Aleppo and Homs, and these stations were connected in the 1970s by the main station through microwave links. The upgrade and expansion of the Syrian television system was strongly motivated by the availability of television signals from other countries, specifically Israel (the two countries were at war in 1967 and 1973), Iraq, and Jordan. In 1975, a decision was made to introduce color television in Syria (Boyd, 1993).

Television in Syria is directly financed by both the government and advertising sales, and most of the programs, such as news, drama, music, and public affairs programs, are designed to promote the political regime, as in other Arab states under mobilization broadcasting.

Iraq. Radio was first introduced in 1935 but the government radio service did not begin broadcasting until 1939. The Iraqi government did not pay much attention to the development of radio until it started receiving hostile radio broadcasting from neighboring states, especially Egypt's radio messages against the Iraqi prime minister, Noury el Said, who was asking for Arab support for the pro-Western Baghdad pact (Boyd, 1993).

In July of 1958, a military coup headed by Abdel Karim Kassem took over the country and started utilizing the power of electronic media to gain political support internally and to communicate with Arab countries externally. The Iraqi revolutionary regime at that time relied on the former Soviet Union for technical assistance as well as for the establishment of broadcast facilities. From the beginning, Iraqi radio broadcast was pro-Nasser, but after the unification between Egypt and Syria it immediately became an anti-Nasser broadcast service. Most of the radio services during the Iran–Iraq war called for Arab support for the Iraqi regime headed by Saddam Hussein, who in 1990 and 1991 during the Gulf crisis allocated most of the services and programs to attack those countries which had helped him before. Other messages primarily focused on claims and issues, such as the historical rights that Iraq has over Kuwait, religious justifications for the invasion, and the occupation of Kuwait. The latter was portrayed as a confrontation between Moslems and non-Moslems. Importance was also given to the imbalance of wealth between the rich Gulf states and the poor Arab countries. The Iraqi media also stressed the linkage between the liberation of Palestine and the withdrawal from Kuwait (Amin, 1992).

Iraqi radio programs consist of the main program, the Voice of the Masses, Kurdish and other minority language programs, and foreign and beamed programs. Most of these services are mobilized for propaganda supporting the Iraqi political leadership.

Television in Iraq started in 1956. Very quickly, the political power structure realized the importance of the medium and ordered an increase in the power of the Baghdad station. However, this era ended when Abdel Karim Kassem was overthrown in 1963 and his body displayed on live television. New stations were opened, however, north of Baghdad, (viz., Kirkouk in 1967 and Mousul in 1968) and south of Baghdad (Basra in 1968). At the beginning of the 1970s, a second television channel was introduced and, in 1967, color television came into being. Like radio, television is a heavily political medium and most of the different kinds of programs carry political messages promoting the image of the Iraqi ruling system (Martin & Chaudhary, 1983, p. 105).

Algeria. Algeria started its radio broadcast services in 1967 as a service to French colonists. Most of the program services were relayed from Paris and the first Arabic radio broadcast channel was introduced in 1940 followed by a Berber channel (KABYLA) in 1948. Politically, these services' main purpose was to provide propaganda and support for the French presence. The main impetus behind the development of Algeria's broadcast system was that the country is relatively large in size and its population scattered (Head, 1985, p. 35).

The French broadcasting organization Radio Diffusion Television Francais (RTF) installed radio transmitters in key cities in North Algeria. In January of 1963, RTF became Radio Diffusion Television Algerie (RTA). The French model of government control influenced the radio broadcast; from the beginning, RTA was under tight control from the Ministry of Information and Culture. Ahmed bin Billa, the first Algerian president, began the establishment of state socialism in Algeria and thought that radio broadcasting would play a major rule in its development. He was followed by Houari Boumedienne, who came into power in 1965 and strove to build up Algeria's national identity and cultural independence away from the West, especially France. He also started a mission to Arabize most of the existing programs. Tremendous investments were made to promote broadcasting technology during the period of 1965 to 1985. There are currently three radio services—two domestic channels and one international service.

Television broadcasting in Algeria began in 1956 but immediately faced a problem of securing television programs. Algeria relied heavily on transmission from Europe via a relay station located on the Balearic islands. Like radio, Algeria started to Arabize the medium and by 1969 had established a televised Arabic literacy pilot project carried by UNESCO (Head, 1974, pp. 31–32). Algeria under President Ben Jadid began to move toward political and economic reform, which resulted in the breakup of RTA into smaller enterprises, thereby decreasing the level of state control and opening the door for private entrepreneurs to get into the broadcasting business. RTA was split into four entities in 1987: (a) the National Enterprise of Television, (b) the National Enterprise for Audiovisual Production, (c) the National Enterprise for Radio and (d) the TDA (an enterprise managing television equipment; Mohammedy, 1993).

Television broadcasting in Algeria is provided through one channel covering the entire country through microwave links and via satellite distribution with a schedule of a variety of program types broadcast approximately 64 hr per week. The system is state controlled and the programs, particularly news and news programs, are designed to promote the policies of the current political regime.

Sudan. Radio broadcasting was introduced in 1940 but Radio Omdurman was unable to cover the entire state until 1972. However, the advancement of the system had a similar problem to that faced by Algeria. Sudan is the largest country in Africa and its population is scattered throughout the state. Sudan gained independence from Britain in 1956 and in May of 1969 a military coup headed by Jaafar Nemeiry took over the country. Radio services in the Sudan are composed of the following programs: the national program, the Koranic station, Voice of the Sudanese Nation, National Unity Radio, and the Juba local service (Head, 1974, p. 50).

Television began in the Sudan in 1962 with the inauguration of a low power transmitter in Omdurman, built with the assistance of the Federal Republic of Germany. The expansion of the television facilities was delayed due to lack of funds and personnel. Later, the government realized that it must develop a national system for mass communication. In 1972, a second television station was introduced, soon followed by a third station in the Nile province. Color television was introduced in 1976. In 1978, the first satellite system, Sudo Sat, was established to link the country and to achieve national integration but faced numerous technical, personnel, and operational problems. The one national color channel broadcasts approximately 52 hr a week (Head, 1974, p. 51).

Libya. Radio broadcasting made its entry in Libya in 1939, and after gaining independence from Italy in December of 1951, El Senousi's government started directing some of the first funds from the newly discovered oil fields to promote and advance the broadcast system. The first national radio service began broadcasting from Tripoli after independence in 1955, followed by a similar radio station in Benghazi. The official inauguration of the national service was not announced, however, until 1957 when the two stations came under the organization defined as Radio Libya (Head, 1974).

When Qaddafi came to power on September 1, 1969, the new military regime stopped all foreign broadcasting within the country. The development of radio in Libya was very similar to Egypt's experience, because Qaddafi was greatly influenced by Egypt's Nasser. He admired the Voice of Arabs broadcast from Cairo and thereafter started to invest huge amounts of money to advance radio broadcasting in Libya. The broadcast enterprise in Libya was restructured on June 2, 1973 when the People's Committees took over control of the radio operation in Tripoli and Benghazi (Katz & Wedell, 1977, p. 95). The National Service of Libyan Broadcasting broadcast 19 hr each day. There are now two radio channels: the European program and the Libyan Jamahiriya broadcast, which include the Holy Koran program (Boyd, 1993).

Libyan television broadcasting started in 1968 with the help of the British Broadcasting Corporation (BBC). Much of the development of the television broadcasting system happened in the 1970s and 1980s. The content of the television broadcast schedules tends to be serious rather than entertaining. News, public affairs programs, and discussion programs represent a good deal of the television schedule. Messages stress Arab unity, Pan-Arabism, and Arab integration (Boyd, 1993).

South Yemen. Radio made its entry to South Yemen, now united with North Yemen, in May 1954, and in August of the same year the Aden Broadcasting Services was officially inaugurated. The radio facilities were greatly expanded in the late 1950s with the help of the British government and, after independence, the Soviet Union. In 1974, a decree was issued establishing government control of all kinds of mass communication.

Television was also introduced in South Yemen with the help of the British government. When the National Liberation Front assumed power from Aden, the quality of the television service deteriorated due to the lack of technical assistance in terms of spare parts and maintenance. The state has continued to operate a monochrome service because its main focus is on radio broadcasting.

The Governmental Broadcasting Type

The governmental broadcasting type in the Arab world tended to be slower in development and the broadcast programming less aggressively political than in the mobilization type. Countries operating under this kind of broadcasting include Bahrain, Kuwait, Jordan, North Yemen, Oman, Qatar, Saudi Arabia, Tunisia, and UAE (Martin & Chaudhary, 1983, p. 163).

Jordan. Radio started in 1948. Jordanian radio, which is officially known as the Hashemite Broadcasting Service, was expanded in the 1950s in order for the Jordanian government to counter broadcasted attacks on the government from Cairo for taking orders from the British. In 1959, King Hussein inaugurated the Amman Broadcasting Service. The service was never very powerful or influential because it did not reach the neighboring countries of Syria, Iraq, Israel, and Saudi Arabia. However, because it was a commercial service, the income it generated helped to pay the broadcast service bill until 1967. One result of the 1967 war was the general cooling of the broadcast propaganda in the Middle East. The Jordanian main broadcast service is now composed of the main Arabic program, the English service, and the FM stereo service (Boyd, 1993, pp. 93–100).

Television made its entry to Jordan in 1968 with a 3-hr transmission on one channel. In the early 1970s, another channel was added carrying foreign programs. Color television was introduced to Jordanian television in 1974 and most program formats are adapted from Western television programming (Boyd, 1993, p. 101).

Tunisia. Radio started when the Tunisian and the French governments signed an agreement establishing the Radio Broadcasting Service in 1939. After independence, the Tunisian government began to develop broadcast facilities and initiated a plan to modernize the system, especially the Arabic service. Tunisia's radio is utilized as a tool to promote national development, especially in the fields of agriculture, industry, and public health (El Gabri, 1974, p. 30).

Television was not introduced to Tunisia until May 31, 1966, Tunisia's national day, and offered both information and entertainment. Programs are mixed, in French and in Arabic, and as in Tunisia's radio service, national development issues are given great attention.

The Gulf States

The Gulf states are composed of six countries: Bahrain, Kuwait, Oman, Qatar, Saudi Arabia, and the UAE. After the 1973 war, these countries became a major international economic force because of their oil exports. It is therefore understandable that they play an important part in the political arena in the Arab world.

Saudi Arabia. Radio began in 1949 after the government debated the issue with the *Ulema*, the religious leaders, who at the beginning rejected the idea of introducing radio broadcasting to the country. Faisal, soon to become crown prince and later king, was put in charge of Saudi Arabian broadcasting. Radio broadcasting in Saudi Arabia progressed during the 1950s and 1960s because of the government's interest in decreasing the size of the audience of foreign broadcasts. After the October 1973 Middle East War, radio broadcasting witnessed a tremendous improvement due to a greatly increased budget arising from the growth of oil revenues. Radio services in Saudi Arabia are composed of the General Program, the Holy Koran Broadcast, the International Foreign Language Program, and the European Services. Radio in Saudi Arabia has a religious tone because Saudi Arabia is considered to be the center of the Islamic World (Boyd, 1993, pp. 137–147).

Officially, television broadcasting in Saudi Arabia began in 1965 but in fact earlier, unofficial broadcast services were initiated in 1955 and 1957. AGLTV went on the air in Dhahran, the eastern province of Saudi Arabia, and was operated by the United States Air Force. Similarly, a second station began broadcasting, also from Dhahran, in 1957. Station HZ-22-TV broadcast from the ARAMCO compound and served the company's American employees.

Like radio, television was also subject to opposition and rejection and earned the antagonism of conservative religious groups. Saudi Arabia initially operated two national television systems. Color television made its entry to Saudi Arabia in 1976. Television programming in Saudi Arabia is similar to radio in the sense that Saudi Arabia is the heart of the Islamic nations. Therefore, religious programming has special importance in the country.

Kuwait. The Kuwaiti radio station began broadcasting in 1961 after independence. Because Kuwait is a small country, introduction of both radio and television broadcasting faced few difficulties in terms of financing, because large terrestrial networks were not required. Kuwaiti radio broadcast services include the main program, the second program, the English program, the Koran program, the music program, and the Persian and Urdu service. Most of the radio broadcast facilities were destroyed during the Gulf War, but immediately after the liberation of Kuwait the Kuwaiti government replaced the facilities.

Television started in Kuwait informally at the end of the 1950s. Radio Corporation of America television started a low power station in Kuwait City to promote the sale of television receivers. At independence in 1961, however, the Kuwaiti Ministry of Information took control of the system after changing it to European standards. The system was advanced and developed during the 1960s and 1970s, especially after the 1973 war because of increase in petroleum revenues. Color television emerged in 1974. The television broadcast in Kuwait includes two channels and programming is a mixture of news and entertainment.

Qatar. Radio broadcasting service started in 1968. Great Britain announced that it would leave the area and grew after the country's independence in 1972. Programming includes the Arabic program, the English services, and the Urdu program, which is directed toward Pakistani expatriates. Most of the radio programs are a mixture of news, entertainment, religious, and educational programs.

Monochrome television was introduced in Qatar in August of 1970 and color television soon replaced it in 1974. The Arabic program telecasts on Channels 9 and 11; the second television service, which broadcasts entirely in English, operates on an ultrahigh frequency and utilizes more than one channel in the spectrum.

Bahrain. Bahrain started its own radio broadcasting service in 1955. The station increased hours of transmission gradually to 14 hr by 1980. Bahrain started an English-language radio service in 1977 because the language is widely spoken in both Bahrain and in the neighboring states. Programs are a mix of news, education and entertainment, and religion.

Color television broadcasting was established in Bahrain in 1973. At the beginning of 1990s, Bahraini television had two channels with a mix of programs, most popular of which are the Arabic serials from Egypt.

UAE. Radio was introduced by British armed forces in the Gulf and Abu Dhabi was first emirate to introduce Arabic radio broadcasting in 1969. On independence, Abu Dhabi Radio changed its name to United Arab Emirates Radio to reflect the country's name change. The federal government advanced and promoted the service during the mid-1970s and also added an English-language program.

Television transmission started in Dubai as a monochrome system in August of 1969 before the formation of the UAE federation. After the formation of the UAE, Dubai's system became the national television channel owned and operated by the federal government. Color television was introduced in 1974. By the mid-1980s, the UAE had added a second national television channel heavily dependent on English programs, especially from the West. Dubai has played a very important role in the UAE in terms of broadcasting services and has offered commercial radio services as well as two color television services that are a mix of Arabic and English (Merrill, 1983).

Oman. Radio was launched in 1970 and was expanded in 1973 with a national Arabic program. In 1980, an English program was added. Just like the rest of the Gulf states, television was considered to be an important tool for development. Television broadcasting began in Oman in 1974 on one channel. Television programs are compiled of news, information, and cultural programs with great dependency on Egyptian broadcast television products (Boyd, 1993).

Yemen. North and South Yemen, now united into one country, developed broadcast systems separately according to the political environment of each country. As was discussed earlier, South Yemen's system developed under the mobilization type of broadcasting while North Yemen's system developed under the governmental type of broadcasting.

Radio was developed in North Yemen in 1947. The three radio stations of Sana's broadcast only in Arabic. In contrast, South Yemen developed its radio services back in 1954 and relied on the BBC Arabic service. Arabic programming was introduced through the Aden broadcasting service.

Television was introduced in North Yemen in September of 1975, when the government formally opened the Sana'a-based television broadcast station, and it was broadcast in color. In contrast, South Yemen's, monochrome television broadcasts started early in 1965 with the help of the British. Since the unification, many plans have been developed to integrate the electronic media of North Yemen and South Yemen and are being evaluated for implementation (El Gamrah, 1982, p. 253).

Lebanon. Lebanon and Morocco are considered the most liberal states in the Arab World in terms of broadcasting. The French government in Lebanon began the country's radio broadcast service in 1937. During the civil war, unofficial broadcasting came to Lebanon and many unofficial stations started to operate. More than 50 of these stations were in use during the war in Lebanon.

Lebanese television started in May of 1959 with one channel. A second commercial channel was introduced in 1962. Tele-Orient was the first television station and was owned by Lebanese interest and the American Broadcasting Company, which later sold its share to the British Thompson Corporation. Lebanese television is a mix of Western and foreign programming, particularly from the United States, Europe, and Egypt. Unofficial television broadcasting started during the Lebanese civil war. These networks included Tele-Lebanon, Star of Hope, Fahi Television, and Lebanese Broadcasting Corporation. Television in Lebanon is a unique case in the Arab world. More than 40 private television stations are now operating in Lebanon; however, a decree was recently issued by the Lebanese Cabinet that will reorganize the radio and television broadcast industry in Lebanon.

Morocco. Morocco began broadcasting by radio in 1928 from Rabat. The system grew during the 1940s and 1950s to offer two radio stations: the "A" program in French and the "B" program in Arabic and Berber. Later, a "C" program in Spanish and English was established. In

January of 1962 after Morocco's independence, an executive order shifted RTM (Radio Diffusion–Moroccan) to the control of the Ministry of Information. RTM radio currently consists of three networks based in Rabat plus nine regional stations scattered throughout the country. The national radio network is the most important service for the lower socioeconomic levels. RTM's programming includes music, news and public affairs programs, and entertainment programs.

Television made an entry in Morocco in March of 1962 . RTM-TV reaches over 80% of the population and in July of 1989 the first private television station, 2M International, was introduced. 2M International is scrambled 10 hr a day and unscrambled for 5 hr.

As was mentioned early in this chapter, the Middle East includes non-Arab nations, such as Cyprus, Iran, Israel, and Turkey. Each of these countries has different broadcast systems and is discussed separately.

Cyprus. Radio Fonikon Idryma Kyprou (RIK; Cyprus Broadcasting Corporation), an independent corporation supervised by a government-appointed board of governors, began radio broadcasting in Cyprus in 1959. The system is funded by advertising and license fees and has two national networks, one broadcasting in Greek and the other broadcasting in Turkish, English, and Armenian. RIK also operates an external service in English and Arabic. In addition, the British Ministry of Defense established the Sound and Vision Corporation in 1948, which operates two radio networks and one television channel (Drost, 1991). Television service was introduced in 1957 and provides a mix of programs, although most are news and news programs.

In 1974, intervention by Turkish troops in Cyprus resulted in the establishment of a separate administration by the Turkish Cypriot minority. The media in Northern Cyprus have since developed completely separately. Radio broadcasting started in 1983 followed by television. Radio and television broadcasting operations are under the Bayrak Radio Television Korporasi (Bayrak Radio and Television Corporation). Bayrak Radio has two networks: a domestic network in Turkish and an international program in four languages. The television service has three channels in Turkish, Greek, English, and Arabic (Drost, 1991).

Iran. In 1979 at the time of the establishment of the Islamic Republic of Iran, the new government put the country's radio and television networks under the control of the Seda Va Sima-Ye Jomhuri-Ye Eslami-Ye Iran (Voice and Vision of the Islamic Republic of Iran). The broadcasting service, which was originally founded in 1954, operates three national radio channels as well as 39 regional radio stations in different languages including Persian, Kurdish, and Arabic in addition to 10 other regional languages. The Iranian radio network also operates an external service in 18 languages including Persian, Arabic, English, French, German, Russian, and Spanish. In addition, underground radio stations which operated from exile in countries such as Iraq and Afghanistan broadcast antigovernment material; the most prominent of these stations were Voice of the Holy Warriors of the People and Radio Iran Toilers. These stations stopped broadcasting in 1990 and 1991, respectively.

The Iranian television service has two networks telecasting approximately 100 hr of television programs a week from the main radio and television center in Tehran and from 28 local television stations (Drost, 1991).

Turkey. Radio and television broadcasting is in the hands of the Turkiye Radio Televizyon Kurumu (TRT), which is a formally independent corporation supervised by a 12-member board appointed by the president. This corporation ensures that the programs do not contradict "the principles of the national policy", an indication that broadcasting in Turkey is under strict government control. The Turkish radio has three national networks in addition to 45 local stations with TRT-1 acting as the general service of news, educational, and entertainment programs (Drost, 1991).

Turkish television, which started its regular broadcasting in 1968 with two channels, is considered to be the major source of news in the country. Two additional channels were introduced in 1989 presenting national coverage in Istanbul and other Turkish cities. A fifth channel has also recently been added.

Israel. Radio and television broadcasting operates under the supervision of the Reshut Hashidur Hayisra'elit (Israeli Broadcasting Authority). Radio and television broadcasting is independent to a large extent and is directed by boards appointed by the Minister of Education and Culture. Kol Isra'el (Voice of Israel) has five national radio networks broadcasting in Hebrew, Arabic, and other minority languages (Merrill, 1983, p. 111). The second program (Reshet Bet) is the main general service and broadcasts up-to-date news items. The external service, which broadcasts news worldwide, is threatened by the need to provide air time for the introduction of a new Russian channel serving the Soviet immigrants. There are also two independent radio stations operating from ships anchored off the coast in the international waters and one radio station (Galei Tzahal) run by the army.

Israeli television broadcasting started in 1968 and currently broadcasts around 40 hr of programming per week. There are more than 1,000 cable television stations in Israel and the occupied territories, and most of them broadcast political issues dealing with support for the Palestine Liberation Organization and propagandizing for the extreme right-wing Kach party (Drost, 1991).

INTERNATIONAL RADIO AND TELEVISION BROADCASTING IN THE MIDDLE EAST

Most countries in the Middle East are transmitting their own messages to others to assert their social, political, and economic positions. This wave of new transmission was led by the First World countries and succeeded by other developing countries. The main reason for Arab states to develop international radio services is to export political and religious philosophies, such is the case in Egypt and its popular international radio service "Voice of the Arabs." Competition in the Arab World with regard to international radio services is dominated by countries of the mobilization type, such as Egypt, Iraq, and Libya.

Middle East global television is witnessing a new wave, especially in the Arab states, because Egypt started its international television service (SpaceNet) through The Arab States Satellite Organization followed by Nile Television. Saudi Arabia, realizing the importance of international television services, launched MBC, a London-based operation, followed by ART services consisting of four specialized international television networks for children, movies, sports, and the general channel. In 1994, the Saudis launched a new service called Orbit operating one international television channel. Other services utilizing Arab Sat are Dubai Television, Omani Television, the Jordanian Satellite Channel, Kuwaiti Space Channel, Moroccan Satellite Channel and Tunisian TV7. Turkish channels are popular in the Arab World to an extent causing Arab officials to ban public viewing in some countries.

REFERENCES

Amin, H. Y. (1990). Mass communication policies in the Arab states. *Journal of Arab Research and Studies.* The Arab League Educational, Scientific, and Cultural Organization (ALESCO), Cairo, Egypt.

Amin, H. Y. (1992). The role and the impact of Egyptian International Television Network during the Gulf crisis. In R. Weisenborn (Ed.), *Media in the midst of war: Cairo reporting to the global village.* Cairo: Adham Center Press.

Amin, H. Y., & Boyd, D. A. (1993). The impact of the home video cassette recorder on the Egyptian film and television consumption patterns. *The European Journal of Communications, 18.*

Boyd, D. A. (Ed.). (1993). *Broadcasting in the Arab world: A survey of the electronic media in the Middle East* (2nd ed.). Ames: Iowa State University Press.

Drost, H. (1991). *The world's news media.* New York: Longman.

El Gabri, A. (1974). Al Maghreb. In S. W. Head (Ed.), *Broadcasting in Africa: A continental survey of radio and television.* Philadelphia, PA: Temple University Press.

El Gamrah, A. S. (1982). Management and administration for radio and television in Yemen. *Darassat wa bahouth izaaiyah [Broadcast research and studies], 25.* Tunis, Tunisia: Arab States Broadcasting Union.

El Halwani, M. (1984). *El-izaat el-Arabiya [Arab Broadcasting].* Cairo: Dar al-Fikr al-Arabi.

Foote, J. S. & Amin, H. Y. (1993). Global television news in developing countries: CNN's expansion to Egypt. *Equid Novi: Journal for Journalism in Southern Africa.*

Head, S. W. (Ed.). (1974). *Broadcasting in Africa: A continental survey of radio and television.* Philadelphia, PA: Temple University Press.

Head, S. W. (1985). *World broadcasting systems: A comparative analysis.* Belmont, CA: Wadsworth.

Katz, E., & Wedell, G. (1977). *Broadcasting in the Third World: Promise and performance.* Cambridge, MA: Harvard University Press.

Labib, S., Kandil, H., & Abu Bakr, Y. (1983). *Development of communication in the Arab states: Needs and priorities.* (Publication No. 95). Paris: UNESCO.

Martin, J. L., & Chaudhary, A. G. (1983). *Comparative mass media systems.* New York: Longman.

Merrill, J. (1983). *Global journalism: A survey of the world mass media.* New York: Longman.

Mohammedy, Y. (1993). Algeria. In D. A. Boyd (Ed.), *Broadcasting in the Arab world: A survey of the electronic media in the middle east* (2nd ed.). Ames: Iowa State University Press.

Napoli, J., & Amin, H. Y. (1994). Press freedom in Egypt. In F. Eribo (Ed.), *Communication and press freedom in Africa.* Boulder, CO: Westview.

Rugh, W. A. (1979). *The Arab press.* Syracuse, NY: Syracuse University Press.

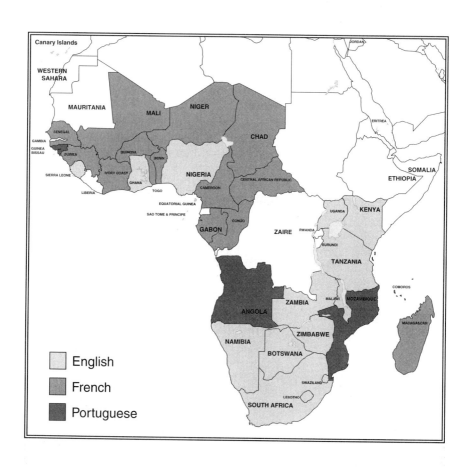

	English
	French
	Portuguese

Chapter 8

Sub-Saharan Africa

**Osabuohien P. Amienyi with
Gerard Igyor on Nigeria**

THE NATURE OF SUB-SAHARAN AFRICA[1]

The Portuguese were the first Europeans to explore Africa in the mid-1400s. In 1884, European countries, such as England, France, and Portugal, began a general scramble for colonies in Africa (The map shows how the area was divided). By 1920, all of the 48 countries in the area called sub-Saharan Africa (also Africa South of the Sahara or Black Africa), with the exception of Ethiopia and Liberia, were under colonial rule. Anticolonial and independence movements developed in the 1950s and new countries were born as each of the colonies became independent (*The New Encyclopaedia Britannica,* 1993).

The peoples of sub-Saharan Africa are culturally diverse. There are wide variations from country to country and within countries. In fact,

---

[1] *Editor's note:* In general, sub-Saharan African countries vary in population, growth rate, geographic size, gross national product (GNP), and media availability (see Table 8.1). Nigeria has by far the largest population in the region. It is estimated that one out of every five Africans is a Nigerian. Nigeria is therefore covered individually by Gerard Igyor. Ethiopia, Zaire, and South Africa are the only other countries with more than 40 million people.

Table 8.1
Sub-Saharan Africa

Country	Population (In Millions)	Growth (%)	Land Area (square kilometers)	GNP/Capita (1992 U.S. Currency)	Radio Sets (In Millions)	Television Sets (In Millions)
Eastern Africa						
Burundi	6.0	2.9	27,834	210	0.30	0.004
Comoros	0.5	3.5	2,235	510	0.06	—
Djibouti	0.6	3.0	23,200	—	0.04	0.02
Eritrea	3.5	2.6	124,993	—	—	—
Ethiopia	55.2	3.1	975,990	110	9.00	0.10
Kenya	27.0	3.3	580,367	330	2.20	0.26
Madagascar	13.7	3.3	587,041	230	2.30	0.13
Malawi	9.5	2.7	118,484	210	2.00	—
Mauritius	1.1	1.5	1,865	2,700	0.38	0.16
Mozambique	15.8	2.7	801,590	60	0.62	0.04
Reunion	0.6	1.8	2,510	—	0.17	0.09
Rwanda	7.7	2.3	26,338	250	—	—
Somalia	9.8	3.2	637,657	(1990) 120	0.30	0.08
Tanzania	29.8	3.4	945,087	110	0.57	0.12
Uganda	19.8	3.0	235,880	170	1.80	0.20
Zambia	9.1	2.8	752,614	290	0.60	0.14
Zimbabwe	11.2	3.0	390,580	570	0.80	0.14
Western Africa						
Benin	5.3	3.1	12,622	410	0.40	0.02
Burkina Faso	10.1	3.1	274,200	290	0.23	0.05
Cape Verde	0.4	2.9	4,033	850	0.06	—
Cote d'Ivoire	13.9	3.5	322,463	670	1.60	0.81
Gambia	1.1	2.7	11,295	390	0.14	—
Ghana	16.9	3.0	238,533	450	4.30	0.25

	Population	Pop. growth	Land surface area	GNP per capita	Radio	TV
Guinea	*6.4*	*2.5*	*245,857*	*510*	*0.23*	*0.07*
Guinea-Bissau	*1.1*	*2.1*	*36,125*	*210*	*0.04*	*—*
Liberia	*2.9*	*3.3*	*111,369*	*(1987) 460*	*0.60*	*0.05*
Mali	*9.1*	*3.0*	*1,240,192*	*300*	*0.35*	*0.01*
Mauritania	*2.3*	*2.9*	*1,025,520*	*530*	*0.30*	*0.001*
Niger	*8.8*	*3.4*	*1,267,000*	*300*	*0.44*	*0.03*
Nigeria	*98.1*	*3.1*	*923,768*	*320*	*18.00*	*6.10*
Senegal	*8.2*	*2.7*	*196,722*	*780*	*0.85*	*0.06*
Sierra Leone	*4.6*	*2.7*	*71,740*	*170*	*0.90*	*0.03*
Togo	*4.3*	*3.6*	*56,785*	*400*	*0.72*	*0.15*
Middle Africa						
Angola	*11.2*	*2.7*	*1,246,700*	*—*	*0.45*	*0.05*
Cameroon	*13.1*	*2.9*	*475,442*	*820*	*1.50*	*0.02*
Central Af. Republic	*3.1*	*2.4*	*622,984*	*410*	*0.18*	*0.01*
Chad	*6.5*	*2.6*	*1,284,000*	*220*	*1.31*	*—*
Congo	*2.4*	*2.6*	*342,000*	*1,030*	*0.24*	*0.01*
Equatorial Guinea	*0.4*	*2.6*	*28,051*	*330*	*0.13*	*0.003*
Gabon	*1.1*	*2.7*	*267,667*	*4,450*	*0.16*	*0.04*
Zaire	*42.5*	*3.4*	*2,345,409*	*(1989) 230*	*3.48*	*0.02*
Southern Africa						
Botswana	*1.4*	*2.7*	*581,730*	*2,790*	*0.14*	*0.01*
Lesotho	*1.9*	*1.9*	*30,355*	*590*	*0.12*	*0.05*
Namibia	*1.6*	*3.3*	*824,292*	*1,610*	*0.23*	*0.04*
South Africa	*41.2*	*2.6*	*1,221,037*	*2,670*	*11.20*	*3.45*
Swaziland	*0.8*	*3.2*	*17,364*	*1,080*	*0.12*	*0.13*

Note. Population (mid-1994 estimates), population growth (natural increase), and Gross national product per capita (1992) in U.S. dollar equivalents are from 1994 *World Population Data Sheet*, Washington D.C., Population Reference Bureau, 1994. Radio and television set figures are from A. G. Sennitt (Ed.), *World Radio TV Handbook*, Volume 49, New York: Billboard Books, 1995. Land surface area figures are from *UN Statistical Yearbook, 1991/2*, New York: UN Statistical Office, 1992. Because of their small size, Ascension Island, Mayotte, St. Helena, Seychelles, Sao Tome and Principe, and Tristan Da Cunha have been omitted.

the region's diversity is so great that it can be said to be sub-Saharan Africa's fascination (Amienyi, 1989). There are more separate and distinct languages in the region than there are in any other continent. Sub-Saharan Africa is also a developing region with all the associated demographic, social, and political problems of the Third World. Efforts at achieving self-sustaining economic development in the region have been plagued by a host of internal and external factors, including political instability, mismanagement of scarce resources, poor policy choices, and external economic domination. The region's main economic activity is agriculture, which accounts for more than three fourths of the GNP of all countries in the area but utilizes only two thirds of the labor force. The area is rich with mineral deposits but they are unevenly distributed among the countries (*The New Encyclopaedia Britannica*, 1993; *The World Factbook*, 1992).

The climate in the region is determined by its position astride the equator. Year-round high temperatures in the northern and southern tropical zones are modified by the elevations in mountain areas or by currents from oceans along the coast. Away from the equatorial rain belts are vaste areas of tropical grasslands, merging into poor scrublands and desert. Much human misery is created as the Sahara desert moves southward.

Politically, the majority of the governments in the area are one-party or military-dominated states. However, since 1992 there has been an increase in the movement toward multiparty democracy. Mali, Togo, Ghana, Zambia, Tanzania, and South Africa have all adopted multiparty governments and for the very first time in its history, South Africa has a multiracial government.

Sub-Saharan African countries control less than 2% of the world's technological research and development capacity. Countries in the region depend on the West for much of their technological hardware and software, including those technologies that relate to broadcasting (Famoriyo, 1988). The manufacturing sector contributes only one eighth of the GNP of the region (*The New Encyclopaedia Britannica*, 1993).

BROADCASTING IN SUB-SAHARAN AFRICA

Broadcasting was introduced to sub-Saharan Africa in the early 1930s by colonial authorities. The first services were monitoring (relay) stations established to bring programs offered by stations in the colonizing countries to colonial settlers in Africa. These relay stations were later converted into distribution (rediffusion) centers and their services were expanded. The rediffusion services were run by private firms on behalf of the government agencies that owned their equipment. By 1935, Madagascar, Nigeria, Sierra Leone, and Ghana had such operations (Martin, 1991).

During World War II, broadcasting facilities were established at a greatly accelerated pace in sub-Saharan Africa. Many countries introduced broadcasting services to keep their citizens informed about the war. These countries included Zaire (formerly Belgian Congo), Cameroon, Congo, Ethiopia, Gambia, Mauritania, Senegal, Somalia, and Zambia. By the end of the war, more than 15 countries had acquired broadcasting facilities. Today, every country in sub-Saharan Africa has some sort of a broadcasting system.

Radio has emerged as the primary means of broadcasting in sub-Saharan Africa. It is certainly the medium that can reach the largest proportion of the population (see Table 8.1). Because of the remote nature of many countries and the high rates of illiteracy, rural Africans have little access to other media options (Wigston, 1994). Radio is popular because it requires less capital and electricity than television and its receivers are cheaper, more available and portable, and can run on batteries. Also, radio broadcasts resemble the oral communication patterns found in many sub-Saharan African cultures more closely. Governments, therefore, guard radio broadcasting as the most effective tool for promoting national development and it is also the first target of insurgents in periods of political strife (Martin, 1991).

Television has begun to flourish in sub-Saharan Africa but it may be some time before it becomes as ubiquitous as radio. All but four (Comoro Islands, Malawi, Rwanda, and Sao Tome and Principe) of the 48 countries in sub-Saharan Africa have a regular television service. Every country operates satellite transmissions, with transponders leased from the International Telecommunications Satellite Organization (INTELSAT). In 1992, the Union of National Radio and Television Organizations of Africa (URTNA) introduced a continent wide satellite news exchange program called AFROVISION. In many countries, the main television transmitters and studios are located in urban centers, and repeaters, relay stations, or both are provided in outlying areas to increase reach and coverage. Television programming heavily emphasizes education and information but many stations are beginning to devote more time to entertainment (Stephens, 1993).

When broadcasting began in sub-Saharan Africa, the degree of dependence on foreign programming was high. For example, in 1983 countries such as Nigeria imported 50% of their television programs; Kenya and Zimbabwe 60%; Mauritius, Zambia, and Senegal 70%:and Madagascar 80% (Price, 1992). In the late 1980s, many countries began to reduce their dependence on foreign programs. This general trend was fostered by the increase in local productions and the emergent awareness of the negative effect of foreign programs on local cultures that was gained during the New World Information and Communication Order Debate (discussed in Chapter 1) of the late 1970s and early 1980s.

In sub-Saharan Africa, the relationship between government and the broadcast media remains tenuous. Even though the economic constraints caused by the global recession of the 1980s forced many governments to divest their interests in the broadcast media, very few countries (e.g., Botswana, Gambia, Mauritius, Tanzania, and South Africa) have explicit policies favoring the free expression of opposing ideas. Several countries have constitutions that provide for a free media but many constraints are implemented to stifle such provisions (Martin, 1991). In several countries, therefore, the broadcast media follow the Soviet model of media use and operate as instruments of government propaganda (Kodjo, 1987). It is for this reason that analyses of trends and audiences are usually unavailable in sub-Saharan Africa.

Eastern Africa[2]

Burundi. Burundi has a unified system of broadcasting. Radio and television are run from the same government department. The service is known as Radiodiffusion et Television du Burundi (Burundi Radio and Television) and it operates one radio and one television channel. The

---

[2] *Editor's note:* The following discussion describes the broadcasting systems in sub-Saharan Africa on a country-by-country basis for each of the four designated United Nations regions (see Table 8.1 for basic statistics).

radio channel is carried by two medium-wave and two FM transmitters. The television service broadcasts on a single transmitter. The principal languages for broadcast are Kinundi, Swahili, French, and English. The services are funded by direct government subsidy.

Comoros. There is no television service on the Comoro islands. The radio service is a sparse system of relay and high-frequency radio communications that serves both the island and its neighbor Madagascar. Radio Comoro operates two medium-wave and one FM station. It is part of the Ministry of Information, Posts, and Telecommunications and depends wholly on government funding. Its programs are offered mainly in French and Comonian but the international service also include broadcasts in Swahili and Arabic (Hunter, 1993).

Ethiopia. There are no private broadcasters in Ethiopia. All of the broadcasting in the country is controlled by the government. The radio service comprises four medium-wave radio channels. There are no FM services in the country. Ethiopia has one television station that is also closely tied to the government. Programs are offered in English and Amharic.

Kenya. Kenya was the first British colony to have a regular public wireless broadcasting service. The service, which began in 1927, was a shortwave station located in Nairobi that relayed BBC broadcasts to British settlers in several parts of Africa. In 1931, Imperial and International Communications Limited (IIC), a private company, took over the station and was put in charge of broadcasting for 25 years. Later that year, IIC was renamed Cable and Wireless Limited and in return for the monopoly of international telegraphic traffic, it agreed to handle all the broadcasting for the colony (Martin, 1991).

Initially, broadcasts were in English and listeners paid a licensing fee. At the beginning of World War II, Asian and African programs were added to the schedule. The English and Asian programs were produced by Cable and Wireless Limited and the Information Department of the government provided the African programs in Luo, Kiswahili, Kikuyu, Kikamba, Nandi, Luhya, Kipsigis, and Arabic languages. The African programs were broadcast from four transmitters owned by Cable and Wireless Limited. The broadcasts were called The African Broadcasting Service and marked the beginning of nationwide broadcasting in Kenya. In 1959, Cable and Wireless Limited was replaced by the Kenyan Broadcasting Service (KBS).

In 1962, the Kenya Broadcasting Corporation (KBC) was created and charged with the responsibility of running the preexisting radio service and planning for the introduction of television. The next year, television was formally begun and the KBC was nationalized and renamed the Voice of Kenya (VOK). The VOK was established as a public service broadcasting organization with the main aim of providing the general public with information, education, and entertainment (Sennitt, 1993). The radio service comprises two nationwide channels: the National Service in Kiswahili and the General Service in English. In addition, there are three channels that are shared by programs in 16 other languages spoken in Kenya. Most of these services are transmitted simultaneously on shortwave, FM, and medium wave. In all, there are 16 medium wave and four FM radio transmitters in the country.

The television service, which broadcasts in Kiswahili and English, is carried simultaneously on four channels. Each of the four channels serves a different part of the country. Aside from direct government subsidy, the KBC receives income as a licensing authority, as the controller of broadcast-receiving apparatus, and as a dealer in receiver repairs and sales. Nearly half of the operating costs of the broadcasting services are paid for by advertising revenues.

Madagascar.   By African standards, there is a highly developed broadcasting system in Madagascar. Prior to 1990, broadcasting was a monopoly of the government. In 1990, a law was passed to allow public and private stations to coexist so as to provide the island nation with an extensive web of radio and television services. The government service is Radio Madagascar and Television Malagasy. The services were inaugurated in the 1930s and depend solely on the government for funding. Radio Madagascar has 17 medium-wave and three FM stations. Television Madagascar operates a single channel that is carried throughout the country via 36 repeaters.

African Television Network and Capricorne Television are the two private services in Madagascar. Both services came into existence in early 1992. African Television Network is owned and operated by an Italian environmental Group. Capricorne TV is run by a local private television company. Both services derive their funding from commercial advertising. It is not clear what percentage of the small audience each commands.

Malawi. The Malawi Broadcasting Corporation (MBC) came into existence in 1946. It is a statutory body that provides broadcasting as a public service for education, entertainment, and information. Its broadcasts are transmitted 19 hr per day in English (the official language) and Chichewa (the national language). The MBC is financed through commercial advertising and direct government subvention. The licensing fee system was discontinued as a revenue source in 1966. Commercial revenue constitutes about one third of the corporation's total income. Subventions make up the difference between the total sum of anticipated revenue from commercial advertising and other sources of revenue. Over the years, subvention has progressively increased to keep pace with the expansion of the corporation. The corporation's capital projects are financed mainly by government loans.

The MBC operates through 22 radio transmitters: 10 AM (three 50 kW, two 10 kW and three 1 Kw), 2 SW (100 kW and 20 Kw), and 17 FM. Most of this transmitting equipment was obtained as a gift from the governments of Germany, Great Britain, and the United States. There is no television service in Malawi (Europa World Yearbook, 1994).

Mauritius. Mauritius is an island located West of Madagascar in the Indian Ocean. It has been settled by peoples from Asia and is ethnically very diverse. The Mauritius Broadcasting Corporation (MaBC), which operates the national radio and television service, was established in 1964. Its television service was inaugurated in 1965 and began color transmission 10 years later using the SECAM system. In 1989, the corporation introduced an FM radio service. A second television channel was created in 1990.

The MaBC offers a mixture of programs in French, English, Creole, Hindustani, Bhojpuri, and other Asian languages. The corporation ensures that its program outputs are balanced on both radio and television and serve the varied needs and preferences of its highly diverse audience. The main programs include musical entertainment, drama, news, current affairs, documentaries, sports coverage, and children's programs. Events of national importance are given live coverage on both radio and television.

On special occasions, international events are relayed to MaBC via communications satellite. Given the large segment of the population that speaks Asian languages (e.g., Hindi, Urdu, Telugu, Tamil, Gujarati, Bhojpuri, Marathi, and Mandarin Chinese), the MaBC schedules special features in these languages including films, plays, musical entertainment, dance, poetic symposia, folklore, news, topical features, and discussions.

The MaBC derives its revenue from both advertising and licensing fees. Although there is no licensing fee for radio sets, a monthly viewer's license fee is charged on the electricity bill of homes possessing a television receiver. A special annual fee is charged for hotels, restaurants, and other public places.

Mozambique. Mozambique was formerly a Portuguese colony and is today the poorest country in Africa. The regulation of broadcasting is carried out in Mozambique by the Ministry of Transport and Communication. The ministry operates the state-controlled Radio Mozambique and Television Experimental and oversees the conduct of the newly inaugurated private radio services. Radio Mozambique was founded in 1975. It operates 29 AM transmitters and provides programs in Portuguese, English, and Tsonga. In addition, there are four private FM stations in Mozambique.

The television service was introduced in 1981 but its progress since then has scarcely gone beyond the experimental stage. It currently transmits for only a few hours a day on Wednesday, Thursday, Saturday, and Sunday. The service is funded by the government.

Reunion. The principal language of broadcasting in the Reunion Islands is French. Both public and private stations exist. The public stations are supported by the government, whereas the private ones are financed by advertising revenues. The major broadcasting organizations are Antenne Reunion, Canal Reunion, Radio Free-Dom and Tele Free-

Dom. The government service comprises 3 medium wave and 13 low-power FM radio stations and three television services linked with 18 repeater stations. In addition, there are over 40 private radio stations broadcasting locally.

Rwanda. Rwanda was scheduled to have begun a television service in 1992 but the status of the service is not clear given the ongoing state of warfare and disorder. Rwanda's national radio service, Radio-diffusion de la Republique Rwandaise, runs two medium and one FM channel. The FM signal is carried simultaneously on seven transmitters. The services are strictly tied to the government. They offer programs in Kinyarwanda, Swahili, and French. Rwanda also plays host to the transmitter that relays Deustche Welle (Voice of Germany) to the rest of Africa.

Somalia. Somalia is another strife torn country. The Somalia Broadcasting Service is the main government service. The service comprises two medium wave stations (there is no FM service in the country): Radio Mogadishu and Radio Hargeysa. Radio Mogadishu was taken over by the warlord General Mohammed Aidid in 1991. It broadcasts in Somali, Arabic, English, Italian, Swahili, Amharic, Galla, and Afar. Radio Hargeysa serves mainly the northern region of Somalia. Its broadcasts are in Somali and it also relays the Somali and Amharic transmissions of Radio Mogadishu. To supplement these services, some radio receivers are used for public announcement purposes in small towns and villages.

Since 1991, a string of other radio stations has emerged on the Somalian landscape. Supporters of Somali President Ali Mahdi established an alternative Radio Mogadishu in 1992. In 1993, the U.S.-led United Task Force created Radio Manta. The same year, the Voice of Peace was established to promote peace and reconstruction in Somalia. The Voice of Peace is supported by the United Nations International Children's Emergency Fund and the Organization of African Unity (OAU; Europa World Year Book, 1994).

In 1983, a limited television service was established in Somalia with funds obtained from Kuwait and the United Arab Emirates. The service transmits for only 2 hr every day of the week, except for Fridays and public holidays when it provides 3 hr of broadcasts. It offers programs in Somali and Arabic and is received only within a 30-km radius of Mogadishu, the state capital (Sennitt, 1995).

Tanzania. The introduction of multiparty democracy has brought some changes to the structure and organization of broadcasting in Tanzania. Since 1992, the government has passed various resolutions favoring private participation in radio and television. These resolutions have in effect democratized the country's information industry. For example, Radio Tanzania (the national radio service) has been stripped of its role as the mouthpiece of the ruling party and is now required to give each political party in the country an equal share of air coverage, as well as to include privately owned newspapers in its review program of national newspapers. Still, it is believed by many that as long as the ruling party subscribes to the socialist ideology, broadcasting will remain closely linked with the government (Ngatara, 1992).

Radio Tanzania is Tanzania's domestic radio service. It was founded in 1951, operates an educational service, and provides programs in Swahili. This service is received by more than 91% of the population. In the same year, Tanzania launched its external service, the Voice of Tanzania-Zanzibar. The external service also offers its programs in Swahili and is received on three separate frequencies (Notebook, 1993c).

Since 1972, Tanzanians have received their television service from the Isle of Pemba and Zanzibar. There are plans to begin television broadcasting on the mainland in 1995. According to the plan, the television service, Television Tanzania, will be run by a commercial government-affiliated corporation, which would strive to be financially independent. Initially, its transmitters will be located in the six largest cities in Tanzania, which would bring the service to just over 20% of the population (Price, 1992).

Uganda. Radio Uganda began officially in 1954, 8 years before the country became independent. Initially, it was a rather limited service that was on the air for just 2 hr a day. In 1956, more vernacular-language programs were added and airtime increased to an average of 6 hr per day. By independence in 1962, there were two national shortwave channels with more than 36 hr of airtime. In 1969, four medium-wave regional stations were added to support the shortwave stations on which two thirds of the country relied. The stations were located in four principal regions—midland, eastern, northern, and western—and each was equipped with a 100 kW high-power transmitter. A fifth transmitter was installed recently to serve the northwest region. These installations marked the introduction of regional broadcasting in Uganda. The regional stations are autonomous in the sense that they originate their own programs and broadcast in the vernacular of the region for about 8 hours per day.

Uganda Television (UTV) was introduced in 1963 as a network comprising nine stations scattered around the country. The main station is in Kampala, the national capital. Individual stations upcountry can opt out of the network to carry regional programs. UTV was converted to color in 1975 (Martin, 1991).

Radio Uganda and UTV are both departments in the Ministry of Information and Broadcasting. Hence, they are funded primarily through an annual subsidy from the government. Both are allowed to carry commercial advertising but revenue from this sources is minimal. The national policy is that the aim of both departments is to educate, entertain, inform, and mobilize the people of Uganda (Sennitt, 1993).

Zambia. Radio broadcasting was inaugurated in Zambia in 1941 by the government of what was then Northern Rhodesia. The main functions of the station were to broadcast news messages to families of members of the Northern Rhodesia Regiment and to convey orders to the people in the event of a grave emergency arising from the war. In 1945, the coverage area of the station was broadened to include Southern Rhodesia (now Zimbabwe), Northern Rhodesia (Zambia), and Nyasaland (now Malawi). Consequently, the station was renamed the Central African Broadcasting Service (CABS).

In 1953, after the creation of the Federation of Rhodesia and Nyasaland, the Federal Broadcasting Corporation (FBC) was established to administer broadcasting matters for the federation. CABS was still operating as an African station even though its control had been shifted to Salisbury (now called Harare). At Zambia's independence in 1964, CABS emerged as the Zambia Broadcasting Corporation (ZBC). In

1966, the ZBC reorganized to become a government department and its name was changed to the Zambia Broadcasting Service (ZBS).

In 1961, a privately owned commercial television station run by Rhodesia Television Limited began operating in Kitwe, on the Zambian Copperbelt. Three years later, its service was extended to Lusaka (Zambia's capital). In 1967, it was taken over by the government and integrated into the ZBS. The 2 decades that followed brought major expansions to Zambia's radio and television services. The installation of microwave links provided the country with a large transmitter network to cover the heavily populated areas and to link all provinces. In 1987, the ZBS was further reorganized to make it self-sufficient and it became a statutory commercial corporation named the Zambia National Broadcasting Corporation (ZNBC).

The ZNBC now operates one television and four radio channels. Radio One provides a 19-hr daily broadcast schedule. It broadcasts in seven Zambian languages (Bemba, Kaonde, Lozi, Lunda, Luvale, Nyanga, and Tonga) on a single time-sharing channel. Radio Two is an FM station. Radio Three, which was the international channel of the corporation, was closed in 1992 having outlived its usefulness because it had been used mainly by the liberation movement in Southern Africa. Radio Four, also known as Radio Mulungushi, was inaugurated in 1989. It operates strictly as a commercial channel on FM stereo, broadcasting 19 hr a day Monday to Thursday, and 24 hr the rest of the week. It covers the populated and industrialized area that stretches along the rail line from the Copperbelt to Livingstone.

ZNBC television operates a single channel for 7 hr during weekdays. On weekends, afternoon broadcasts are added to extend the broadcast time to 9 hr, and in late 1989 morning television was introduced to further extend broadcast hours.

Zimbabwe. The earliest broadcasting service in Zimbabwe (formerly Southern Rhodesia) was a radio transmitter at Belvedere in Salisbury (now Harare). It was installed by Imperial Airways of Britain and used to provide radio guidance and weather reports to airplanes flying from England to South Africa. Three engineers at the national Post Office were permitted to use this transmitter to originate programs to the population. During

World War II, the development of broadcasting was accelerated. Radio studios were set up in the old Post Office building in Harare, primarily to make war news readily available to Zimbabweans (Martin, 1991).

Until the mid-1950s, broadcasting in Zimbabwe was an arm of the Civil Service. In 1955, Sir Hugh Greene (of the BBC) headed a commission that examined the broadcast needs of the newly formed Federation of Central African States. This body recommended the creation of an independent statutory corporation. The resultant FBC was formed in 1958 and lasted until 1963 when the Federation of Central African States was dissolved. A year later, it was replaced by what is now known as the ZBC. The ZBC is a public corporation funded entirely by advertising revenues derived from its broadcasting services.

The corporation operates six national broadcasting services, four radio, and two television. Radios 1, 2, and 3 operate daily from early morning to midnight. Radio 1 broadcasts exclusively in English, whereas Radio 2's programs are presented in Shona and Ndebele (the languages of two of the major ethnic groups in the country) and other minor languages. Radio 3's programming is mainly youth oriented. Radio 4, the latest of the radio services, began operation in 1982. Patterned after BBC 4 in Britain (see chap. 3), Radio 4 is essentially an educational channel with an audience base of listeners' clubs, made up mainly of women. The clubs have been funded in part by private money but the ZBC has plans to take full control of funding in the next few years (Winbury, 1992).

Radios 1, 2, 3, and 4 operate on the medium-wave (AM) band. Alongside the AM service, there are 18 very high-frequency (FM) and five SW stations. Together, these stations provide a radio service that covers a small percentage (20%) of the country.

When television began in Zimbabwe in 1960, it was controlled by a private company under a franchise granted by the ZBC. This service was taken over by the ZBC in 1976 and remained the only television service (Television 1) in Zimbabwe until 1986, when Television 2 was inaugurated. Television 1 carries advertising and generates the largest portion of ZBC's revenues. Its programs include soap operas, features, comedies, musical shows, documentaries, magazine shows, panel discussions, sports, and news. Television 2 is also commercial but because it is mainly an educational service it is subsidized by the government (Europa World Year Book, 1994; Sennittt, 1993).

Western Africa

Benin. Despite the fact that the system and philosophy of government the of Benin changed from Marxism to multiparty democracy in 1989, broadcasting remains a government monopoly. The Office de Radiodiffusion et de Television du Benin, which runs the country's radio and television stations, is a department within the country's Ministry of Culture and Communications. The office operates two AM, two FM and two television channels. These services offer programs in French, English, and 18 vernacular languages.

Burkina Faso. Burkina Faso has a relatively small broadcasting industry. The country has two medium-wave stations, one FM station, and two television stations. The main broadcasting organizations are Radiodiffusion-Television Burkina, Radio Bobo-Dioulasso, and Radio Horizon. These stations offer programs in French, English, and eight other vernacular languages. The television stations are called Television Nationale Burkina. Burkina Faso broadcsting is run by the government.

Cote d'Ivoire (Ivory Coast). The government's monopoly of broadcasting in the country ended in 1991, when legislation was enacted to permit the establishment of private broadcasting. However, it was not until 1993 that the first private radio station was established. The private stations are operated by foreign companies, mostly based in France. These companies have been able to establish their own FM stations in Abidjan either directly or through partnership with local stations. The private stations include Radio Phoenix FM, Frequence Horizon, BBC French Service, RFI (Radio France International, Radio Pulsar, and Radio Nostalgie (partly owned by SOFIRAD, a commercial French broadcasting company). Licenses have also been awarded to Jeune Afrique Musique and Africa Number 1 (partly owned by SOFIRAD).

   The government still controls the main radio service, Radio-diffusion Ivoirienne (Ivorian Radio), and the main television service, Television Ivoirienne. The national radio service offers 3 medium-wave, 2 FM and 12 shortwave services. The stations are run by the Ministry of

Communications and provide programming in French, English, and a host of vernacular languages.

Television Ivoirienne is the national television service. Like its radio counterpart, it is government supported and run by the Ministry of Communications. It operates a single channel that relays via 14 transmitters. Its broadcasts are in French and English. SOFIRAD-owned Canal Horizon has been granted a license to operate a private television station.

Equatorial Guinea. There are six main radio stations. Five are shortwave stations and the remaining one is an FM station. Two of the SW stations are owned by the government and run by Radio Nacional de Guinea Ecuatorial. Two others are run by private companies under the names Radio Africa and Radio East Africa. These offer mostly religious programs in English. Africa 2000, a cultural group, runs the remaining two stations (one AM and one FM) for the purpose of relaying the services of Radio Nacional. The television station, TV Nacional, is also government dependent. The government services (both radio and television) offer programming in Spanish, French, Fang, and Bubi.

Gambia. Gambia, perhaps because of its small size, is one of the few remaining African countries without a television service. Radio Gambia was established in 1962 after 20 years of experimentation. Its broadcasts were initially carried by transmitters leased from a private company, Cable and Wireless Limited. In 1976, Radio Gambia acquired two 10-kw and two 1-kw AM transmitters and located them at both ends of the country. With these, the station offered an average of 12 hr of broadcasting a day. In 1979, following the commencement of Schools Broadcasting and the expansion of Rural and Adult Broadcasting Services, the broadcasting hours were increased to an average of 15 hr a day.

In the early 1990s, Gambia established a second radio channel. This channel operates through four FM stations, three of which are used to serve the rural areas of the country. One is devoted to Schools Broadcasting and General English programs. Another carries all local language programs and also rural broadcasting and adult education. These stations presently broadcast an average of 15 hr per day. (There is also a Swedish-owned commercial station, Radio Syd, which broadcasts in Swedish for tourists from November to April; Sennitt, 1995.)

Ghana. National broadcasting began in Ghana after a new Broadcasting House was completed in 1940. The new Broadcasting House, equipped with a 1.3 kW SW transmitter, offered programs to Ghana and neighboring West African countries. In 1954, an autonomous corporation, Gold Coast Broadcasting System (GCBS), was formed. From then onward, broadcasting became entirely independent of the Government's Information Services Department. The GCBS was renamed Ghana Broadcasting Service (GBS) when the country adopted its new name on the eve of its independence in 1957. Since then, the corporation has undergone many structural reorganizations (Notebook, 1993b).

Presently, the Ghana Broadcasting Corporation (GBC) operates through seven divisions: radio, television, engineering, accounts, administration, public affairs (comprising publications, public relations, audience research, and reference library), and commercial services. The Radio Division runs the corporation's national networks, which comprise Radio 1, Radio 2, and the External Service. Radio 1, considered to be the most effective unit of the GBC, broadcasts programs in six languages widely spoken in Ghana, Akan, Dagbani, Ewe, Ga, Hausa, and Nzema; and three languages of the upper east and upper west regions, Gurenne, Dagaari, and Kusaal.

Commercial broadcasting was introduced on Ghanaian radio and television in 1967. Radio 2 is the main channel for commercial broadcasts. Its primary audiences are business and commercial interests but its music, talk, feature, and discussion programs are enjoyed equally by the entire public. The External Service resumed broadcasting in 1987 after having been off the air for about 10 years due to technical inadequacy and economic hardship. It broadcasts in English, French, and Hausa to the rest of West Africa.

GBC-TV was inaugurated in 1965. It operates on four channels and transmits programs in six Ghanaian languages. More than 75% of GBC programs are produced locally. Of this, 42% are classified as entertainment, 33% as information, and 25% as education or culture. Since 1986,

GBC-TV transmissions have been in color. The GBC derives its funding from commercial broadcasting (radio and television), TV licensing fees (which are being phased out), and direct government subsidy.

The first private television network began operating in Ghana in October of 1993. The network, called Multichoice Ghana is essentially a subscription service and mainly televises event outside Ghana, via satellite. It rebroadcasts the services of M-NET International of South Africa and the BBC World Service Television, and also programs movies, sports, and children's shows (Notebook, 1993b).

Guinea. There are three medium-wave, one FM, and three shortwave radio stations in Guinea. These stations and one television service constitute the country's national broadcasting system. Guinean broadcasting is a monopoly of the government. It is funded entirely by the government and run by the Ministry of Communications, which uses it primarily to promote national policies and development.

Guinea-Bissau. Guinea-Bissau is a small country with a population of a little more than 1 million people. Its radio and television broadcasts are operated as a national service. Its single radio channel is carried by two medium-wave and three FM transmitters. There is only one television channel and transmitter in the country. Radio and television are a government monopoly in Guinea-Bissau. Their main programming objective is to promote national goals through the dissemination of information and education.

Liberia. Liberia is one of the few sub-Saharan African countries that did not inherit its broadcasting system as a colonial legacy. A religious group from the United States, the Sudan Interior Mission, brought broadcasting to Liberia in 1954 when it founded the station ELWA. The noncommercial station carried religious and a few development-oriented programs on both mediumwave and shortwave to West, Central, and North Africa. Its broadcasts were in English, French, Arabic, and 42 West African languages. The station was destroyed in the early stages of the Liberian civil war but it has since been revived by the West African

Peace Keeping Forces (ECOMOG) through help provided by the United Nations.

The government established its own radio station, ELBC, in 1964 but its services were never extended beyond the capital, Monrovia. In 1981, the U.S. Agency for International Development established three stations that formed the Liberian Rural Communication Network (ELNR). The stations were used primarily to promote development in the rural areas of Liberia. Its signals covered 80% of the country. When USAID discontinued its funding to these stations in the late 1980s, the Liberian government assumed sponsorship.

In addition to ELWA, ELBC, and ELNR, there are Radio Baha'i (a high-powered AM station operated by the Baha'i Faith) and a low-powered AM station operated by the Catholic Church (Europa World Yearbook, 1994).

ELTV is Liberia's only television service. Founded in 1964, it is a government-owned service that is run on a commercial basis. It offers mainly news and current-affairs programs for 5.5 hr per day on weekdays and 9.5 hr per day on weekends. It can only be received in the capital city of Monrovia.

Mali.   In 1992, a law was passed to allow private radio and television stations in Mali. The following year, six independent AM stations began broadcasting in the capitalcity, Bamako. In 1993, Radio International and the Gabonese-based Africa Number 1 began FM services in the country.

The government's own radio and television service is integrated and run by Radiodiffusion et Television du Malienne (Mali Radio and Television). The national radio service began in 1957 and remains closely linked with the government. There is also a regional station in the western part of the country. The radio services offer programs in French, English, Bambara, Peulh, and a host of other local languages. The television service offers 37 hr of broadcasts per week in about the same number of languages as radio.

Mauritania.   Mauritania has one of the poorest broadcasting services in sub-Saharan Africa. It has no FM radio service, only two AM radio stations that are carried through five transmitters, and one television channel. The only broadcasting organization is the Office of Radiodiffusion-Television de Mauritania (ORTM or the Office of Radio and Television of Mauritania), a branch of the Ministry of Interior, Posts, and Telecommunications. Founded in 1958, ORTM broadcasts in Arabic, French, Sarakote, Toucouleur, and Wolof. Its principal source of funds is the government.

Niger. The operation and financing of broadcasting is a government monopoly. The national radio and television service is provided by a government department, the Office de Radio-diffusion Television du Niger. The radio service is La Voix du Sahel (The Voice of Sahel). Its service is concentrated in the Southwestern area of the country and it operates 15 AM and five FM transmitters.

The television service is Tele Sahel (Sahel Television). The service was founded in 1950 and is carried by 18 transmitters scattered throughout the country. The main language for broadcasting is French, but minority languages such as Hausa, Djerma, Kanuri, and Arabic are also used.

Nigeria by Gerard Igyor

The political entity known today as Nigeria came into being in 1914 when the two British territories, Northern Nigeria and the Southern Protectorates, were amalgamated into one colony with a federal structure of government and the capital at Lagos. The northern and southern protectorates (western and eastern regions), however, maintained their various regional Houses of Assemblies, in addition to the Federal House of Parliament. Nigeria became an independent nation on October 1, 1960 (Coleman, 1963).

Nigeria has had military governments with only two trials of democratically elected government since its independence from Great Britain. The First Republic lasted from 1960 to 1966 and was overthrown by a military regime that ruled the country from 1966 to 1979 (Omu, 1968). The Second Republic lasted from 1979 to 1983 and was overthrown by the present military government on December 31, 1983 (Butari, 1994).

Nigeria's political disintegration and its ethnic diversity (the country has over 250 ethnic groups and nearly 400 mutually unintelligible languages) are reflected in the development of its broadcasting system. Once the country had gained its independence, the three regions kept pulling away from the federal structure of government and believed that regional radio and television development was important in the establishment of their separate identities (Egbo, 1982). The multistate structure that replaced the former tripartate regional division threatened to make the broadcasting situation more complicated, as each of the new states strove to start its own broadcasting system.

The developed and developing worlds of broadcasting do not confront one another more starkly than in Nigeria. The Nigerian broadcasting system is as unpredictable and hard to analyze as the country's politics. From the inception of Nigerian broadcasting in the early 1930s, the system had been a struggle between federal, regional, and later state monopolies until 1977, when the military government of the day took over all television stations in the country. A body known as the Nigerian Television Authority (NTA) was created in 1977 to operate the system. Henceforth, the development of new television stations was the sole responsibility of this authority. NTA carried out its assigned duties until 1983 when some state governors decided to established their own television stations to promote their states' identities and programs.

Radio Broadcasting

Restructuring of the radio industry came in 1978 with the dissolution of the old Nigerian Broadcasting Corporation (NBC) and the creation of a new organization, the Federal Radio Corporation of Nigeria (FRCN). The government dissolved NBC and handed over 20 of its radio stations to the state governments (which had became 19 states instead of the three regional adminstrations). The only NBC stations retained were those in Lagos, Ibadan, and Enugu which were then merged with the former Broadcasting Company of Nothern Nigeria (BCNN) Kaduna to constitute the FRCN. The chief executive officer of FRCN is the Director General who is assisted by professionals heading specialized departments, such as the secretariate, public affairs, audit, corporate planning, finance, training and manpower development, educational, and adminstration, programming and engineering (FRCN, 1993).

The structure of the FRCN is presently based on zoning of the country along liguistic lines with emphasis on 12 Nigerian languages—Edo, Efik, Fulfulde, Hausa, Igala, Igbo, Ijaw, Kanuri, Nupe, Tiv, Urhobo, and Yoruba. By this arrangement, over 90% of the population of Nigeria is effectively covered by FRCN's programs in these languages in addition to English. The new order also influenced the state radio stations by drastically reducing their permitted transmission power, thus limiting them to broadcasting within the confines of their own state.

The FRCN operates a transmitter in each state to disseminate regional and national programs. The federal stations in each zone have some autonomy to program according to the composition of the region. Nigerian radio, therefore, has a four-tier structure: (a) federal national service whose network news must be carried in all the states; (b) zonal broadcasts along broad regional lines; (c) local grassroot services from the state stations; and (d) as of August 24, 1992, private commercial stations.

The Lagos National station of the FRCN operates three channels: Radio Nigeria I, Radio Nigeria II, and Radio Nigeria III. It broadcasts in English on its Radio I and II. Radio Nigeria I is a station with a nationwide reach catering to a variety of interests and tastes. It is an embodiment of national values and aspirations. It combines the attributes of public service radio with that of a viable commercial outlook, producing programs in attractive and sponsorable formats. Its slogan is: "We are the one; The first before the rest." Radio I broadcasts on both SW and AM frequencies. Radio Nigeria II, the first stereophonic radio station in Nigeria, provides general entertainment services for its mainly urban listeners. Radio II is very innovative and trendy in its programming. It is the highest revenue earning radio station in Nigeria. Known as the "Sunshine Station," it broadcasts in both FM and and AM stereo. Radio Nigeria III is a station with special grassroots appeal. It broadcasts in Hausa, Igbo, Yoruba, and Pidgin English and goes by the slogan "We speak to the people in the language of the people."

The other National Stations are Enugu ("The station on your side"), Kaduna ("Your credible companion"), Ibadan ("Fun and Entertainment All the Way"), and Radio Nigeria Abuja ("Capital Radio-The Voice of Unity"). With the creation of more states in 1990 (30 states and the new federal capital Abuja), Nigeria has more than 70 FM and AM radio stations. Presently, each of the 30 states has at least one AM and one FM radio stations. All radio sets sold in Nigeria are also capable of receiving foreign international broadcasts services like the BBC, Voice of America (VOA), Radio Moscow, Radio Canada, and so on.

Radio broadcasting tends to provide a heavy diet of entertainment, mainly music. In 1983, Radio Nigeria I broadcast about 65% of foreign music, primarily from the United States, while only about 26% was Nigerian and the rest from other African countries. A study before the proliferation of FM radio in Nigeria had revealed that about 54% of music played on Nigerian radio was of Nigerian origin and 46% was foreign. These differences are accounted for by the new FM formats which tend to play more imported music than the traditional SW and AM radio stations. Surprisingly perhaps, American country western music is very popular with the Nigerian radio audience (Gross, 1995). The only private radio station, Ray Power 100 FM, is gaining popularity because of its overwhelmingly foreign music content. In particular, its rap and reggae music are very popular with younger audiences.

External broadcasting began with the establishment of the Voice of Nigeria (VON) in 1962. Its services were initially in English and French, but it soon added Arabic and other African Languages. The service currently broadcasts about 140 hours per week in Hausa, English, Arabic, French, and German. Its programming is mainly news and current affairs, with some music and developmental and cultural programs. It is a valuable tool for the Nigeria government to communicate with Nigerians living overseas and presents its political programs to the entire world. VON's programs target audiences in Africa, Western Europe, the Middle East, and North America.

Television

The pioneer television station in Africa started at Ibadan, the capital of the Western Region of Nigeria in 1959, as a result of a joint investment by the regional government of Western Nigeria and a British company, Rediffusion Overseas (WNTV-WNBS, 1959). It was to be financed by advertising (Public Relations Unit of NTA, 1977). The station later became a solely government corporation when Rediffusion withdrew due to the station's unprofitability. The government of Eastern Nigeria formed the Eastern Nigeria Broadcasting Service to handle its radio and television services in 1960.

The BCNN went on air with its radio and television on 1962, in partnership with two British companies, the Electrical and Music Industries (EMI) Limited and the Granada Company. After heavy financial losses, the regional government was forced to rescue the service and buy out the foreign companies (Katz & Wedell, 1977). Thus by the end of the second year after independence all three regional administrations had established their own brodcasting services to offer alternative channels of mass communication for their people.

The Federal Government of Nigeria began television service in 1962. For the first 5 years, it was operated under contract by the American company National Broadcasting Corporation (NBC) International. Unlike its British competitors, NBC International refrained from investing in government-owned stations (Makay, 1963).

The creation of states in the 1970s meant that the new state administrations could set up television services in their areas. The government of the Mid-Western state in 1973 established Mid-West Television. Benue-Plateau Television followed in 1974 telecasting in black and white. The following year it began transmitting in color, the first television station in the country to do so (Salama, 1978).

The intense competition that resulted in several regional television stations in the 1960s resurfaced again in the 1970s as each state rushed to establish state-owned and controlled television stations. During this period, Nigerian spending on development projects was estimated at about $30 million a day. A significant proportion of this expenditure found its way into the mass media field, mainly television (Mytton, 1983).

On March 23, 1977, Lieutenant General Olusegun Obasanjo, head of the then Federal Military Government and commander-in-chief of the armed forces of the Federal Republic of Nigeria, went on both radio and television to announce the takeover of all existing television stations in the country. Henceforth, the establishment of further television stations was taken away from state governments and made the exclusive responsibility of NTA (Gazette, 1977).

The number of television stations continued to grow under the NTA monopoly. In 1992, there were 25 stations and 84 transmitters, with two more transmitters planned for 1993. These facilities have established NTA as Africa's largest television network and it ranks among the world's biggest television organizations, broadcasting about 85,000 hr of different programs annually. Each station transmits an average of 7 hr on weekdays and extra hours on weekends. Today, over 30 million people from Nigeria and neighboring countries receive NTA signals (NTA, 1993, p. 6).

Broadcasting in Nigeria entered a new era with the government's decision to allow private ownership of radio, television, cable, and satellite broadcasting. On August 24, 1992, it promulgated Decree 38, establishing the National Broadcasting Commission, which is similar to the Federal Communications Commission in the United States. It is now been possible for private individuals and corporate bodies to establish radio, television and cable systems in Nigeria. In June of 1993, the National Broadcasting Commission granted licenses for 14 private television stations, 13 cable and satellite and retransmission operators, as well as one private radio station. Thus, Nigeria now has federal, state, and private organizations involved in the broadcasting industry with the National Broadcasting Commission as the regulatory body (NTA,1993, p. xxv).

According to the rules and guidelines of the National Broadcasting Commission, the minimum standard of operation for any broadcast station other than cable or satellite shall be 60% local and 40% foreign. For cable and satellite redistribution organizations, the local programming content shall not be less than 20% on any channel (National Broadcasting Commission, 1993). The NTA's network target, however, is for no more than 30% of programs to be imports. Presently, 69% of NTA's programs are locally produced, with 31% coming from the United States, Western Europe, Brazil, and Asian countries.

Although virtually all the feature films are still imported into the country, the ability to produce some local programs is certainly a significant development in any national television system. Currently, some private production of programs is done on a contract basis but this usually represents only a small part of the local production. In the near future, the Nigerian Film Village should boost domestic production.

Meanwhile, imported programs like the *Cosby Show, Golden Girls, Rosanne, Amen, Sanford and Son, Family Ties,* and *The Jeffersons* are very popular on the television schedules. Although Nigeria imports many television programs, it also produces more local programs than any other African country. The NTA (1993) reported an annual airing of 85,000 hr of programming.

Network news is broadcast on NTA three times a day beginning at 7:00 p.m. for 30 min and at 9:00 p.m. for 1 hr and news cap at 11:00 p.m. for another 30 min. The local stations also broadcast their own news mostly at 7:00 p.m. followed by translations into the various languages of their coverage areas. NTA news contains segments from the Cable News Network (CNN), SkyNews, BBC, and Visnews. Before the introduction of private broadcasting in Nigeria, NTA had a contract aggreement with CNN to carry its signals when NTA was off the air, but with cable and satellite licences granted to private individuals, the National Broadcasting Commission cancelled the CNN–NTA aggreement. The national news is only broadcast in English. Network sports are offered to affiliates every weekend. Soccer, track and field, and wrestling are the most popular sports on Nigerian television (NTA, 1993).

A "public enlightenment" category of programs includes children's (game shows, *Sesame Street*, Nigerian cultural displays), women's, religious, public service, and educational programs. Most of these programs are geared toward developmental uses, such as education, agriculture, and improved health and living conditions. Religious programs are mostly scheduled on Fridays for the Muslims and Sunday mornings for the Christians.

Shows produced by NTA affiliates and state stations are mostly in local languages. Nigerian dramas and plays tend to portray the hardships and different living conditions between the urban and rural dwellers, the rich and the poor. Network programs are more and more like U.S. daytime soaps and prime time programs, with the actors trying to act and speak like Americans or Britains.

With the creation of the National Broadcasting Commission and the allocation of cable and satellite retransmission licences to private individuals, the former illegal proliferation of multichannel satellite services is highly regulated. Because of the cost associated with these methods of broadcasting, only affluent Nigerians can afford the satellite receivers and pay for a decoder in order to receive the services offered. In major metropolitan areas of Lagos, Ibadan, Kano, Kaduna, Enugu, Benin, Jos, and Port Harcourt, most housing estates have been wired, making television viewing in these cities possible around the clock. The services offer a range of channels such as CNN International, C-Span, Canal Horizon (French), MM Abatho TV, Bophuthatswana (Bop TV), South African, MTV Europe, Angloan TV, M-Net, VOA Europe, K-TV/Super Sport, Algeria TV, BBC International, and a host of local television stations (*Multichoice*, 1994). With the introduction of private enterprise in broadcasting, these satellite services may create financial problems for domestic broadcasting. As of mid-1995, 14 private licenses for radio and TV stations had been issued, and the company that launched the first private FM radio station in Lagos in 1994 was awarded the country's first satellite TV license (Reuters, 1995). In addition, VCRs are widely used in Nigeria, as pirate copies of film and music videos are openly sold in the stores and on the streets.

Senegal. The broadcasting system is operated by a government-controlled corporation called Societe Nationale du Radiodiffusion Television Senegalese (RTS, formerly called Office de Radio–Television du Senegal). The system comprises two networks, with the main station in Dakar (the capital) and four regional stations broadcasting 132 hr a week, mainly in six vernacular languages. The networks also offer programs in French, Portuguese, and English. In all, there are 10 medium-wave stations in the country. The two FM stations in Senegal are also affiliated with the government. FM 92 was founded in 1991 as a joint venture between RTS and Radio France International. It operates 24 hr a day and serves mainly the Dakar metropolis. FM 94 (Dakar FM) was founded in 1990. It transmits 8 hr of local broadcasts per day.

Officially, television began in Senegal in 1990 but it was not until 1991 that Canal Horizon Senegal (CHS) began transmissions. CHS is a private coded channel in which RTS and the French private television company, Canal Horizon, participate as part owners. RTS owns about 19% of the company and Canal Horizon (France) runs about 15%. The station is carried by 10-kW transmitters in five locations in the country. In 1989, Senegal reached an agreement with France to receive direct programming from French television. After this, TV 5 Afrique was formed in 1992. This station is operated by French- based TV 5 to transmit direct satellite programs to Francophone Africa (Europa World Yearbook, 1994).

Sierra Leone. The Sierra Leone Broadcasting Service (SLBS) was created from the Freetown Rediffusion Service in 1934. It is the oldest of the English-speaking broadcasting services in West Africa and has two stations in Freetown (the capital of Sierra Leone) with two shortwave transmitters (250 kW and 10 kW) for national coverage, a 10-kW medium-wave transmitter, and two 50-kW medium-wave transmitters for provincial coverage. The stations are on the air for 110 hr per week and broadcast regularly in English and four of Sierra Leone's national languages: Mende, Temne, Limba, and Krio. There are also weekly features for other local languages and a weekly program in French (*Television and Cable Fact Book,* 1994).

The television service is on air for 5 hr daily. It began in 1963 as a pilot service operated in cooperation with private commercial interests. The service is mainly in English but there are weekly discussion and magazines programs in Mende, Temne, Krio, and Limba. The service was upgraded in 1978 when a 10-kW color compatible television transmitter was added. This extended television coverage to 7 out of 12 districts and marked the start of color television in Sierra Leone.

The SLBS is a government department existing within the Ministry of Information and Broadcasting. As such, its services are funded mainly by government subsidy. Commercial advertising began on both radio and television in 1963. It now provides about 25% of the corporation's revenue.

Togo. The principal broadcasting organizations in Togo are the Radiodiffusion du Togo and Television Togolaise. Both are financed by direct government subsidy. There are two radio services. The first was established in 1953, the second in 1974. Both are medium-wave stations, offering programs in French, English, and vernacular languages. There are no FM stations in Togo. Togo's television service was established in 1973. It is a single channel relayed by three transmitting stations.

Middle Africa

Angola. Although the inauguration of religious broadcasting brought the first private radio station to Angola in 1992, the government still remains the dominant broadcaster in the country. The main government radio service, Radio Nacional de Angola (RNA or Angolan National Radio) was already in existence prior to 1975 (the actual date of its founding is unknown). It broadcasts mainly 24 hr a day on 11 medium-wave and one FM channels. These channels are supported by 16 medium-wave provincial stations, 8 of which are relayed through 13 additional shortwave transmitters. Its programms are are offered in Portuguese and nine vernacular languages: Chokwe, Kikongo, Kimbundu, Kwanyama, Fiote, Ngnagela, Luvale, Songu, and Umbundu (Sennitt, 1995). The External Service programs in Portuguese, Spanish and French.

The second FM service in the country is a private, religious station that was established in 1992. It operates three channels. Televisio Popular de Angola (Angolan Popular Television) is Angola's national television service. It was founded in 1975 and operates a single channel through six transmitters located in major centers of the country. The service is entirely state controlled. It broadcasts for 4.5 hr Monday through Friday, 9 hr on Saturdays, and 14 hr on Sundays.

Cameroon. Radio and television are state controlled in Cameroon and operated as a unified service by the Office de Radiodiffusion-Television Camerounaise. The radio service is made up of one channel carried by 11 medium-wave and 11 FM transmitters. The programming is in French and English and focuses on information, education, and entertainment. The television service is also a single channel but it is carried by 26 transmitters.

Central African Republic. The broadcasting system is practically nonexistent. There is only one medium-wave, one FM, and one television transmitter serving a population of 3 million. The system is entirely state controlled and funded.

Chad. The main medium for broadcasting is radio. Tele-Chad, the country's national television system, provides only a limited service. Its single transmitter serves the capital, N'Djamena. The main radio service is the government-controlled Radiodiffusion Nationale Tchadiene (Chadian National Radio), which operates three stations. Each of these stations are received on two different channels. A fourth station is run by the political party in power. There is also one FM station in the country.

Congo. Although private broadcasting has begun, there are still very few radio and television stations. There are only four medium-wave, one FM, and four television transmitters in the country. The majority of these are controlled by the government-owned La Voix de le Revolution Congolaise (Voice of the Congolese Revolution) and Television Nationale Congolaise (Congolese National Television). These stations broadcast principally in French but programs are also offered in Lingala, Kikongo, Subid, English, and Portuguese. Less than 2% of the population receives the country's television service, which mainly serves the capital, Brazzaville.

Gabon. Commercial radio stations are now permitted but the operation of television remains the exclusive preserve of the government. Presently, there is one government (the national) and one commercial radio station in Gabon. The national radio station comprises a network of two stations in Libreville (the capital) and four provincial stations. The private station is a small FM service operated by Africa Number 1. It serves mainly Gaborone and broadcasts in English and Setswana.

The Gabonese government recently acquired 13 new television transmitters to make television available to all Gabonese. The service offers pay television and French is the main broadcast language.

Zaire. Broadcasting began in the former Belgian Congo in 1937. In that year, the Jesuit Fathers installed two transmitters in Kinshasa to carry educational stations to the country. One of the transmitters was taken over by Belgian authorities in 1940. The broadcasts were initially aimed at European listeners exclusively and were delivered in English and Flemish. In 1950, the programming schedule was broadened with the addition of African programs (Martin, 1991).

The principal radio organizations in Zaire are the Voix du Zaire

(Voice of Zaire–the External Service), Television Zaire, and Radio Candip. The Voice of Zaire is composed of three AM, four FM, and nine SW stations. Radio Candip is the main educational radio channel. It operates three 1-kW AM stations and one FM station. There was a new private religious radio station operating in Kinshasa, the capital city of Zaire, at the beginning of 1994. Its service was discontinued by the government in March. The station, Radio Sango Malamu (Radio Good News), programmed Christian music and teachings and community development tips. Its service was discontinued because the totalitarian regime of Mobutu Sese Seko feared that rebels could use it to subvert the government.

Television Zaire operates a total of 18 stations. Nine of these provide regular daily broadcasts on a full-time basis; six provide regular daily broadcasts on a part-time basis and the remaining three provide irregular services (Sennitt, 1995).

Southern Africa

Botswana. The Department of Information and Broadcasting is the sole provider of broadcasting. As a government department, the main function of Radio Botswana (formerly Radio Bechuanaland) and the newly introduced television service is to publicize government policy, and the programming is geared mainly toward national development. Airtime is provided to other government ministries and departments (e.g., Agriculture, Commerce and Industry, Education, and the University College of Botswana), which all produce radio and television programs to meet their individual needs.

Prior to 1992, Radio Botswana had seven AM stations, 12 FM stations, and one television station. In 1992, a second FM channel was established bringing the total of FM stations in the country to 13. The new channel, RB2 (FM 103), is strictly commercial and serves mainly Gaborone, Botswana's capital city. The channel puts out 17 hr of broadcasts per day on weekdays and 20 hr per day on weekends. There is one television station in Botswana operated by the Gaborone Television Corporation but specific details about its existence are not available.

Lesotho. Since its early stages, broadcasting has been closely linked with the government. Radio Lesotho was established in 1964 with a transmitter power of only 600 W. Its primary function was to educate, inform, and entertain its audience. When Lesotho became independent from Britain in 1966, Radio Lesotho became the Lesotho National Broadcasting Service (LNBS). LNBS's three new transmitters (one 10-kW medium wave, one 10-kW shortwave and one 1-kW FM) provided adequate coverage of the country's major, densely populated lowland areas. However, many villages in the mountain areas could not receive its transmissions. In 1976, high-power medium-wave transmitters were installed that covered the whole of Lesotho as well as a large portion of South Africa with their combined 100-kW output. A 100-kW shortwave transmitter was installed in 1980 to carry Radio Lesotho to all of Southern Africa.

LNBS has also taken the first steps toward a nationwide FM network with its FM transmissions on a more powerful 10-kW stereo transmitter. A 5-kW FM transmitter was installed to bring LNBS signals to the segment of the population that lives in the rural and mountain areas. The FM network was further extended to other areas in 1990 when a 250-W VHF and FM transmitter was installed on a high peak to serve two very remote areas.

Lesotho began television broadcasting in 1988. The Lesotho Television Service reaches most of the country's lowland areas. The service currently broadcasts a daily news magazine supplemented by occasional programs of national interest (Europa World Yearbook, 1994).

Namibia. The early days of broadcasting were characterized by language broadcasts offered by the South African Broadcasting Corporation. These broadcasts provided nine "ethnic" services to rural communities in one or more dialects and were basically fragmented. In 1990, the old South West Africa Broadcasting Corporation was replaced by the Namibian Broadcasting Corporation. Today, the Namibian Broadcasting Corporation broadcasts on four medium-wave and four FM channels that include the Namibian language services as well as the national service. The language services broadcast 12 hr per day, the remaining 12 hr are taken up by the National Service and the All-night

Service. The radio services reach about 90% of the population.

Namibian Broadcasting Corporation television service broadcasts an average of 5.5 hr per day. The service, which originally began as a relay from South Africa, offers locally produced bulletins as well as programs imported from many other countries. Its local productions include a 20-min magazine program and certain sports programs. The service has 10 transmitters but its programs reach only about 25% of the population at this time (*Combroad Handbook*, 1993/94). Eighty percent of Namibian Broadcasting Corporation's funds are derived from government subsidy. The remaining 20% comes from license fees and advertising.

South Africa. South Africa was the first country in sub-Saharan Africa to introduce radio broadcasting. South Africans began experimenting with radio broadcasting in 1920. In 1923, the government asked prospective broadcasters to apply for licenses. The next year, the first three official stations were established in Johannesburg, Durban, and Cape Town. The stations were owned by the Association of Sciences and Technical Societies, the Durban Corporation, and the Cape Peninsula Broadcasting Association, respectively.

The South African Broadcasting Corporation (SABC) was created in 1936. It has a near monopoly on broadcasting in South Africa and has the best developed, most modern, and highest capacity media infrastructure among sub-Saharan African countries. Its authority covers the areas of licensing, control, and direction of the vast majority of broadcasting services in South Africa. Prior to recent political developments, the SABC was controlled exclusively by Whites. Since the move toward majority rule was initiated a few years ago, dramatic changes have occurred in the organization including the appointment of a Black female Director-General (Notebook, 1993a).

SABC radio comprises 22 international radio services providing broadcasts in 11 languages and a foreign service offered in seven languages. The first few community radio stations are presently being established with help from public broadcasters in the United States. SABC's external service is called Channel Africa (formerly Radio South Africa). It broadcasts in seven languages to the entire continent for a total of 29 hr each day. According to a recent BBC survey, awareness of Channel Africa is high in sub-Saharan Africa. For example, the survey reports that more than 72% of Zambia's 8 million people know about Channel Africa. In Tanzania, one fifth of the country's 24 million people listen to the station's Swahili service. The Channel's television service resumed daily satellite transmissions to 25 countries in Africa in 1993 after a 6-month trial period that ended in March of the same year (Notebook, 1993a).

SABC television operates three channels broadcasting in seven languages. TV 1 is the main English and Afrikaans service. The second channel (CCCV-TV) is the main language service offering programs in northern and southern Sotho, Tswana, Xhosa, and Zulu. The third channel (TSS-TV) is the main public affairs channel, offering mainly documentaries and educational and sports programs.

The private media sector in South Africa revolves around the satellite subscription service called M-NET. This provides not only a domestic service, but also an international service to countries such as Angola, Algeria, Ghana, Lesotho, Namibia, and Sudan. M-NET is funded exclusively by advertising (Report of the Africa Group Meeting, 1993).

Swaziland. Radio and television are operated as a national service in Swaziland by two separate statutory corporations that are part of the Information Department of the government. Radio is operated by the Swaziland Broadcasting Service (SBS), which provides both an information and an educational service. The information service began in 1966. Its single 10-kW transmitter provided just 2.5 hr of service in the evening. Today, the service provides over 10 hr of programming.

The Educational Service began as an experiment by the Ministry of Education in 1967 but its operation was integrated into the Information Department in 1970. The informational and educational services broadcast for 85 hr per week and over 100 hr per week when schools are session. The SBS has a second 10-kW transmitter that serves as a backup to its primary transmitters. The service also has six VHF/FM transmitters. Two new VHF/FM transmitters have been added to increase coverage in the northern and western parts of the country.

There are two private radio stations in Swaziland. One is Swaziland Commercial Radio, a private channel offering music and religious programs to Southern Africa in English and Portuguese. The second channel is Transworld Radio. Founded in 1974, Transworld Radio offers evangelical broadcasts to Southern, Central, and Eastern Africa and the Far East. The station operates in 23 languages through six transmitters.

Television is provided by the Swaziland Television Authority (STVA). The STVA (or "Swazi TV" as it is now called) was established in 1983 and incorporates the Swaziland Television Authority Rentals. Swazi TV transmits 42 hr of mostly imported programs per week. It operates 10 transmitters. Like the SBS, STVA is funded solely by the government.

THE PROBLEMS OF BROADCASTING IN SUB-SAHARAN AFRICA

Broadcasting faces a number of social, economic, and technological problems in sub-Saharan Africa. The main social problem is language and there are two dimensions to the problem. The first is the existence of a plurality of languages on the continent. This plurality presents broadcasting with the dilemma of how to fulfil the natural desire of every community to be addressed in its own language or dialect. This is a challenge that broadcasting has been unable to meet simply because governments have not acquired the additional hardware and programming needed for its realization. So, many countries offer services only in a limited number of major languages. However, the placement of emphasis on the language of a few majority group leads other groups to clamor for equal recognition. It is thus difficult to use broadcasting to cultivate any sense of national unity.

The second dimension is related to the first. It concerns the use of a common language. Because of the presence of multiple languages in sub-Saharan Africa, broadcasters have had no choice but to program in a common language. In all but a few East African countries (e.g., Kenya, Tanzania, and Zambia), the common language is the foreign language that was inherited as a colonial legacy (French, English, Portuguese, or Spanish). The problem with using this foreign language is that it limits the potential to use broadcasting for education and development. The broadcasts tend to cater only to urban elites who have acquired the educational preparation to comprehend these languages. It isolates the masses who actually need the services.

Another major problem of broadcasting in sub-Saharan Africa is the inadequacy of capital. In many countries, the money to acquire and operate adequate broadcasting facilities, modernize obsolete technologies, and produce satisfactory programs is just not available. In fact, countries such as Somalia, Tanzania, and Zimbabwe would not even have a system if not for donations made by international philanthropic bodies such as the Thomson Foundation of Britain or the Friedrich Ebert Stiftung of Germany. Most government stations operate on a shoestring budget. Licensing fees are difficult to collect because people do not report radio purchases and listening is often done in groups at the community level. Advertising is barred from many stations and if it is allowed its revenues usually account for less than 10% of the total budget. All of this means that sub-Saharan African broadcasting stations operate from a poor revenue base, which usually means a lack of money to produce programs.

The main technological problem is the lack of indigenous know-how. This means that equipment used by African broadcasters has to be imported. In Africa, imported technology often suffers a high mortality rate. It is usually not adaptable to African climatic realities and many countries do not have the qualified maintenance staff to keep it operational. There is also the choice of the medium-wave as the principal channel for radio broadcasting. The medium-wave band is preferred because it is less susceptible to atmospheric interference and easier to receive. However, it covers only a limited area. Therefore, to blanket a country with medium-wave signals, several stations must be installed (Martin, 1991). This has not been possible in Africa where economic and technological capacities have been lacking.

THE PROSPECTS OF BROADCASTING IN SUB-SAHARAN AFRICA

Economic stagnation forced many African governments to accept the deregulation of broadcasting as inevitable in the early 1990s. Accordingly, some countries introduced advertising as a source of broadcast revenue, whereas a few others adopted regulations to allow private broadcasting media to coexist with public ones. Yet, the future for broadcasting is far from being a professional, self-reliant media operation.

In many countries, governments will probably continue to carefully watch both public and private broadcast media and will not hesitate to close private stations that are not found to be operating in accordance with the aims for which broadcast media are established in sub-Saharan Africa. Future policies may be formulated to ensure that all broadcasting stations, public or private, operate as a tool for national development and unity, a way of promoting cross-cultural awareness, and an avenue for increased political participation. It is in the interest of these aims that broadcasting will continue to develop and grow in sub-Saharan Africa.

REFERENCES

Amienyi, O. P. (1989). Obstacles to broadcasting for national integration in Nigeria. *Gazette, 43*, 1–15.

Buhari, M. (1994). Explanation for the military intervention on December 31, 1983. *Africa,150* (February).

Coleman, J. S. (1963). *Nigeria: Background to nationalism*. Berkeley: University of California Press.

Edbo, M. I. (1982). Television broadcasting in Africa, *Television Journal*, a publication of NTA, Lagos, Nigeria.

Europa world yearbook 1994. (1993). London: Europa Publications Limited.

FRCN (1993). *Bulletin No 3*. Lagos, Nigeria: Federal Radio Corporation of Nigeria.

Famoriyo, S. (1988). Perception of technology in Nigeria. *International Journal of Technology Management, 3*, 515–527.

Gazette. (1977). Federal Ministry of Information Official publication of the Federal Military Government of Nigeria, No. 14, Vol. 64, Part A.

Gross, L. S. (1995). *The international world of electronic media*. New York: McGraw-Hill.

Hunter, B. (Ed.). (1993). *Statesman yearbook* (130th ed.). London:Macmillan

Katz, E., & Wedell, G. (1977). *Broadcasting in the third world*. Cambridge: Harvard University Press.

Kodjo, E. (1987). *Africa tomorrow*. New York: Continuum.

Martin, L. J. (1991). Africa. In J.C. Merrill (Ed.), *Global journalism: Survey of international communication*, (pp. 155–204). New York: Longman.

Mackay, I. (1963). *Broadcasting in Nigeria*. Ibadan: Ibadan University Press.

Multichoice Kaleidoscope. (1994). Program Schedule (December), agents for M-Net, BBC World Television, and Canal Horizons. Johannesburg, South Africa.

Mytton, G. (1983). *Mass communication in Africa.* London: Edward Arnold.

Ngatara, L. A. (1992). Tanzania: A cry from a hen to a hawk. *Intermedia,* 20, 31.

Nigerian Television Authority. (1993). *Annual reports & accounts, 1993.* Lagos, Nigeria: Academy Press.

Notebook. (1993a). Channel Africa: Research effort. *Combroad, 100,* 22.

Notebook. (1993b). Ghana: New private Ghanaian TV network to carry M-NET and BBC WSTV. *Combroad, 101,* 27.

Notebook. (1993c). Television Tanzania. *Combroad, 98,* 34.

Omu, F. A. (1968). The dilemma of press freedom in colonial Africa. *Journal of African History, 9* (2).

Price, G. (1992). Television for Tanzania? *Combroad, 95,* 23–24.

Public Relations Unit of NTA. (1977). *Some notes.* Lagos, Nigeria: NTA.

Report of the Africa Group Meeting. (1993). Satellite above and the challenge face of broadcasting below. *Combroad, 100,* 4–5.

Reuters. (1995). Nigeria's military government has approved a licence.. June 15, Internet.

Salama, G. (1978). *Television in a developing nation.* Jos, Nigeria: NTA Publication.

Sennitt, A. G. (Ed.). (1993). *World radio / Television handbook.* Billboard Books.

Stephens, S. G. (1993, February). *Broadcasting in Sub-Saharan Africa: Evolving toward an exchange with the world.* Paper presented at the Intercultural and International Communications Conference, Miami, FL.

Television Journal, 4 (1984). Lagos, Nigeria: NTA Corporate Publication.

The New Encyclopedia Britannica: Micropaedia-Ready Reference. (1993). Chicago: Encyclopedia Britannica.

The World Factbook. (1992). Washington, DC: Central Intelligence Agency.

WNTV-WNBS. (1959). *First in Africa daily service.* Ibadan, Nigeria: Western Nigeria Ministry of Information and Social Services.

Wigston, D. (1994, February). *The challenge of international radio broadcasting: What's in it for Africa?* Paper presented at the Intercultural and International Communication Conference, Miami, FL.

Winbury, R. (1992). Zimbabwe puts its women on air. *Intermedia, 20,* 31.

NICARAGUA

PANAMA

VENEZUELA

GUYANA

SURINAME

FRENCH
GUIANA

COLOMBIA

ECUADOR

PERU

BRAZIL

BOLIVIA

CHILE

PARAGUAY

ARGENTINA

URUGUAY

Chapter 9

Latin America and the Caribbean

Donnalyn Pompper

In countries characterized by political strife, low per capita income, and terrain separated by mountain ranges and miles of sea, the broadcast media in the Latin American and Caribbean nations lag significantly behind those in their continental neighbors to the north: the United States and Canada. Geographically, the scattered islands, rugged mountains, and sheer distances pose significant interference and transmission problems. Broadcast media within each country have had limited success, sometimes cutting across barriers of language, culture, and economy, in aiding education and development efforts in Latin American and Caribbean nations. However, it is a region most influenced from the outside.

Broadcast technology was introduced first in the United States and Europe before being imported into Latin America and the Caribbean. Today, broadcast media programming powerhouses in the United States, Mexico, and Brazil face anticulturalism criticisms for significantly influencing the entire region and determining what a "developing" population of 359 million will listen to on the radio or watch on television. The broadcasting systems in Brazil and Mexico are among the world's largest and most sophisticated and are competing fiercely for global markets. Mexico's Televisa and Brazil's TV Globo (discussed in

Table 9.1. North and Latin America

Country	Population (In Millions)	Growth (%)	Land Area (Square Kilometers)	GNP/Capita (1992 U.S. Currency)	Radio Sets (In Millions)	Television Sets (In Millions)
North America						
Canada	29.1	0.7	9,976,139	20,320	26.88	17.40
United States	260.8	0.7	9,372,614	23,120	524.20	215.00
South America						
Argentina	33.9	1.3	2,766,889	6,050	21.50	7.17
Bolivia	8.2	2.7	1,098,581	2,210	4.25	0.05
Brazil	155.3	1.7	8,511,965	2,770	55.00	30.00
Chile	14.0	1.7	756,945	2,730	4.40	2.00
Colombia	35.6	2.0	1,138,914	1,290	5.40	5.50
Ecuador	10.6	2.5	283,561	1,070	3.24	0.90
French Guiana	0.1	3.5	90,000	—	0.07	0.01
Guyana	0.8	1.8	214,969	330	0.39	0.02
Paraguay	4.8	2.7	406,752	1,340	0.70	0.35
Peru	22.9	2.0	1,285,216	950	5.30	2.00
Suriname	0.4	1.6	163,265	3,700	0.26	0.04
Uruguay	3.2	0.8	177,414	3,340	1.85	0.60
Venezuela	21.3	2.6	912,050	2,900	8.30	3.70
Central America						
Belize	0.2	3.3	22,965	2,210	0.11	0.03
Costa Rica	3.2	2.3	51,100	2,000	0.76	0.34
El Salvador	5.2	2.7	21,041	1,170	2.08	0.50
Guatemala	10.3	3.1	108,889	980	0.57	0.48
Honduras	5.3	3.1	112,088	580	1.91	0.16
Mexico	91.8	2.2	1,958,201	3,470	21.00	56.00
Nicaragua	4.3	2.9	130,000	410	0.93	0.21
Panama	2.5	1.8	77,082	2,440	0.53	0.20

Note. Population (mid 1994 estimates), population growth (natural increase), and Gross national product per capita (1992) in U.S. dollar equivalents are from 1994 *World Population Data Sheet,* Washington D.C., Population Reference Bureau, 1994. Radio and television set figures are from A. G. Sennitt (Ed.), *World Radio TV Handbook,* Volume 49. New York: Billboard Books, 1995. Land surface area figures are from *UN Statistical Yearbook,* 1991/2. Because of its small population, Greenland has been omitted.

Table 9.2. The Caribbean

Country	Population (In Millions)	Growth (%)	Land Area (square kilometers)	GNP/Capita (1992 U.S. Currency)	Radio Sets (In Millions)	Television Sets (In Millions)
Antigua and Barbuda	0.07	1.2	440	4,870	0.07	0.03
Bahamas	0.25	1.5	13,878	12,020	0.13	0.06
Barbados	0.26	0.7	430	6,530	0.22	0.07
Bermuda	0.07	1.6	53	—	0.08	0.03
Cuba	11.1	0.8	110,861	—	3.61	2.50
Dominica	0.07	1.3	751	2,520	0.05	0.01
Dominican Republic	7.8	2.2	48,734	1,040	1.18	0.73
Grenada	0.09	2.5	344	2,310	0.05	0.03
Guadeloupe	0.33	1.2	1,705	—	0.09	0.03
Haiti	7.0	2.3	27,750	380	0.27	0.03
Jamaica	2.5	1.8	10,990	1,340	1.00	0.48
Martinique	0.33	1.1	1,102	—	0.07	0.07
Netherland Antilles	0.17	1.2	800	—	0.21	0.04
Puerto Rico	3.6	1.0	8,897	6,610	2.48	0.83
St. Lucia	0.12	2.0	622	2,900	0.10	0.03
St. Vincent / Grenadine	0.98	1.7	38	1,990	0.07	0.02
Trinidad / Tobago	1.3	1.2	5,130	3,940	0.58	0.25
U.S. Virgin Islands	0.1	1.4	342	—	0.10	0.03

Note. Population (mid 1994 estimates), population growth (natural increase), and Gross national product per capita (1992) in U.S. dollar equivalents are from *1994 World Population Data Sheet*, Washington D.C., Population Reference Bureau, 1994. Radio and television set figures are from A. G. Sennitt (Ed.), *World Radio TV Handbook*, Volume 49, New York: Billboard Books, 1995. Land surface area figures are from *UN Statistical Yearbook*, 1991/2. Countries with populations below 65000 people have been omitted.

the next chapter of this book) even battle for market share in their rival's own backyard. TV Globo, for many years king of Latin American television broadcasting, now also competes with Univision, based in Miami. Univision markets program packages to 14 Latin American affiliates, including television stations in Puerto Rico, Venezuela, Ecuador, Peru, and Chile.

From Nassau to Tierra Del Fuego, the power of radio and television impacts millions (see Tables 9.1, 9.2). Despite high poverty levels in countries like Mexico, for example, it is not unusual to see huge, white satellite dishes tottering on dirt-floor hut roofs (Ellison, 1993). A cursory survey of the region reveals that broadcast media often have a chaotic organization with varying levels of sophistication, are too commercial, and rely heavily on imported programming. Some countries subscribe to public ownership in the European tradition with subsidized funding and government control. Other Latin American nations enjoy a mix of public and private broadcast station ownership and management. Following the U.S. lead in private ownership and commercial funding, most broadcast media owners are in business to make a profit rather than to serve the public interest. The result is commercially produced entertainment programming.

Strong British and U.S. influence is evident throughout the chain of small Caribbean islands where the broadcast media are generally controlled by minority wealthy classes. In the early 1990s, Cable Satellite Network, based in Miami, began transmitting programming similar to the U.S. music channel, MTV, throughout the Caribbean. Critics accuse broadcast advertising, primarily on television, in developing Latin American and Caribbean countries of reinforcing class distinctions between the small wealthy class and the majority poor class. Only the rich can afford to purchase most of the products and services advertised.

The "big four" international news agencies, the Associated Press and United Press International of the United States, Reuters of the United Kingdom, and Agence France-Presse of France, dominate international news coverage in Latin America and the Caribbean (Salwen, Garrison, & Buckman, 1991). These powerful news organizations are accused of failing to meet the needs of the Latin American and Caribbean nations and often are charged with "media imperialism." In 1971, several newspapers formed a privately owned news cooperative and a 1976 UNESCO conference identified a need for regional news agencies. In 1983, representatives from nine Latin American and Caribbean nations formed the Agencia Latinoamericana de Servicios Especiales de Informacion headquartered in Mexico City.

Latin American and Caribbean governments have used radio and television as a tool of suppression and propaganda for many years. Military coups and ousted governments have left their mark on broadcast media development. Cuba has served as a Cold War battleground, between the United States and the former Soviet Union. The United States created Radio Marti and TV Marti in the 1980s, designed to provide Cubans with a non-Communist flow of information. The Cuban government, however, views this strategy as propagandistic and has fought hard to scramble both systems ("America and Cuba," 1993). In Haiti, the Catholic Church transmits Radio Soleil from studios in the Dominican Republic to affect political and human rights changes.

Listening to the radio during the 1920s and 1930s and later watching television in the 1950s was a pastime for only the wealthy in Latin American and the Caribbean. Now, even the poorest of Latin American and Caribbean nations boast of high radio and television set ownership relative to their populations. Although the broadcast media provide mostly entertainment, educational and sociocultural programs are available in some areas. Experimental televised and radio "escuelas," or schools, have achieved limited success in educating and elevating literacy among the lower classes. In Ecuador and Bolivia, low-powered rural radio takes on a special significance by strengthening local culture and religion with programming that broadcasts traditional music, education, and social services information.

BROADCAST INTRODUCTION

The introduction of radio in Latin America and the Caribbean during the 1920s and television in the 1950s is the product of entrepreneurial spirit, pioneering, and piracy. Radio, a forerunner in communications technology, was relatively inexpensive to launch and it single-handedly aided in binding each nation's villages and cities. Television, however, developed far more slowly than radio because of high equipment and technology costs.

Regular radio broadcasting began in the United States in 1920; radio broadcasting in Mexico, Brazil, and Argentina followed only 2 years later. In Mexico, radiotelephony, a point-to-point communications vehicle comparable to the telephone, preceded radio broadcasting. It engrossed hobbyists during the time of the Mexican Revolution from 1910 to 1920 (Alisky, 1988b). In 1922, citizens of Brazil celebrated 100 years of independence and President Epitacio Pessoa was the first voice Brazilians in Sao Paulo and Rio de Janeiro heard on radio. The first radio station in Brazil opened the following year, a private venture without commercial revenues (Oliveira, 1988). The station operated as a club and listeners paid membership fees.

To the west, Peruvians listened to neighboring nations' radio waves with shortwave receivers and Peru's government established the first radio station in 1925. Venezuela experienced growth of broadcasting comparable to that in Peru (Alisky, 1988c). The public sector pioneered broadcasting in Uruguay but private stations soon entered the arena (Salwen et al., 1991).

Mexico and Brazil led development of the television medium in Latin America in the 1950s. Two creative Cuban entrepreneurs, brothers Goar and Abel Mestre, proclaimed the "Pearl of the Caribbean" the third nation in Latin America to inaugurate television broadcasts following their successful launch of the show *Radio Reloj* (Radio Clock). This may have been the first all day, every day all-news station. In the 1950s, the Mestres made CMQ-TV technologically comparable to networks in New York. The Cubans' love for baseball encouraged the Mestre brothers to become the first to transmit a live international television broadcast during the World Series in 1953 (Salwen et al., 1991). A DC-3 airliner over the Florida Keys picked up the signal. Later, Goar Mestre launched broadcast stations and coordinated program distribution in Argentina, Venezuela, and Peru.

CONTROL, REGULATION, AND POLITICS

As compared to television, radio broadcast ownership and management are significantly less costly. Radio has successfully communicated politically motivated messages inexpensively over mountains, through jungles, and across towns in a myriad of languages and dialects. Although private interests and governments vie for radio and television broadcast ownership, stations in some Latin American and Caribbean countries are owned and controlled by political parties, religious factions, unions, and universities ("America and Cuba," 1993; "Argentine Channels," 1992; Avirgan, 1992; Salwen et al., 1991). In Mexico, Argentina, and Brazil, reliance on commercial advertising is heavy ("Argentina Is Prime," 1992; Besas, 1993; "Buenos Aires Private," 1987).

The history of Latin America is fraught with military coups and broadcast station seizures, yet the broadcast media have survived and, in some countries, prospered. Propaganda-motivated radio stations broadcasting guerrilla warfare strategies have prospered in El Salvador, Peru, and Colombia ("TV Or Not TV," 1990). Uruguay enjoys free press and information. Paraguay, conversely, lacks press freedom.

During the 1960s and 1970s, governments could and did use economic pressures to close print and broadcast media. Many advocated violence against writers and directors ("Argentine Channels," 1992). In Nicaragua and Cuba, Marxist ideologies opposing organized religion led to prohibition of programming with religious themes. Even Catholic Church publications were forbidden in some nations and governments censored foreign correspondents.

Next is a look at selected individual countries. This is followed by a discussion of programming throughout the regions and of satellite and cable development.

Central America

Mexico. Mexico is the "giant" of the region as indicated in Table 9.1. The public sector in Mexico pioneered broadcasting there despite the socialist tendencies of the Mexican constitution of 1917 (Alisky, 1988b). By late 1922, Mexicans could receive radio transmissions from the United States, Cuba, and Puerto Rico. The Mexican government allowed private stations to enter the field along with the state's educational, cultural, and propaganda programming. The Law of General Ways of Communication of 1940, comparable to the U.S. Federal Communications Act of 1934, declared that the public owns the airwaves and that foreign ownership of radio stations is forbidden.

By the mid-1950s, under President Miguel Aleman, the state had sold many stations to private investors and granted many other new licenses. Aleman embraced the electronic media and authorized private television broadcast in 1950 (Salwen et al., 1991). When he left office, he actively worked in the television broadcast arena and was involved in the launch of Televisa. This station enabled Mexico to produce its own programming and end a dependence on imported U.S. programming. The secretary of the government, a powerful assistant to the president, enforces the Law of Radio and Television. This law passed in 1960 and has been amended several times. The law specifically outlines guidelines for broadcasters, which include affirming "respect for moral principles, human dignity, and family relationships."

Currently, Mexico's government keeps a sharp eye on broadcasting despite private ownership. Reportage is objective and the Mexican government permits some criticism, provided the news does not embarrass government officials. The Internal Affairs Ministry regulates broadcast programming content. In 1985, the United States and Mexico ended 3 years of negotiations by agreeing to mutually address problems of AM radio broadcasting, especially interference.

Many broadcasting stations and networks in Mexico are privately owned but the state operates its own facilities as well. Televisa, comparable to the monolithic TV Globo in Brazil, is the parent company of the Spanish-speaking network, Univision. It dominates the market and exports "telenovelas," or soap operas, and other programming throughout Latin America.

The other nations of Central America, Nicaragua, Costa Rica, Honduras, El Salvador, Guatemala and Panama have experienced a variety of politically motivated government upheavals, often characterized by violence and media censorship.

El Salvador. El Salvador, with a 3.5 million population, is the poorest Central American nation. Historically, a handful of wealthy landowners owned the broadcast and print media. Today, the majority poor population still has a very small voice. Nearly all media in Central America, except those in Costa Rica, are owned and controlled by the government or the wealthy classes with close political ties.

Nicaragua. In 1979, the revolutionary Sandinista government closed almost all print and electronic media including Radio Catolica, a radio station owned and operated by the Catholic Church (Avirgan, 1992). Radio transmitters financed by the U.S. Catholic Bishop's Conference have a "past shrouded in CIA secrecy" (Avirgan, 1992, p.13), according to the *National Catholic Reporter.* Radio Impacto was a private station that played music and anti-Sandinista propaganda. The Nicaraguan government requires broadcast operating licenses and closely scrutinizes distribution.

Some radio stations returned to the airwaves following the Central American peace accord signed in August 1987. It stated that all countries must have complete freedom for the press, radio, and television by November of that year. Although the February 1990 elections left the Sandanistas defeated, Nicaragua's economy struggles under continued military leadership.

Costa Rica. In Costa Rica, the most democratic nation in Central America, nearly all media are privately owned and controlled by the wealthy class (Salwen et al., 1991). Costa Ricans enjoy a high standard of living relative to their neighboring countries and press freedom is the norm there. During the Nicaraguan revolution, two radio transmitters in San Jose sent anti-communist messages via Radio Costa Rica to Nicaraguans. The ultra right-wing Costa Rica Democratic Association, funded by the U.S. Central Intelligence Agency (CIA), formed Radio Impacto in 1982 (Avirgan, 1992). The CIA faxed broadcast editorials from Washington. Radio Impacto supported the Contras, headquartered in Honduras. Its broadcasts of popular music found an audience in southern Nicaragua, even among the Sandinistas.

Panama. In 1988, many radio station owners spoke out against dictator Manuel Noriega ("TV Or Not TV," 1990). Independent television studios were closed for reporting on opposition rallies. Noriega closed the independent print and broadcast media and Panama's citizens were hungry for news in their native language. Underground broadcasts filmed in the United States aired in 18-min segments of "guerrilla television" on the Liberty Network. Longer broadcasts jeopardized the lives of all in the studio if the signals could be traced by Noriega's army. Liberty Network viewers, however, looked for real news about their country, not U.S. supported propaganda.

South America

Colombia. Privately owned radio is more popular than the one government network but the Colombian government controls television broadcasting. Political strife and the narcotics industry have made the road for Colombian broadcasting development a rocky one. Private investors introduced radio but by 1948 the military government revoked nearly all radio licenses and strictly censored news and political reporting ("Will The Air," 1992).

Colombian television began in 1954 under dictator Gustavo Rojas Pinilla who made television a state monopoly run by the Instituto Nacional de Radio y Television, also known as Inravision (Salwen et al., 1991). Rojas's ouster in 1958 kept television under state control. Inravision broadcasts one education channel and two commercial channels. The commercial channels air advertising and the government brokers airtime to independent programmers. Television may slowly return to private ownership by the end of the 1990s but the government actively censors it. Colombia's Vice Minister of Communications Felipe Tovar de Andres told *Variety:*

> "The new constitution establishes a fulltime autonomous state entity— one that will work independent of the ministry to oversee the regulation, control and vigilance of all TV activity. This organization will develop all future policies, including the possibility of privatizing emissions." ("Will The Air," 1992, p. 84)

Programmers can no longer get time slots on both channels. This encourages competition between channels and lays the groundwork for creating private ownership. Now, soap operas compete against soap operas and comedies against comedies.

Venezuela. Broadcasting is primarily a private venture interrupted periodically by military dictatorships. Television grew parallel to the oil industry, positively influencing Venezuela's economy. During the 1980s, programs on the three government channels were prescreened to assure cultural and educational emphasis (Salwen et al., 1991). With a return to democracy came interest in private television. However, studios were in a state of dilapidation.

In late November of 1992, Venezuelan revolutionaries captured the national television system for 3 hr. The failed coup attempt killed 10 people, including two station managers. On two television channels and one radio channel, the rebels urged Venezuelans to take to the streets and join the insurrection while the rebels bombed the presidential palace of Andres Perez and a military airport. One television station and the major cable supplier, Omnivision, unscrambled Cable News Network (CNN) coverage of the coup.

Peru. Peru pirated the radio waves with shortwave receivers until President Augusto B. Leguia's minister of defense built a shortwave station for military patrol reports and weather reports (Alisky, 1988c). When Peru celebrated its first 100 years of independence from Spain in 1921, construction of two stations began. Broadcast medium development took a back seat to military and civilian government power shifts in Peru. The public sector pioneered broadcasting here, enabling private stations to enter the field. When the socially conscious Peruvian military government seized power in 1968, it ordered 51% public ownership of broadcast facilities. The handful of wealthy families who had maintained a monopoly for many years criticized the policy. Most of them lived in the capital city of Lima and most stations were based there. Peruvian broadcast media did not serve the majority population of Indians.

The Law of Telecommunications of 1980 enables remote communities with meager resources to carry network programming provided they produce their own local news. A minister of transportation and communications enforces the laws and supervises licensing. Another administrator within the Communications Ministry monitors stations to ensure that they comply with the regulations requiring at least some cultural or educational programming. A law passed in 1985 requires local production for all television advertising.

Brazil. Brazil is by far the largest country in Latin America, both in land area and population (see Table 9.1). It is also a leader in broadcasting. Radio was the first medium used to unite the country and cut across its diverse class structure. It carried cultural, social, and political messages using the national language of Portuguese. Getulio Vargas, a fascist dictator who strictly censored radio broadcasting from 1930 through 1945, used radio broadcasts as a propaganda weapon. Creation of the Comissao Tecnica do Radio to control broadcasting personified the state's view that broadcasting was its privilege.

Relaxed censorship characterized the period between Vargas's fall and the 1964 military coup (Oliveira, 1988). The military siege lasted until 1984 and broadcasting could be censored any time in the name of national security. Today, with a return to civilian rule and more relaxed democratic regulations, Brazil's broadcasting is mostly private. Brazil boasts one of the world's largest broadcasting systems, that maximizes state-of-the-art technology. A detailed account of Brazilian television and the part played by TV Globo is given in the next chapter of this book.

A Sao Paulo-based vice president of a communications company reported that "Brazilians are TV crazy" (Ellison, 1993, p. 10A) and said that families watch an average of 7 hr per day, more than those in the United States. More Brazilian families own televisions than refrigerators, (Ellison, 1993, p. 10A). CONAR, Brazil's self-regulatory advertising body, monitors imported ads and prefers those produced locally. The state of broadcasting in Brazil does not satisfy everyone, however. In Sao Paulo, several homemade, illegal pirate stations transmit music and programming aimed at the small rural communities uninterested in the commercial programming targeting cities and wealthier groups.

Chile. Chile's population is literate and educated. Early radio was nearly all private and commercially supported. The government's interest in the airwaves lay in encouraging and guaranteeing educational and cultural programming. Television was a latecomer in the 1960s, the product of an experiment of technicians at the University of Chile and the Catholic University of Santiago. President Jorge Alessandri in 1963 refused the request for private commercial television. The Broadcast Law of 1970, developed under the Christian Democratic administration of Eduardo

Frei, enabled the government to set up a third station. Chilean television grew slowly, amid leadership changes, coups, overthrows, deaths, and new ideologies. Chilean universities now own four of the country's five television stations. The government owns the other (Alisky, 1988a).

Argentina. Argentina broadcasting was dominated for most of its existance by military regimes and their propaganda. The country returned to civilian rule in the early 1980s and a renaissance in cinema and television followed as broadcast media exiles returned. Radio is predominantly private, with 75 independent stations and 37 controlled by the national government, 4 by provincial governments, 3 by municipal governments, and 3 by universities (Salwen et al., 1991).

Entrepreneurs were the leaders in television broadcasting and the government set up rival stations to promote educational and cultural programming. In 1992, Argentine President Carlos Menem signed a law to reprivatize Buenos Aires television Channels 11 and 13, two of the three main competitive forces in production and broadcasting. Owners of Argentina's largest circulation morning newspaper, *Clarín*, scooped up Channel 13. Financiers from publishing and other communications media obtained a license for Channel 11.

The Caribbean

Jamaica. Inflation has outpaced the local advertising market and growth has been flat. Media competition is fierce. The government-owned Jamaica Broadcasting Service and Radio Jamaica in 1992 sold its remaining 25% stake in the advertising market. The government awarded a license for a private television station in 1993 but the owners have not yet raised the required start-up capital.

Dominican Republic. Father Pedro Riquoy runs a Creole-language radio station, Radio Enriquillo. By playing the guitar or bongo drum and singing the news, the Catholic priest can skirt government restrictions (Slavin, 1992). The program became known as "Radio Resistance" and could be picked up in the island's sister nation of Haiti.

Haiti. In 1978, the Catholic Church launched the award-winning Radio Soleil to serve as a "voice for the voiceless," defying a tradition of 34 years of military dictatorship. It promotes literacy and human rights education. The station is the first Creole-language station in Haiti and has experienced periodic shutdowns by Haitian government authorities. Facilities have been shot at and ransacked. Radio Soleil encouraged voters to come out in March of 1987 and later reported the noticeable absence of voters in the flawed January 1988 election. Programming has fluctuated from messages for political change to exclusively religious programming.

Puerto Rico / Virgin Islands. Broadcasters from these U.S. territories have petitioned the Federal Communications Commission to grant higher power to override interference from other Caribbean nations not included in communications treaties. Puerto Rico has about 70 radio stations, most struggling to stay on the air.

Cuba. Cuba was the first Third World country to claim nationwide print and electronic media coverage. U.S. financiers and private Cuban investors influenced Cuban broadcast development. Before the revolution, when Havana's broadcast media were unregulated and often chaotic, the forum was available to all. The airwaves boasted a highly competitive mix of print and electronic media and broadcasters were responsible for controversial programming and often irresponsible reporting. Finally, the Cuban government enacted the world's first "right-to-reply-to-radio" laws and dictator Fulgencio Batista and his officials instituted a strict censorship code (Lent, 1988).

Radio played a major role in Fidel Castro's revolution throughout the 1950s, linking guerrilla units and "informing" Cubans of his military program. The legendary Che Guevara launched Radio Rebelde in 1958, which quickly gained popularity among Cuban civilians as Batista increased censorship efforts. Castro also communicated by television with passionate speeches to garner support for his Communist campaign, sometimes for 4 to 6 hr without interruption.

The 1959 revolution that ended with Fidel Castro in power saw drastic changes in Cuba's media. Broadcast become an arm of the propaganda machine. In 1961, the Cuban government took control of CMQ broadcasting, the last independent broadcasting system in Cuba. Today, broadcast media are completely under state or Communist Party control. Cuba's technological gains since the revolution have been slight. Because of U.S. trade embargoes on all shipments to Cuba, replacement parts are scarce and nearly all electronic equipment is imported from Russia and assembled in Cuba.

The U.S. government accuses the Cuban government of jamming U.S. broadcasts. Cuba can interfere with radio broadcasts from California to New York and as far north as Iowa. The United States officially filed complaints in 1987 with the International Frequency Registration Board in Geneva ("Cuban Radio," 1987). Conversely, the U.S. Information Agency fueled the Cold War by funding Radio Marti in 1985 and TV Marti in 1990. Their stated purpose is to ensure "balanced and accurate" programming. The stations were named for Cuban national hero Jose Marti. TV Marti has experienced several technical problems as well as criticism in the United States. Castro's government jams the 3-hr daily 3 a.m. to 6 a.m. transmission and denounces the United States for invading Cuban airwaves. President George Bush's White House spokesman Marlin Fitzwater responded in a prepared statement in 1990:

> "We regret the Cuban regime's decision to attempt to deny the free flow of information by jamming, but we recall the experience of Radio Free Europe and Radio Liberty, in which the broadcasts were jammed for years yet people were able to listen." ("President OK's," 1990, p. 51).

TV Marti broadcasts its signal from a transmitter and antenna attached to a balloon floating 10,000 feet above Cudjoe Key in Florida.

Radio Marti, which transmits on the AM airwaves, has gained moderate acceptance among Cubans and served as the model for TV Marti. However, according to a report in The Economist, American officials at the U.S. Interests Section in Havana complained that Radio Marti is "staffed by liberals who oppose the American economic embargo against Cuba" and is alienating "hardline anti-Castro radio stations" ("America and Cuba," 1993, p.28). Similarly, the Castro government has won back listeners by increasing the amount of formerly forbidden rock and roll music.

PROGRAMMING

Although the United States boasts the world's three largest commercial networks, Brazil comes in fourth with the TV Globo Network and Mexico comes in fifth with Televisa, the parent company of Univision which is the Spanish-language network in the United States. In Latin America and the Caribbean, the most popular type of broadcast programming is entertainment. Radio broadcasts of traditional music underscore cultural identity, Mexico's ranchero music, the Islands' reggae, Brazil's samba, Bolivia and Peru's Andean flute music, Argentina's tango, and Paraguay's harp music. The government in Paraguay requires a specific percentage of native music broadcasts (Salwen et al., 1991).

There is, however, some emphasis on information as well as educational and cultural programming. Literacy is high throughout Latin America but in rural areas where illiteracy still can be found radio serves as a learning aid. Languages range from Spanish to Portuguese to native Indian tongues. Educational programs highlight agricultural techniques, health, and animal husbandry. Some church-owned stations even air literacy classes.

Television programming in Latin America before the 1970s relied heavily on U.S. imports such as *I Love Lucy*. Even today, you can see reruns of *Dynasty, Dallas,* and *The Addams Family,* (Oliveira, 1988; Salwen et al., 1991). Audiences, like those in the United States, enjoy situation comedies, adventure shows, variety shows, and prime-time soap operas called telenovelas. Many of the telenovelas produced in Mexico and Brazil are now exported to other countries in the hemisphere and to Europe.

In Cuba, government control of the airwaves allows for music, entertainment, news, and sports. Radio Habana Cuba airs daily programs in eight languages. The high cost of producing local programming has forced Cuba to become involved in television program exchanges with Nicaragua, Mexico, and Spain. The Communist Party has tried to stop the Western influence of rock music and television programs but with geographic proximity to the United States this proves difficult. Popular programs in Cuba include a public information call-in question show with bureaucrats, a nutritional information cooking show for housewives facing food shortages, coverage of foreign news as it relates to Cuban politics, a magazine-format program featuring personalities and music, and educational programs. The controversial TV Marti features news, sports, and entertainment.

Although U.S. programming dominates the airwaves in Mexico, television is the medium of choice for promoting Mexican culture as well as nationalism. Mexico is the only non-Communist Latin American nation that forbids religious programming. Believing in strict separation of church and state, men and women of the cloth cannot wear their garb in public and cannot grant broadcast interviews (Alisky, 1988b). Political campaigning by individual candidates cannot arbitrarily find its way to the airwaves. The government sanctions time periods for all competing political parties to present their views.

Radio Nacional in Peru, the nationwide government network, boasts the largest radio audience for news. Listeners tune in to privately owned stations for popular, jazz, rock, and folk music. On the television screen, sports programming, soccer matches in particular, and soap opera dramas are extremely popular. Over half of all Peruvian television programming is imported. Spanish-language programming from Mexico and Argentina and dubbed programming from the United States run repeatedly. For example viewers can watch a variety of vintage programs such as *The Three Stooges, The Little Rascals, Laurel and Hardy, The Flintstones, Cannon,* and *The Partridge Family.* Children's programming includes cartoons and wildlife programs.

In Brazil, government regulations require that at least 5% of programming on radio and television be information and education (Oliveira, 1988). However, radio stations primarily air music and news, whereas television focuses on variety shows and telenovelas.

Although Costa Rican law limits imported programs to 75 %, estimates show nearly 90% of broadcast schedules feature nonlocal programming. The state has one television channel that presents educational programming but viewers are few. Costa Ricans prefer to watch Venezuelan and Mexican soap operas, soccer matches, and dubbed U.S. program reruns. Costa Rican intellectuals criticize television programming, complaining about the negative influence of violent U.S. programs aired there. Programs such as *Los Magníficos (A-Team)* and *Koyak (Kojak)* may erode Costa Rican culture and its traditional pacifism. A coalition of Costa Rican writers, artists, and former government ministers, called CODELI, criticizes media control by elitists who act as censors, limiting the information made available to Costa Ricans.

Nicaraguan television begins transmissions in the morning with cartoons and concludes the programming day at midnight. Programs range from telenovelas, to old movies, to reruns of U.S. programs. About 1 hr per day features educational and public service programming, including information about AIDS, personal hygiene, and news and weather. Radio programs feature music as well as radionovelas. Video sales and rentals have escalated in popularity, leading to the demise of Nicaragua's cinema business.

Cable and Satellite

According to a 1993 report in *Variety* on Latin American cable television prospects, there were an estimated 3.5 million cable homes in Latin America, 1.5 million in Mexico alone, and nearly 24 cable channels to satisfy the demand (Besas, 1993). The two major cable markets are Mexico and Brazil. The key satellite for beaming programs throughout Latin America is Panamsat I.

Television has grown as countries traded microwave for satellite transmission. Called the "global television age," in which technology knows no political alliances or geographic borders, satellite dishes successfully bring television programming to formerly isolated Latin Americans. Mexico has an estimated 1 million satellite dishes. Nearly all of Latin America belongs to Intelsat. Argentina, Mexico, Venezuela, Brazil, Colombia, and Chile lead the pack in broadcast technology (Ellison, 1993). All have their own orbital communication satellites. Satellite uplinks are crucial for mountainous regions and countries like Chile which cover vast land masses. In fact, cable television throughout Latin America may expand to include international home shopping, interactive banking, and global religious networking (Ellison, 1993). Although the U.S. market is flat, industry experts see Asia and Latin America as the growth markets for television.

In Mexico, five cable networks carry U.S. Programming: CBS, ABC, NBC, PBS, and a movie channel. Satellite dishes dot the Mexican metropolitan landscape. Brasilsat 1 was Brazil's first communications satellite launched in 1985. MTV arrived in Sao Paulo, Brazil in 1990. U.S.-based Home Box Office (HBO) and Omnivision, a Venezuelan pay-television company, launched HBO-Ole in 1991. The 24-hr network is a first of its kind because there are no commercials. The Spanish-language service airs popular feature films, children's programs, sports, and concerts that reach the Caribbean and most of Latin America, except Brazil. Subscribers pick up HBO-Ole via the Panamsat satellite to cable operators and direct-broadcast services to backyard dishes (Besas, 1993). From the United States, Panamsat also transmits TNT, CNN, and ESPN. Caracas-based HBO-Ole plans to use 10% of programming originated from Latin America.

Cable industry experts view Argentina as the prime cable market in Latin America. Cablevision and Video Cable Communication began operations in Buenos Aires during the mid-1980s ("Argentina Is Prime," 1992). Its viewers receive approximately 10 cable channels and a locally produced channel called Space, which is also carried in Paraguay.

In 1992, the Caribbean Satellite Network (CSN), based in Miami, began broadcasting Caribbean-and West-Indian-oriented music and cultural programming on the Galaxy 3 satellite ("President OK's," 1990). The 24-hr transmission may be picked up with a home satellite dish by viewers across the United States, southern Canada, Mexico, Central America, northern South America, the West Indies, and the Caribbean. Its primary investor, Delroy Cowan, has spent millions of dollars on the project ("President OK's," 1990). It represents his latest entrepreneurial venture following successes in a Caribbean import company, a small airline, and the Caribbean's largest amusement complex, Coney Park. The ad-supported network is programmed for an international audience. The format is comparable to that of MTV from the United States. The network has initially attracted Caribbean-based advertisers promoting tourism and travel-related businesses. A morning news show, *The Caribbean Sunrise*, headlines the CSN program day followed by a mix of music videos featuring jazz, gospel, rap, blues, and reggae concerts. On the weekend, CSN features a live dance party staged in its Miami studios and a top-10 countdown show.

New government regulations in the Bahamas opened doors for the first privately owned radio station there in 1993. Thirty investors also submitted applications to set up a cable television system. Prime Minister

Hubert Ingraham said that the Bahamian market cannot support more than one cable network and the government expects a company licensed to bring cable television there to work with the state-owned Broadcasting Corporation of the Bahamas (*Latin America*, 1993).

The African–Caribbean Satellite Channel entered an informal program supply agreement with Black Entertainment Television of the United States but is responsible for raising launch capital. It is having a hard time getting cash from the United Kingdom, United States, or the Caribbean (Satellite TV Finance, 1993).

According to a *Forbes* magazine report in 1993, 10 major media companies are looking to launch global satellite news programs ("All-news," 1993). The British Broadcasting Corporation and Reuters are beginning plans for a partnership for all-news programming in Latin America. As economies grow, industry experts predict the satellite broadcast business could revolutionize broadcast media throughout Latin America and the Caribbean.

REFERENCES

Alisky, M. (1988a). Chile. In P. T. Rosen (Ed.), *International handbook of broadcasting systems* (pp. 61–68). New York: Greenwood.

Alisky, M. (1988b). Mexico. In P. T. Rosen (Ed.), *International handbook of broadcasting systems* (pp. 215–224). New York: Greenwood.

Alisky, M. (1988c). Peru. In P. T. Rosen (Ed.), *International handbook of broadcasting systems* (pp. 237–242). New York: Greenwood.

America and Cuba off the screen. (1993, July 3). *The Economist*, p. 28.

Argentina is prime as cable market. (1992, March 23). *Variety*, p. 80.

Argentine Channels 11, 13 reprivatized. (1992, December 7). *Variety*, p. 45.

Avirgan, T. (1992, March 13). Beam them up, Costa Rica: Church-funded transmitters once used for U.S. propaganda. *National Catholic Reporter*, p. 13.

Besas, P. (1993, March 29). Yanks seek TV El Dorado. *Variety*, pp. 47, 74, 80.

Buenos Aires private TV channel leaves state TV eating its dust. (1987, March 25). *Variety*, p. 116.

Cuban radio causing interference. (1987, July 27). *TV Digest*, p. 5.

Ellison, K. (1993, May 14). Dish antennas signal trend in Latin America. *Journal of Commerce*, pp. 1A, 10A.

Fuhrman, P. (1993, November 22). All-news orgy, anyone? *Forbes*, pp. 54–59.

Latin America. (1993, September). Caribbean Update, Inc. [On-line].

Lent, J. (1988). Cuba. In P. T. Rosen (Ed.), *International handbook of broadcasting systems* (pp. 79–88). New York: Greenwood.

Oliveira, O. (1988). Brazil. In P. T. Rosen (Ed.), *International handbook of broadcasting systems* (pp. 35–46). New York: Greenwood.

President OK's TV Marti funding. (1990, September 3). *Broadcasting*, p. 51.

Salwen, M. B., Garrison, B., & Buckman, R. T. (1991). Latin America and the Caribbean. In J.C. Merrill (Ed.), *Global journalism* (pp. 267–310). New York: Longman.

Satellite TV Finance. (1993, March 18). *Broadcasting and Publishing* [On-line].

Slavin, J. (1992, April 3). Radio Enriquillo sending Haiti bad news blues. *National Catholic Reporter*, pp. 15–16.

Taylor, R. (1988, October 17). Church to change Radio Soleil line. *National Catholic Reporter*, p. 13.

The new global customer. (1993, Autumn/Winter). *Fortune*, pp. 68–77.

TV or not TV? (1990, February 10). *TV Guide*, pp. 27–30.

Will the air become free in Columbia? (1992, March 23). *Variety*, p. 84.

Chapter 10

Globo TV: The Growth of a Brazilian Monopoly

Venicio A. De Lima

Brazilian television appeared in 1950 with the inauguration in Sao Paulo of TV Tupi, a station belonging to the Diarios e Emissoras Associados, a pioneer communication enterprise led by Assis Chateaubriand. Brazil became the first country in Latin America and the fifth country in the world to have commercial television. From 1950 to the mid-1960s, however, the country was not able to surpass a total of 2 million television sets. Starting in 1968, with the establishment of a domestic electric and electronic industry and encouraged by a program of direct consumer credit, television sales grew so rapidly that at the end of that year Brazil had about 4 million television sets (Ortiz, 1988).

An important aspect of Brazilian television during this period was its exclusively regional character. Until 1967, only three microwave systems existed in Brazil, linking Rio de Janeiro to Sao Paulo, Belo Horizonte, and Brasilia. Nationwide direct television broadcasting was initiated only after 1969, with the inauguration in Rio de Janeiro of the first television center of Empresa Brasileira de Telecommunicacoes (Brasilian Enterprise of Telecommunications) that made possible the interconnection of television stations to the National System of Telecommunications. Neither the installation of the electric and electronic industry nor the existence of a national telecommunications system would have been possible without the decisive participation and support of the authoritarian regime (Frederico; 1982, Ortiz, 1988).

The necessary preconditions existed for the Emissoras Associadas—TV Tupi to become the first national television network. The network was already operating in several states and had the support of a radio network and of several newspapers. The death of its founder, however, intensified the internal dispute over the power to control this pioneer media group. It never became national and it was surpassed by the Globo Organization, which was linked to the leading Brazilian newspaper *O Globo* in Rio de Janeiro. This group was to become the most powerful organization in Brazilian television.

In 1965, 15 years after the introduction of television in Brazil, TV Globo, Channel 4 from Rio de Janeiro, was inaugurated. This station appeared in the wake of a scandal that was the object of an investigation that same year by a *Comissao Parlamentar de Inquerito* (CPI; Parliamentary Investigative Commission) in the Brazilian House of Representatives. TV Globo had been made possible only through an agreement of technical and financial cooperation signed with the North American group Time-Life, an agreement that represented a flagrant violation of Brazilian legislation.

The agreement between Globo and Time-Life had been finalized in 1962, before the military coup d'etat that overthrew President Joao Goulart. After the coup, despite findings of the CPI that had clearly demonstrated the illegal involvement of the Globo Organization with its North American partner, the Brazilian authoritarian regime chose to ignore not only the final report of the CPI, but also an opinion put forth by the National Telecommunications Council. After a tortuous legal procedure, President and General Costa e Silva put an end to the affair, using his legal authority to settle the case in September of 1968 (Herz, 1987).

The reciprocal commitment between the authoritarian regime and the Globo Organization, which was already clear during the CPI hearings and the settlement of the Time-Life scandal, became even stronger during the terms of President and General Medici (1969–1974) and President and General Geisel (1974–1979). By the time of President-General Figueiredo (1979 -1985), the already consolidated TV Globo network became a true "ministry of communications," powerful to the point of challenging the fading authoritarian regime.

THE AUTHORITARIAN REGIME

Garrastazu Medici was an Army general and the president of Brazil from 1969 to 1974, the third of a series of generals who ruled the country from April of 1964. Chosen by a military junta, which had taken power to prevent a civilian vice president from taking office during the illness of President and General Costa e Silva, Medici came into office armed with an exceptional legal instrument that had no precedent in Brazilian political history: the Institutional Act Number 5. This instrument, which prevailed until 1978, provided the president of the republic with power to strip legislative powers from elected representatives, confiscate private wealth, fire state officials, promulgate decree laws, install a state of siege without consent of the national congress, and suspend the basic guarantees of free speech and free expression.

From the time the Institutional Act Number 5 was decreed in 1968 until 1980, there was vigorous official censorship in Brazilian media, especially television. The tentacles of censorship stretched from the content of soap operas to newscasts. The main target was the leader in viewing audience, TV Globo's *Jornal Nacional*. From 1980 on, television stations no longer received regular messages from censoring agencies (Marconi, 1980).

The country was also under a new constitution, imposed by the junta in 1969, which redefined the attributions of the three branches of government by giving excessive power to the executive to the detriment of the legislature and the judiciary. Furthermore, Brazil was experiencing the most unsettled period of its recent history. There was growing social unrest, partially restrained by repression of the labor and student movements, which were expressing themselves through several urban guerilla actions. Political analysts are unanimous in considering the Medici period (19691–974) the most repressive of Brazilian history, surpassing even the dark days of the Vargas dictatorship during the *Estado Novo* from 1937 to 1945 (Stepan, 1973).

On the economic level, it was during the Medici period that Brazil experienced the false euphoria of the so-called "Brazilian miracle." From 1967 to 1972, the country showed impressive rates of growth. The gross national product grew at a rate of 10% a year and inflation was controlled at around 15%. The foreign press went to the extreme of comparing such growth to the Japanese and German miracles of the post-World War II period ("Brazil Plans Trading," 1972, p. 15) but failed to take into consideration the cruel fact that the miracle was the result of a model that was politically authoritarian and economically exclusive, benefitting only 5% of the Brazilian population (Furtado, 1981).

Thanks to vigorous repression and to rigid censorship of the press and broadcasting, plus an efficient propaganda campaign launched by the Special Public Relations Office of the Presidency, it was not too difficult to create a climate of euphoria and silence any popular resistance to the authoritarian regime. An observation made at the beginning of 1973 by then President and General Medici became a symbol of media censorship in those hard times:

> I feel happy every night, when I turn on the TV to watch the news. While the news tells of strikes, agitation, assassination attempts and conflicts in several parts of the world, Brazil marches in peace, on its road to development. It is as if I took a tranquilizer after a day's work. (Carvalho, Kehl, & Ribeiro, 1980, p.31).

Some years later, in a special edition about the 1970s, the weekly magazine *Veja*, which has the largest circulation in the country, summarized the climate of the period:

> "Like in a room full of mirrors, the country which General Medici, more than anyone else, embodied, was the reflection of its own image, which the official propaganda projected over a dark background of censorship. Medici himself seemed to sincerely believe in the mirage. ("Os Anos 70," 1979, p. 32)

Nothing symbolized this climate of euphoria better than the feeling of national pride, celebrated by the whole country and promptly manipulated by the government, that came from Brazil winning its third World Soccer Championship in June of 1970. This much acclaimed victory also marked the first time that Brazil saw a direct television broadcast of an international event. The broadcast of the World Soccer Championship from Mexico was the first concrete result of the deliberate government effort to provide Brazil with a modern telecommunications infrastructure, indispensable to its project of "national integration" under the doctrine of "security and development" that prevailed during the authoritarian regime (Mattos, 1980).

TV GLOBO'S MONOPOLY

When the Globo scandal with Time-Life ended, the Brazilian group already had franchises in the three main Brazilian markets: Rio de Janeiro (Channel 4), Sao Paulo (Channel 5), and Belo Horizonte (Channel 12) . In the next 4 years, Globo obtained franchises in Brasilia, the capital of the country, and in Recife, the most important city in the northeast, besides having three affiliated stations in 1972. From then on, Globo would launch an aggressive campaign of affiliation contracts. In 1973, there were six affiliated stations, a number that more than doubled in the next year, reaching 13. In 1982, the total number of affiliated stations reached 36, 12 times the number of 10 years before.

By 1986, Globo had a television network, the fourth largest in the world, consisting of seven network stations, 36 affiliates, and six repeating stations for a total of 49 channels, covering 3,991 of the 4,063 Brazilian municipalities which is more than 93% of the country's total population and 95% of the 17 million homes with television sets. The potential audience of the network is more than 100 million viewers and covers 98% of Brazilian territory ("Globo Has Brazil," 1987).

Considering that, according to 1980 data, 75% of this immense audience were captives of Globo programming, it becomes evident that the network maintained a de facto monopoly in Brazilian television. *Jornal Nacional*, for example, was watched daily by an average audience of more than 60 million people, which represents almost three times the number of viewers mobilized by similar newscasts in Japan and more than four times the number of viewers who watched the BBC nightly news in Britain ("30 Anos de TV," 1980).

The audience monopoly and the concentration of the advertising budgets eliminates any possibility of competition. Data extracted from the specialized magazine *Propaganda* ("Os 15 Anos da Globo," 1980), in a special edition about the 15 years of the Globo network, show that, for a total budget of approximately $500 million (U.S. currency) injected into Brazilian television, $350 million (70%) went to the Globo network. By 1986 *Variety* ("Globo has Brazil in its Pocket," 1987) estimated that around $600 million (U.S. currency) of the Brazilian advertising pie went to TV Globo. At the same time, in order to further this gigantic commercial scheme, TV Globo inaugurated a computerized system of commercialization, the Sistema de Apoio a Comercializacao (SISCOM; Commercialization Support System), which has been in operation in the largest Brazilian markets since 1980. This technology allows advertising agencies and clients, through their own terminals, to find out in a matter of seconds the availability of advertising space in the national programming of the network. Furthermore, SISCOM furnishes a list of programming sponsors at any given date, information about the products by brand or by the name of the manufacturer, and even the name of the advertising agency.

Nowadays, nothing illustrates the power of Globo better than its expansion into new areas of the cultural industry and into other fields of the economic and financial sectors. This has turned Globo into a typical conglomerate of monopoly capitalism: a conglomerate that owns TV Monte Carlo (airing in Italy) and that has become the third largest exporter of television programming in the world, behind only the United States and Britain. Globo's programming sales totaled $12 million (U.S. currency) and involved 128 countries outside Brazil in 1986 ("Globo Has Brazil," 1987; "Os Anos 70," 1979) and more than $25 million sales in 1992 (Lamb, 1993).

The conglomerate encompasses, in addition to the TV Globo network and the newspaper *O Globo* (with the largest circulation in the country), the following enterprises: Globo Radio System (with 20 AM and FM stations), a publishing house (Rio Grafica), the Globo System of Recording and Audio–Visual enterprises including a recording company (Som Livre), a video company (Globo Video) and a commercial production company, (Globotec), TELECOM-Electronic Industry, a show-business company (VASGLO), a promotion firm, and art galleries. Besides these holdings, Globo includes the Roberto Marinho

Foundation, which, among other activities, currently takes on a questionable leadership role in the field of television education that used to be the sole responsibility of a network of state-owned stations ("Globo Has Brazil," 1987).

THE AUTHORITARIAN REGIME AND TV GLOBO

The consolidation of TV Globo's virtual monopoly in the 1970s was paralleled by the consolidation of an exclusive economic model, supported by the authoritarian regime, which had in the Globo Organization a crucial ally and accomplice. From an economic point of view, TV Globo had an indispensable role in the integration of a country with continental dimensions through the integration of its consumer market (Caparelli, 1982). From a political point of view, Globo's programming was indispensable as a medium for a national message of developmental optimism, "positive messages" in the official discourse, fundamental to the legitimation, and maintenance of authoritarianism.

In January of 1972, Minister of Communications Higino Corsetti, on the eve of introducing color television in Brazil, made clear what the regime expected from the television stations:

> In the case of Brazil, TV is not only a medium in action, with its communicative power. We need not forget that today TV is also a factor of development, a precious instrument of social and economic integration. It is necessary to reconcile the interests of the stations with what must be done in terms of the national interest and the interest of the viewers. My concern with the quality of the programming, therefore, is still further justified; the new viewers that we are incorporating need to be well informed and need to receive *positive messages*. [Italics added] ("A Opiniao do Ministro," 1972, pp. 49–50)

About 2 years later, in December of 1973, that same authority admitted that Globo had been the only television station that had fulfilled, up to that point, the demands of the regime: "the electronic transmission of recreation, information and education, by a private enterprise, founded in the solid structure of a modern enterprise" (Carvalho et al., 1980, p. 13).

The optimism cherished by the regime found its highest programming expression in the so-called *Padrao Globo de Qualidade* (Globo Pattern of Quality). It was characterized by visual opulence, the sanitizing of pictures, and the expulsion from television screens of any facts that could be viewed as expressing a negative view of life of the country. TV Globo in the 1970s, a perfect mirror of the regime, presented a Brazil without social conflict, repression, or poverty. Nothing sums up this Brazil of TV Globo better than the words of the 1970 New Year's message of the network that were aired throughout the decade:

> Today is a new day of a new time which has started. On these days of course, happiness will be for all, it suffices to wish. All our dreams may become true; the future has begun. Today the party is yours, the party is ours. It is for whoever wants it, for whoever comes. (Carvalho et al., 1980, p. 11)

Years later a top executive of the Globo network, referring to the Medici period (1969–1974), admitted that

> a nice marriage happened between Globo and the image of Brasil Grande [Great Brazil]. Globo became the representative of the ideals and dreams of the miracle, of the developmental pride, of the glamour, over and above the crises of the regime, over the ups and downs of the military system during these 15 years. Globo became a bastion of the middle class, floating above reality and selling to the viewer a pretty Brazil, a well-succeeded country, a Brazil of the miracle. It was affinity, it was not a Machiavellian plan put forth by somebody. Globo is, without any doubt, the best-finished product, the biggest success of the dictatorship. Globo made concrete an abstraction: Order and Progress. (Carvalho et al., 1980, p. 31).

Such was the success of this marriage that the Globo network was able to announce at the end of the 1970s that Globa had the 10 most popular programs in Rio and Sao Paulo. ("Os 15 Anos da Globo," 1980).

As early as the mid-1970s, however, TV Globo's virtual monopoly was beginning to worry even those in the regime who became aware of the economic and political power that was being concentrated in the hands of a single private cultural industry. Without referring specifically to the Globo network, Colonel Euclides Quandt de Oliveira (1975), then the Minister of Communications, affirmed:

> The concentration of powerful media of mass communication in the hands of a group with commercial ideological interests constitutes a great danger, because they are a significant instrument of support or dissent: they may become beyond control of any controlling or moderating institution, thus turning into the hydra of today. The monopoly, both of channels in the hands of one group, and of audience, is highly detrimental. It is convenient to provide options to the viewers in the field of television, taking into consideration not only national and regional values, but also those originating from other sources. (pp. 11–12)

Such concern with the virtual monopolization of television began to assume an even more defined configuration. In March of 1979, President and General Joao Figueiredo came into power and included breaking the television monopoloy in his platform of government. This platform states that "the formation of national networks will be stimulated, especially in the field of television, as a means of supporting the goal of national integration and of assuring the economic and financial stability of the enterprises, within a competitive and balanced regime" ("Figueiredo: Radiodifusao," 1979, p. 10).

The disproportionate growth of the Globo Organization, therefore, worried its own partners in the authoritarian regime. The regime's concerns became even clearer about 1 year later. In a hearing of the Communications Committee of the House of Representatives, Minister and Chief Said Farhat of the Office of Social Communications of the Presidency contended that "the services of television in the country are presently in a stage of pre-monopoly, due to the concentration of audience in the programming of the Globo Network" ("Farhat Confirma Monopolio," 1980, p. 5). It was the first time that the regime, through its main spokesman, admitted publicly the power and the domination of the Globo television network. As a consequence of the regime's visible concern with the virtual monopoly of the Globo network, in an unprecedented decision all seven franchises of the Diarios Associados–TV Tupi network were revoked in 1980. With the opening of bids for new franchises, the stations of that pioneer network were divided in the next year between two groups in the hope they would be better able to compete with Globo: The Silvio Santos Group, thus strengthening the Sistema Brasileiro de Televisao (Brazilian Television System), and the Bloch Group, which now controls the Rede Manchete (Manchete Network) ("Agora e com," 1981). Those measures, however, have had no major effect on TV Globo's audience leadership or enormous economic edge in relation to the other networks.

POLITICAL INSTITUTIONS

Analysts of Brazilian life agree that traditional institutions, such as political parties, labor unions, and professional politicians, have been extremely weak in Brazil's political history. The lack of democratic tradition was reinforced with the 1964 coup. The political parties were dismantled and the main labor unions, which had a history of government patronage and interference, suffered new interventions. All but a few working-class leaders escaped imprisonment or exile but elected politicians were stripped of their political rights during the following years and most were automatically eliminated from professional political life (Skidmore, 1967, 1988).

In such a social environment, not few institutions of civil society can survive with any sort of relative independence and autonomy. In Brazil, some would argue that the important alternative institutions are the business community, the Catholic Church, and the media (Dantas Mota, 1987). The Brazilian state, however, has a number of different ways to control the media, specifically broadcasting. It has the licensing power. It is one of the main advertisers. It regulates the industry. It makes decisions about the importation of euipment, video, and film. It owns and operates most of the physical infrastructure necessary to the functioning of radio and television stations (phone lines, microwaves, satellites). Still, there is a general consensus among Brazilian media institutions that the Globo Organization's newspaper, magazines, and radio and television networks are by far the most politically powerful, independent, and autonomous. Globo's media were able to benefit from their reciprocal commitment and identity with the authoritarian regime during the 1970s and grew economically and politically to the point of having a uniquely important role in Brazilian civil society.

One also has to consider that Globo President Roberto Marinho, one of only three Brazilians included in Forbes list of the richest men in the world, personifies a particular type of entrepreneur (Seneker, 1987). He took over the newspaper *O Globo* at the age of 21 years, after the death of his father in 1925, and has since directed the transformation of the Globo Organization into one of the biggest Brazilian private conglomerates. However, he has done so with a deep sense of a particular mission, trying to run his conglomerate not only as a business, but also, as he likes to put it, as a "public service."

At the inauguration of the first Globo radio station in 1944, Marinho emphasized that "this is not only a radio station we are launching. It is a new way Globo has found to serve the country" ("Globo Has Brazil," 1987, p. 131). More than 20 years later, in an interview with of the *New York Times* (Riding, 1987), he adhered to the same kind of perspective:

> Yes, I use [Globo's] power, but I always do so patriotically, trying to correct things, looking for the best paths for the country and its states. We would like to have power to fix everything that doesn't work in Brazil. We dedicate all power to this. If power is used to disrupt a country, to destroy its customs, then it is not good, but if it is used to improve things, as we do, it is good. (p. A4)

This particular "missionary" vision of Roberto Marinho, coupled with the weakness of traditional political institutions and in spite of Brazil's omnipresent state, helped to transform TV Globo into an extremely powerful institution in the political process. TV Globo came to occupy a space that is now used in accordance with its own economic and political interests.

TV Globo's Connection

As Dreifuss (1981) convincingly argued, the 1964 coup was planned and executed by representatives of the interests of industrial and financial capital, multinational and associated, articulated over the years to take control of the Brazilian state. Contrary to previous historical situations,

Brazilian empresarios (business owners) have led the political process and have even used an association, the Instituto de Pesquisas e Estudos Sociais (Institute of Social Study and Research), to meet formally with other class factions and institutions (politicians, the military, professionals, sectors of the church, etc.). Dreifuss listed hundreds of people who were actively involved in this process. What is more revealing, however, is that several of the key figures in this process had some kind of relationship with the Globo Organization. When several of these same people later became high officials in the authoritarian regime, they were extremely instrumental in acting in Globo's interest, first in the Time-Life scandal and then during the consolidation of TV Globo's virtual monopoly (Herz, 1987).

Since the Globo Organization took an active part in the actual planning of the April 1, 1964 coup, its role as ideological mediator between the new dominant group and the dominated classes emerged naturally. The consolidation of TV Globo as a strong and modern capitalist enterprise served the state and the regime, inasmuch as they had identical interests. Of course the Globo Organization was, and remains, a Brazilian capitalist conglomerate that has important contacts with multinational capital (e.g., through advertising). Nevertheless, as the contradictions within the dominant group increased and TV Globo consolidated itself as a virtual monopoly, the political differences between the regime and the Globo Organization became more visible.

While Institutional Act Number 5 lasted (1968–1978), there was a double identification of Globo with the authoritarian regime. First, the TV Globo network represented the model of an efficient and modern capitalist enterprise well adjusted to the exclusive, concentrationist, and transnationalized economic policy. Second, in its news and other programming, the Globo Network was instrumental in creating, maintaining, and reproducing the hegemonic climate of euphoria through a distorted view of life in the country—a view that legitimated the socioeconomic structure in which the network itself was inserted. In serving the regime through misinformation, TV Globo was serving itself, working to consolidate its monopoly and the conglomerate of enterprises to which it belonged.

There was, of course, the excuse of censorship in the period from

1968 to 1978. However, after 1980 the political role of TV Globo, distorting, suppressing, and promoting information, went much beyond the direct official censorship of the authoritarian regime. The enormous growth of TV Globo during the 1970s, the historical weakness of Brazilian traditional political institutions, and Roberto Marinho's peculiar notion of "public mission" managed to transform the network into an economic and political institution so powerful that it became an eventual threat to the authoritarian regime itself. It was not without reason that Minister of Communication Oliveira (1975) expressed, as early as 1975, his fear that television monopoly constituted a "great threat" because it was an "instrument of support or dissent" threatening to "get out of the reach of any controlling or moderating institution [and] thus becoming the hydra of today" (pp. 11–12). Such concern makes transparent the contradiction in which the authoritarian regime had immersed itself: It helped to create the monster that eventually defied it.

PROSPECTUS FOR THE FUTURE

Globo TV was a key institution in the transition from military to civilian rule in Brazil from 1984 to 1985. Through its enormous power of articulation within the dominant group, the Globo Organization was able to dissociate from authoritarianism and to reestablish itself as a leading institution in the new "democratic" regime (Lima, 1988).

Globo TV's lasting political influence was quite visible during all the years of the "New Republic" (1985–1990) and it undoubtedly played a central role in the 1989 presidential electoral process, among other reasons, by publicly supporting the candidate that eventually was elected (Lima, 1993).

As Brazil faces the difficult process of consolidating a fragile representative democracy in the 1990s, all indications point to the increasing role of the Globo Organization, and especially the Globo TV network, in Brazilian political life.

REFERENCES

Agora e com o ibope [Now it is with the ratings]. (1981, April 1). *Isto E'*, pp. 56–62.

A opiniao do ministro [The ministry's opinion]. (1972, January 12). *Veja*, pp. 49–50.

Brazil plans trading companies—Gigantic "economic miracle" is goal. (1972, July 30). *New York Times*, Section 3, p. 15.

Caparelli, S. (1982). *Televisao e capitalismo no Brasil* [Television and capitalism in Brazil]. Porto Alegre: LP&M.

Carvalho, E., Kehl, M. R., & Ribeiro, S. N. (1980). *Anos 70/televisao* [70s/television]. Rio de Janeiro: Europa.

Dantas Mota, L. (1987). *Quem manda no Brasil?* [Who gives the orders in Brazil?]. Sao Paulo: Atica.

Dreifuss, R. (1981). *1964: A conquista do estado* [1964: The conquest of the state]. Petropolis: Vozes.

Farhat confirma monopolio na TV [Farhat ratifies the existence of the TV monopoly]. (1980, October 15). *Correio Braziliense*, p. 5.

Figueiredo: Radiodifusao e privada e de Brasileiros [Figueiredo: Broadcasting is private and belongs to Brazilians]. (1979, March 28). *0 Globo*, p. 10.

Frederico, M. E. B. (1982). *Historia da comunicacao —Radio e TV no Brasil* [History of communication —Radio and TV in Brazil]. Petropolis: Vozes.

Furtado, C. (1981). *O Brasil pos-milagre* [The post-miracle Brazil]. Rio de Janeiro: Paz e Terra.

Globo has Brazil TV in its pocket. (1987, March 25). *Variety*, pp. 131–144.

Herz, D. (1987). *A historia secreta da rede Globo* [The secret history of Globo network]. Porto Alegre: Tche.

Lamb, C. (1993, May 18). Programa "voce decide," da Globo, ja esta em 120 paises, *Gazeta Mercantil*, p. 3.

Lima, Venicio A. de. (1988). The state, television, and political power in Brazil. *Critical Studies in Mass Communicaton, 5*, 108–122.

Lima, Venicio A. de. (1993). Brazilian television in the 1989 presidential election: Constructing a president. In T. Skidmore (Ed.), *Television, politics, and the transition to democracy in Latin America*. Washington/Baltimore: The Woodrow Wilson Center Press/The Johns Hopkins University Press.

Marconi, P. (1980). *A censura politica na imprensa Brasileira: 1968–978* [The political censorship in the Brazilian press: 1968–1978]. Rio de Janeiro: Global.

Mattos, S. (1980). *The impact of Brazilian military government on the development of TV in Brazil*. Unpublished doctoral dissertation, University of Texas at Austin.

Oliveira, E. Q. de (1975). *A televisao no Brasi* [Television in Brazil]. Brasilia: Ministerio das Comunicacaoes.

Ortiz, R. (1988). *A Moderna tradicao brasileira.* Rio de Janeiro: Paz e Terra.

Os anos 70 [The 70's.]. (1979, December 26). *Veja,* p. 32.

Os 15 anos da Globo [Globo's 15 years]. (1980, April). *Propaganda,* pp. 20–22, 36–42.

Riding, A. (1987, January 12). One man's views color Brazil's TV eye. *New York Times,* p. A4.

Roberto Marinho: O fazedor de reis [Roberto Marinho: The king maker]. (1984, December 12). *Isto E',* pp. 18–21.

Seneker, H. (1987, October 5). The world's billionaires. *Forbes,* pp. 81–170.

Skidmore, T. E. (1967). *Politics in Brazil.* New York: Oxford University Press.

Skidmore, T. E. (1988). *The politics of military rule in Brazil: 1964–1985.* New York: Oxford University Press.

Stepan, A. (Ed.). (1973). *Authoritarian Brazil: Origins, policies and future.* New Haven, CT: Yale University Press.

30 anos de TV, 15 anos de monopolio [30 years of TV, 15 years of monopoly]. (1980, April 27). *Jornal do Brasil,* p. 1.

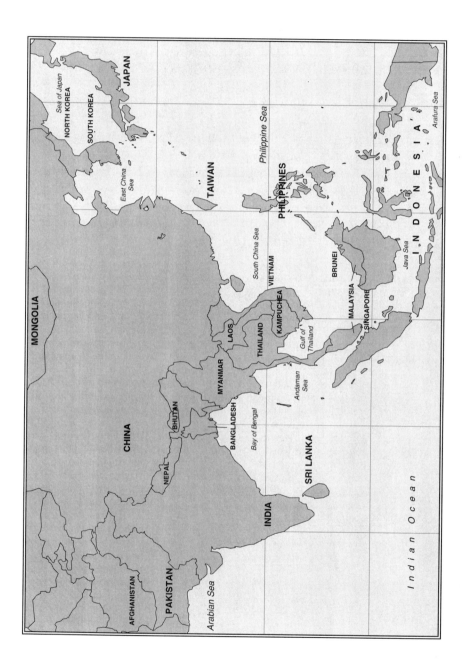

222

Chapter 11

Asia

Hsiang-Wen Hsiao

Asia contains nearly two thirds of the earth's population. It is a culturally diverse region of the world. There are great contrasts in different parts of the continent. In some countries, there are many different cultures, languages, and dialects but in others there is relative uniformity. The broadcasting media are mainly national, controlled either by government departments or by public corporations. Most of the poorer developing countries in the region stress the use of the media for political control as well as for education, change, and economic growth. Especially in Communist countries, such as China and North Korea, broadcasting is the voice of the party and reflects the policy and thinking of its leaders. Broadcasting has also been recognized as a major tool in developing national unity in multiracial, multilingual, and multireligious societies.

The region contains some of the world's richest countries (Japan, oil rich Brunei, Hong Kong, and Singapore), and others that have grown to medium world economic ranks (South Korea, Taiwan, Malaysia, and perhaps Thailand). Most of Asia's population, however, even in fast growing China, lives at a very low economic level (see Table 11.1).

With technological improvement and some economic growth in recent years, broadcasting has expanded considerably in most countries. The region as a whole had an average of 10 radio and 2.5 television receivers per 1,000 people in 1985 (Merrill, 1991). By 1994, receiver set ownership

Table 11.1.
Asia

Country	Population (In Millions)	Growth (%)	Land Area (Square Kilometers)	GNP/Capita (1992 U.S. Currency)	Radio Sets (In Millions)	Television sets (In Millions)
East Asia						
China	1192.0	1.1	9,596,961	380	206.00	227.88
Hong Kong	5.8	0.7	1,045	15,380	3.70	1.75
Japan	125.0	0.3	377,801	28,220	110.00	100.00
Korea, North	23.1	1.9	120,538	1,427	2.50	2.00
Korea, South	44.5	1.0	99,016	6,790	42.57	10.48
Macau	0.4	1.6	16	—	0.12	0.07
Mongolia	2.4	2.7	1,566,500	—	0.28	0.14
Taiwan	21.1	1.0	36,000	—	8.62	7.00
Southeast Asia						
Brunei	0.3	2.6	5,765	—	0.06	0.07
Cambodia	10.3	2.9	181,035	200	0.86	0.07
Indonesia	199.7	1.6	1,904,569	670	26.00	11.00
Laos	4.7	2.9	236,800	250	0.50	0.08
Malaysia	19.5	2.3	329,749	2,790	7.46	2.00

	Population	Growth	Land area	GNP	Radio	Television
Myanmar	45.4	1.9	676,578	—	3.30	1.00
Philippines	68.7	2.4	300,000	770	8.30	7.00
Singapore	2.9	1.2	618	15,750	0.82	0.65
Thailand	59.4	1.4	513,115	1,840	10.00	3.30
Vietnam	73.1	2.3	331,689	—	7.00	2.50
South Central Asia						
Afghanistan	17.8	2.8	652,090	—	1.67	0.10
Bangladesh	116.6	2.4	143,998	220	4.60	0.35
Bhutan	0.8	2.3	47,000	180	0.02	—
India	911.6	1.9	3,287,590	310	65.00	20.00
Maldives	0.2	3.2	298	500	0.03	0.01
Nepal	22.1	2.4	140,797	170	0.63	0.25
Pakistan	126.4	2.8	796,095	410	10.20	2.08
Sri Lanka	17.9	1.5	65,610	540	3.30	0.70

Note: Population (mid 1994 estimates), population growth (natural increase), and Gross national product per capita (1992) in U.S. dollar equivalents are from *1994 World Population Data Sheet*, Washington D.C., Population Reference Bureau, 1994. Radio and television set figures are from A. G. Sennitt (Ed.), *World Radio TV Handbook*, Volume 49, New York: Billboard Books,1995. Land surface area figures are from *UN Statistical Yearbook, 1991/2*. North Korea GNP per capita is taken from *Statistical Abstract of the United States, 1992*, Washington, D.C.: US Dept. of Commerce, Bureau of the Census, 1992, p. 831.

had grown to 168 radios and 128.6 television sets per 1,000 (calculated from the data in Table 11.1). Clearly, these averages mask wide divergences. The figure of 128.6 television sets per 1,000 Asians includes media-rich Japan, with 800 sets per 1,000 people, and media-poor Bangladesh, with 3 sets per 1,000 people.

Japan, China, and India are the giants of Asian broadcasting and are dealt with in the next three chapters. The remainder of this chapter gives a very brief description of broadcasting in other Asian countries. The basic source used for information on contempory radio and television organization was Sennitt (1995). Lent (1978) and Merrill (1991) were consulted for earlier periods.

EAST ASIA

Hong Kong. Hong Kong is a territory leased from China by the United Kingdom. It has been governed as part of the former British Empire. Radio was started in 1928 by Radio Hong Kong, who's monopoly came to an end when a commercial station started to transmit signals in 1959. In 1967, Television Broadcasts, limited (TVB) on a television service license and began broadcasting Chinese and English programs subject to governmant regulation (Merrill, 1991). Hong Kong has become the production center for overseas Chinese-language films and television programs that are exported to ethnic Chinese around the world.

Hong Kong is radio rich. The government service programs seven channels in English and Cantonese, with some Mandarin on Radio 5. There are also two private commercial corporations that each operate three channels from multiple transmitters. Television service is provided by TVB's Jade and Pearl networks and two channels from another private company, Asia Television (Sennitt, 1995).

Star TV, Asia's powerful satellite station, is based in Hong Kong. It is now part of Rupert Murdoch's media empire and can be received in most of Asia. The Chinese government has made tuning in illegal for its citizens and it has provoked cultural controversy in India.

Korea. Korea was a Japanese colony until the end of World War II, at which time it was divided into North Korea and South Korea.

Broadcasting began in 1927 when the Seoul Broadcasting Station, a legal corporation, started to operate. The Korean Broadcasting Corporation (KBC), a public corporation, is the largest electronic media organization in South Korea. Before the 1960s, broadcasting was government operated, except for two Christian radio stations. Broadcasting has greatly expanded since 1970 when only 20% of the households had television sets, 91% of them centered around urban areas (Lent, 1978). By 1994, radios had increased to 42.57 million and television sets to 10.48 million (see Table 11.1).

South Korea now has numerous radio stations operated by KBC, a nationwide commercial network (Munhwa Broadcasting Corporation) and several military, educational, and religious outlets. Television service is also provided by KBC, Munhwa, a government educational system, and a commercial station in Seoul. In contrast to the broadcast diversity in the South, North Korean radio and television remain under the control of the government (Sennitt, 1995).

Macau. Macau radio was initiated by the government in 1936 and a commercial station began broadcasting in 1951 supported by Hong Kong advertising (Lent, 1978). Two private commercial companies now operate the country's broadcasting. Radio Vila Verde programs MW and FM stations in Cantonese. Teledifusao de Macau competes with similar Cantonese radio stations and a Portuguese language FM station. It also runs Macau's Chinese and Portuguese television channels (Sennitt, 1995).

Mongolia. The government operates on all radio bands domestically and provides an external service in five languages. Television is on two channels, one of which relays programs from Moscow (Sennitt, 1995).

Taiwan. Radio began in 1925 when the country was part of the Jananese empire but because of the dislocation before, during, and after World War II, Taiwan's broadcasting development was slow. In 1947, the number of radios in Taiwan was fewer than 1.5 for every 1,000 people (Lent, 1978). After the nationalist (KMT) government retreated from mainland China to Taiwan in 1949, Taiwan's economy and broadcasting have grown rapidly. Currently, there are 408 radios and 332 television sets per 1,000 people (calculated from Table 11.1).

The Broadcasting Corporation of China is nominally a private enterprise under government contract. It broadcasts on MW, SW and FM from major cities in Mandarin and Taiwanese. There are numerous other public and commercial stations. Television service is provided by three commercial networks (Sennitt, 1995).

SOUTHEAST ASIA

Brunei. Brunei is one of the world's richest countries thanks to its oil reserves. The government's Radio Television Brunei provides MW and FM radio programming in Malay, English, Chinese, and Gurkha, and runs the country's television service (Sennitt, 1995).

Cambodia. Cambodia is a very poor country that has been devastated by war. Its limited broadcasting is controlled by the government.

Indonesia. Radio dates to the Dutch colonial period before World War II and television began in 1962. Stations are financed by license fees on sets, advertising, and government subsidies. The mountainous terrain of the countriy's far-flung islands and the lack of electricity in rural areas have provided servere challenges to the broadcasting service. In 1994, Indonesia still had only 130 radios and 55 television sets per 1,000 people. None the less, with its large population there are more than 600 government and commercial radio stations. The government television offers limited service on a single channel (Sennitt, 1995).

Laos. The first radio station was established in 1950 and was donated by France. Lao National Radio is the only official broadcasting system in the country. Broadcasting has increased rapidly during the past decade. In 1971, there were only 50,000 radios and about 40 television sets capable of tuning in the Thai station at nearby Nang Khai (Lent, 1978). By 1994, radios had increased to 500,000 and television sets to 80,000, many tuned to signals from Thailand. The government remains the only broadcaster in the country.

Malaysia. Commercial radio broadcasting was introduced in 1962 and television was established in 1963. Broadcasting is recognized as a significant tool for national development in Malaysia. The Ministry of Information and Broadcasting set guidelines for broadcasters specifing how they must treat government policies, public interest, Malaysian art, popular education, and Malaysian culture and identity. Residents of southern Malaysia can receive programs from the multilingual Singapore Broadcasting Corporation. Television is growing rapidly even in rural areas. In 1994, there were approximately 382 radios and 102 television sets per 1,000 people (Table 11.1).

Myanmar. Myanmar's limited broadcasting is controlled by the military government.

Philippines. Radio began during U.S. occupation in June of 1922. By the time of World War II, the Philippines had four stations, used mainly for demonstration purposes. After the declaration of martial law in September 1972, radio and television stations were controlled by the military and carried a heavy load of propagandistic broadcasts. In the 1980s, broadcasting changed significantly after the new democratic government stressed a policy of free access for broadcasting. There are now 123 radio stations affiliated to either the Association of Broadcasters or the Federation of Catholic Broadcasters and about 30 television stations programmed by 12 companies (Sennitt, 1995).

Singapore. The Singapore Broadcasting Service is a semipublic broadcast monopoly with strong ties to the Singapore government and its Ministry of Culture. All imported programs are previewed by officials in the Department of Broadcasting. Radio and television broadcast four main languages: Malay, English, Mandarin, and Tamil. Radio used to broadcast in Hokkien, Cantonese, Teochew, Hakka, Foochow, and Hainanese—the dialects spoken by the ethnic Chinese in Singapore. This practice was discontinued in line with the government's "Speak Mandarin" policy launched in 1980.

Thailand. The government began radio broadcasting in 1931. Broadcasting is governed by the 1955 Radio Communications Act and the 1965 Radio Broadcasting Act. Television reception is mainly concentrated in the major urban areas, particularly the Bangkok–Thonburi region. There is little or no television in rural areas. During the Vietnam War years, the United States helped Thailand build a radio system that reached isolated rural areas (Lent, 1978). The country now has many radio stations, all operated or supervised by the government. There are five television networks, one of which is government owned and another run by the army (Sennitt, 1995).

Vietnam. Broadcasting came to Vietnam in the French colonial period but was greatly expanded in the south by the American military and U.S. aid during the Vietnam War from the 1960s to early 1970s. After the North Vietnamese reunified Vietnam in May of 1975, broadcasting media became a major tool to promulgate political ideology, and broadcasting was linked to the Soviet Interspuntnik system (Merrill, 1991). The government operates two television channels from Hanoi using the SECAM system and one channel in southern cities on NTSC, the pre-unification American system. Radio is also a state monopoly consisting of two national networks and regional and provincial stations. The latter broadcast in local tribal languages as well as Vietnamese (Sennitt, 1995).

SOUTH CENTRAL ASIA

South Central Asia represents one of the most populated areas in the world with 1213.4 million people, 911.6 million of whom reside in India which is the world's second largest nation (see Table 11.1). Because the region is economically poor, radio is more important than newspapers or television. Radio remains the major broadcast medium in the region for spreading government policy, education, information, and entertainment. In most countries, television remains an impossible luxury for the mass of the population. In 1994, the region had about 70 radios and 19 television sets per 1,000 people.

Afghanistan. Radio broadcasting began in 1925. During the former Communist regime, Radio Afghanistan was a highly centralized bureaucracy. Television was started in 1978 and used mainly for government propaganda (Lent, 1978). Radio now operates on medium wave from Kabul in Pushtu and Dari languages. Other transmitters and the sw service are listed as inactive by Sennitt (1995). Television from the government service is reported to be operating in nine provinces.

Bangladesh. Broadcasting is a government monopoly and is used extensively to promote the government and mobilize the people for its policies. The first radio station was established in 1939. In 1975, there were six radio stations located in the major cities (Lent, 1978). Radio Bangladesh now operates 12 stations in AM (3 in Dhaka), six FM stations, and a SW overseas service. A single-channel television service is broadcast from 11 cities (Sennitt, 1995).

Bhutan. The government operates a limited radio service in this economically and media-poor country. Bhutan is the only country in Asia with no television service (Sennitt, 1995).

Maldives. The government broadcasts on AM and FM radio in the local language, Dhivehi, and beams an SW signal to India and Sri Lanka. It operates a single television station for limited hours (Sennitt, 1995).

Nepal. Broadcasting came late to Nepal—radio in 1952 (Lent, 1978) and television in 1982. Radio Nepal is a semigovernment commercial organization that operates six medium wave stations and an short wave service. The government operates a single, low-power television station (Sennitt, 1995).

Pakistan. Radio began under British colonial rule in the mid-1920s.

Broadcasting is now a state-owned system supported by license fees, government subsidies, and advertising, operated by the Pakistan Broadcasting Corporation. Radio traditionally broadcast programs for political socialization, reflecting only official viewpoints. (Lent, 1978). There are now 28 MW stations, domestic and external SW services, and Azad Kashmir Radio directed at the revolt-torn neighboring province ruled by India. There are 22 television states and production centers in five cities (Sennitt, 1995). The main difficulty is that few people can afford to own television sets. In 1994, Pakistan had about 80 radios and only 16 television sets per 1,000 people (see Table 11.1).

Sri Lanka. The Sri Lanka Broadcasting Corporation is a public corporation that broadcasts on AM, FM and SW primarily in Sinhala, Tamil, and English. It also operates the country's external radio service and a limited-hours television channel. Another television channel is operated by the Independent Television Network (Sennitt, 1995).

CONCLUSION

In their early decades, broadcasting systems in most Asian countries were under strict government control and regulation. Rapid progress in some countries' economies and technical innovations have resulted in the expansion of broadcasting. In most Asian countries, broadcasting has been growing to reach an increasingly large audience and has become more competitive over the past decade. Every Asian nation has its own domestic broadcasting service, each with radio and television (except Bhutan).

Obviously, broadcasters also have a much greater capacity than earlier for the production of radio and television programs designed to meet the needs of their own countries, whether in news, information, education, or entertainment. Each country apparently recognizes the importance of preserving its own culture. Programs appear to be more and more directed to local cultural matters as broadcasters move away from their past dependance on foreign programming.

REFERENCES

Lent, J. A. (Ed.). (1978). *Broadcasting in Asia and the Pacific: A continental survey of radio and television*. London: Heineman.

Merrill, J. C. (Ed.). (1991). *Global journalism: Survey of international communication*. New York: Longman.

Sennitt, A. G. (Ed.). (1995). *World radio TV handbook* (Vol. 49). New York: Billboard Books.

Chapter 12

Japan

Hiroshi Tokinoya

Since broadcasting began in Japan in the 1920s, the country has become one of the world's leaders in broadcasting. It ranks among the top in the world in terms of number of radio and television stations established, coverage, diffusion of receiver sets, length of broadcasting time, news gathering and transmission networks, and size of audience. Audience charactoristics are also well known because in the more than 40 years since television broadcasting began, an enormous quantity of survey data has been accumulated. The purpose of this chapter is to examine the Japanese broadcasting system, its operation, broadcast programming, and its audience.

THE BROADCASTING SYSTEM

The first radio broadcasting stations in Japan were opened in 1925 in Tokyo, Osaka, and Nagoya. The following year, the Japan broadcasting corporation Nippon Hoso Kyokai (NHK) was established with the nationwide diffusion of radio as its aim. Over the next 25 years, NHK, Japan's sole broadcasting enterprise, was administered centrally and monopolistically under strict supervision and regulation by the Ministry of Communication. During World War II, NHK was turned into a propaganda machine under the government's control. After Japan's defeat in 1945, NHK was placed under the Allied Occupation Forces' control. Once the new constitution of Japan had been adopted, the Broadcasting Act and the Radio Act were passed in 1950, putting an end to NHK's monopoly of the broadcasting industry. These acts set the basic direction of public administration of broadcasting in postwar Japan. Broadcasting's diffusion and its impartiality are determined by these broadcasting acts, which were influenced by American broadcasting ideology. Freedom of expression is guaranteed by a clause that states that broadcast programming shall not be regulated or interfered with by any person, unless such authority is determined by law. NHK has also established its own Standards for Domestic Programming and Basic Guide for Program Production, whereas commercial broadcasting has established a Japan Commercial Broadcasting Standard, all of which provide guidelines for independent regulation and freedom in program editing.

In accordance with these broadcasting acts, a license is necessary to set up a broadcasting station and such licenses must be renewed every 5 years. Japan's broadcasting system consists of two kinds of enterprises that derive operating funds through different means: NHK, which is a special corporate entity, and commercial broadcasting. These systems coexist and both are subject to regulation in regard to management, finance, programming, and control.

NHK is a public broadcaster charged with the responsibility of broadcasting throughout Japan. It is required to (a) meet audience demands for broadcasting covering all areas of information, culture, education, and entertainment; (b) to carry out research surveys in aid of broadcasting's progress and development; and to (c) provide international broadcasts.

NHK has a board of governors appointed by the prime minister and approved by the Diet (parliament). Approximately 98% of NHK's financial resources are provided by the receiver fee that the public is required to pay. NHK receives no direct government funding. The receiver fee is levied on every household that receives NHK programming, including satellite broadcasting. Changes in the license fee charges require the approval of the Diet.

Commercial broadcasting is carried out in accordance to the general broadcasting enterprises provisions in the broadcasting acts and is not subject to government control. Its operations are financed by advertising revenues that consist of charges for transmission and production and network fees paid for by the advertiser. All commercial broadcasters today are joint stock corporations that carry out operations in a particular region (metropolitan center or prefecture) on specific radio frequencies authorized by the Ministry of Posts and Telecommunications. Commercial broadcasters must satisfy the needs of particular regional communities and compete with other broadcasters in their regional markets.

In addition to the dual broadcasting system consisting of NHK and commercial broadcasters, the University of the Air commenced broadcasting in 1985. Its objective is to provide educational program with college credits for both students and older citizens. This university is financed by tuition and government subsidy.

RADIO

The first period of radio diffusion in postwar Japan was from 1945 until 1961 and was radio's peak period. It was the time before television made its appearance, when radio was the sole broadcasting medium. NHK made a fresh start with the institution of a new broadcasting act. In 1951, provisional licenses were granted to 16 commercial broadcasting enterprises, the first in Japan. By 1953, commercial radio had made its appearance in major centers throughout the country.

During this period, radio produced information programs, dramas of home life, melodramas, listener-participation programs, quiz and variety programs, and music programs. These program genres still form the basis of television program production today. Radio gained popularity and the number of listeners skyrocketed. The early 1950s period was undoubtedly the golden age of radio in Japan with the number of NHK receiver contracts peaking in 1955. However, radio's golden days were to last only 5 years until the television industry began to expand.

From 1962 to 1971, because of a sharp decrease in radio listeners as television's growth began to accelerate, advertising revenue declined. Television absorbed radio's audience because the broadcasting content handled by both media and their mass media functions were similar. Radio could not compete with the visual attraction of television.

A revival of radio began in 1966. It was a period during which commercial radio's countermeasures against television succeeded. These countermeasures included targeting specialized rather than mass audiences and pioneering new types of programming. Radio began live information and entertainment programs ("wide shows"), celebrity and community sports, talk shows, disk jockey programs, and audience participation. Radio stations aimed late-night programming at young people who made up more than half of radio listeners. They introduced news bulletins, news flashes, and sporting news programs in response to the needs of listeners. They also increased programs aimed at the rapidly increasing number of Japanese motorists. Finally, radio was reorganized with the establishment of nationwide commercial radio networks and formation of NHK's JRN and NRN networks.

In response to television's growth, commercial radio changed to attract a listening audience and also to reduce the cost of program production. The number of news specials and cultural program decreased. Both NHK and commercial radio ceased production of entertainment programs, such as quiz programs and dramas. NHK intensified its production of news and current affairs programs and lifestyle information programs. Beginning in the 1980s, commercial radio increased its focus on entertainment programming, leaving quality news and public affairs programming to NHK.

FM test broadcasting was carried out by NHK from 1957 and by Tokai University from 1958. Other new FM stations were soon on the air and because of good quality and specialized presentation of music, profits have been growing smoothly ever since. These FM stations in Japan took off as music-centered stations but programming is less specialized than in the United States. Programming content for FM stations in Japan typically covers general interests that range from classical music to traditional folk songs. In terms of listening audience size, morning broadcasts rank highest, followed by midday, and then evening broadcasts.

Japan has also introduced AM stereo broadcasting that began in Tokyo and Osaka in 1992. In the same year, small-scale community FM stations, with a broadcast radius of a few kilometers, also began operating. As elsewhere in the world, it seems, radio continues to grow.

TELEVISION

Yoshida (1986) divided the development of television broadcasting into three periods: (a) Period 1 (1953–1961), the early development of television broadcasting; (b) Period 2 (1962–1971), the rapid growth of television broadcasting; and (c) Period 3 (1972–present), the stabilization (saturation) of television broadcasting.

Period 1 saw the establishment and multiplication of television broadcasting stations. The curtain went up on the television era in 1953 when NHK's Tokyo television station began broadcasting and the first commercial television station was opened in the same year. However, because this was the golden age of radio and television sets were so expensive, television was not to become a part of everyday life until 1957 when television licensing policy had been settled and the Ministry of Posts and Telecommunications simultaneously granted VHF licenses to 34 television enterprises. The established policy was one television enterprise per prefecture and two to four enterprises per major urban center.

The national transmission network's main trunk line was completed in 1956. With this line as an axis, cross lines were then built and became the basis for the creation of a fully national network. In 1959, NHK began another national network (channel) for educational broadcasting. For commercial television in the early period, region-based companies were the general rule but partnerships eventually lead to national broadcasting networks. The first national network was the JNN network that began in 1959.

During Period 2, of development, the mass opening of VHF stations continued. By 1967, the Ministry of Posts and Telecommunications had issued UHF station licenses to 15 television enterprises, completing the framework for commercial television's two stations per prefecture system. The UHF prefectural and regional bureau, which had as its purpose the elimination of any disparity in the number of commercial stations between regions, established stations in rapid succession between 1969 and 1970. By 1971, 33 new television stations had come into being and an era of multiple-station television (both VHF and UHF) had begun.

Between 1966 and 1970, Japan's major commercial broadcasting networks were completed. Including the previously mentioned JNN, four network groups were formed: (a) NNN, centered on NTV; (b) FNN, centered on Fuji Television; (c) ANN, centered on NET (!ater ANB); and (d) JNN. Most Japanese television stations belong to one or another of these networks groups that center on Tokyo-based key stations. Networking takes the form of a business arrangement in which powerful Tokyo-based television stations supply news and programs to regional commercial stations and also oversee production of regional news and programs because, apart from program editing, local commercial television stations lack proficiency in program production. Although this results in a reduction of program diversity, it has the advantage of creating a national advertising medium. As a result of networking, competition between networks contributes to the elimination of differences in information content that existed earlier and stations have rushed headlong into intense competition for audience ratings.

During Period 3, ownership of receiver sets almost reached total saturation and the size of the television audience reached a plateau. However, the number of television stations continued to increase. In 1986, in order to average out reception of commercial television so that the major commercial networks could be received in every region nationwide, a multiple-station system consisting of four commercial television channels was established. Television, therefore, passed from metropolis-centered commercial television stations into a more stable period of nationwide network broadcasting.

NHK Broadcasting Corporation is still the largest broadcast organization in the country, transmitting five radio and television networks nationwide. Its hardware includes 3,501 "general" television stations, 3,424 educational television stations, 200 Class 1 and 140 Class 2 radio stations, two short-wave (SW) stations (for international broadcasting), and 512 FM stations (NHK, 1993). Commercial broadcasting now consists of five network groups, 47 AM radio companies, (225 stations), 39 FM radio companies (182 stations), one SW company (2 stations), 48 VHF and 67 UHF television companies (7,090 stations). Altogether, there are 14,015 broadcasting stations in Japan.

When television was established, the price of a television set was twice the average annual income. Because of a high degree of technological innovation and rational business management, Japanese industry was soon able to produce inexpensive sets that consumers could afford. Incomes kept pace with the high economic growth of Japan and radical changes have transformed the country and its economy. The centralized power structure of Japan's public administration system has influenced broadcasting along with most other areas of Japanese life. According to Matsumae (1990), it was largely responsible for the spread of Western culture throughout Japanese society. Broadcasting is subsequently modern and shares the practices of other advanced industrial countries.

FINANCE

In money terms, the broadcasting industry has expanded rapidly and vigorously. In 1965 (Tamura, 1977), the combined size of industry for NHK and commercial broadcasting came to approximately 180 billion yen. With the growth of advertising the color television, the figure grew to almost 500 billion yen in 1974. Television advertising revenue for the same year was 23.8 billion yen and radio advertising revenue amounted to 16.2 billion yen. Thus, television advertising revenue overtook radio advertising revenue in the 7th year after television broadcasting began. In 1992, NHK's receiver fee income alone amounted to 551 billion yen, whereas commercial broadcasting company revenues amounted to 2.1456 trillion yen. NHK, however, has experienced a continuous decline in its share of total broadcast revenues since 1970. Broadcasting represents 0.6% of the gross national product and by 1992 television had become the top advertising medium (Dentu, 1993); (advertising takes about 18% of total weekly broadcasting time).

TELEVISION PROGRAMMING

Looking back over the history of broadcast programming in Japan, the 1950s was a period of trial and error for television programming. During this early period, the production structure had not yet been fully consolidated and broadcasters were forced to rely on live telecasts, such as sports and theater productions. American television films were also imported and gained popularity. These American-produced programs introduced American culture and lifestyle to Japan and provided models for Japanese people's lifestyles as the country became affluent. At the beginning of this early period, news programs were scarce but such programs were attempting to produce an original reporting style.

In 1961, the Ministry of Posts and Telecommunications issued a notification of the scheduling of television programming in Japan. This government circular to the industry remains the basis of present-day programming. It stated that information programs (including news reports) are indispensable and programmers are required to provide more than 10% educational and 20% cultural content within programming schedules. This is enforced through a system by which each television station must submit a report detailing the proportion of these program genres in its schedule.

During the 1960s, the prototypes of present-day television program genres were developed. These included information programs (e.g., news and current affairs), dramas (e.g., home life, melodramas, and action), entertainment programs (e.g., variety, quiz and game shows), recreational programs (which cover professional and amateur sports and music), educational programs, cultural programs, utility programs, and a genre perhaps unique to Japan: the wide show (an information and entertainment program).

In news and information programs, a great amount of new technology has been introduced, making news reporting on real time possible and creating the basis for a golden age of information programming. When the Emperor of Japan visited the United States in 1975, electronic news gathering (ENG) was introduced in earnest and its lightweight and mobility brought about various innovations to program production, including news reporting. When satellite news gathering (SNG) came into operation in 1989, a wide range of live broadcast transmissions became possible and television's function of reporting and providing information was further enhanced.

From the 1980s onward, news programming in Japan has intensified and Japan is now entering the "information age," an age with the following characteristics. First, the proportion that news and information programs occupy within over all television programming is enlarging, from 8% in 1980 to 17% in 1992. Since 1985, news has been popularized by commercial television networks and news programming has been put into prime-time broadcasting slots. Second, the global scope of programming content has become the norm. In November of 1963, the first transmission via communications satellite between the United States and Japan brought the news of President John F. Kennedy's assassination, and in the following year, the 1964 Tokyo Olympic games were the first to be carried internationally on live television. Satellite news sharing agreements have been made by Japanese television stations and the big three American networks and CNN. These international arrangements demonstrated their usefulness during the Persian Gulf War when all Japanese networks had access to U.S. television coverage around the clock.

With the adoption of satellite news gathering by Japanese television, the information age has begun. The collapse of the Soviet Union, the Tiananmen Square incident in 1989, and political upheavals in Eastern Europe have, through satellite relay, been broadcast in real time and as a natural consequence television's power has been further strengthened. Domestically, ongoing scandals within the political and financial worlds and a change in government after 30 years of conservative rule have resulted an increase in the proportion of political reporting in television news broadcasts.

Television has influenced Japanese society in various ways and television journalism has contributed to the democratization of Japanese society. On the other hand, the number of politicians who appear on television to enhance their personal appeal has increased. If a politician does not appear on television, recognition by the general public is difficult. People are increasing assessing politicians and their policies on the basis of their media images.

We next examine entertainment programming since the 1970s. Faced with program saturation, an intense battle for audience rating developed. In an attempt to establish stable audience ratings, long-running serial programs became popular. In Japan, ratings are the absolute yardstick for commercial broadcasting. Programs with low ratings are quickly discontinued. Each television company tends to produce its own programs and technology used in program production is state of the art. The entertainment component of television programming has increased. In 1974, dramas made up 26% of television programming content, entertainment 9%, sports 6%, and music 4%. By 1992, drama's proportion had decreased to 21%, whereas entertainment programs, such as quiz and variety shows, had increased to 14%.

The trend of bringing more laughter, light excitement, and amusement into the home through television has continued. This reliance on entertainment programming is creating a number of problems, including the creation of a television generation, a decrease in literacy, and confusion in the Japanese language. Furthermore, in Japanese programs, sexual and violent acts are tolerated and restrictions on language use appear to be comparatively few.

Dramas are the most popular programs as measured by audience ratings. In 1992, the top 20 programs were 7 television dramas; 2 professional baseball telecasts, 5 variety and other forms of entertainment programs, 4 news programs, 1 music program, and 1 wide-show program. Television dramas in Japan are frequently produced to reflect current or desired social changes. Compared to television dramas in other countries, each drama runs for only a short time, usually a few weeks. Thus, within the ranks of these high-rating programs, there are few long-running serial programs.

There are some commercial television entertainment programs that have run for over 15 years: three dramas, three music programs, two cartoons, two talk shows, one sports program, and amusement program. At NHK, there has been an annual music special at year's end for over 40 years that attracts an audience rating of around 50% and two serial television dramas that have continued for over 30 years. Among the previously mentioned long-running television dramas, three are Samurai (historical costume) and two deal with contempory household matters.

An item-by-item comparison of programming and audience size for NHK and the average of five Tokyo-based key commercial stations in 1990 (Tomura, 1990) showed that NHK general television allocated 41% of its programming to news and current affairs and 29% to entertainment. On average, commercial television allocated 13% of programming to news and current affairs and 59% to entertainment. Television viewers, however, spend 58% of their NHK viewing time watching news and current affairs and 67% of their commercial channel viewing time watching entertainment programs. In other words, NHK broadcasts a large number of news and current affairs programs so its viewers spend most of their viewing time watching such programs. Conversely, in the case of commercial television, more entertainment programs are broadcast and their viewers spend most of their viewing time tuned into those programs.

If only prime-time viewing is considered, commercial television provides mostly entertainment programs, such as dramas and game shows. In other words, programming is concentrated on a small number of program genres. Regional commercial stations rely on the networks to supply programs. Such programming makes up around 80% of regional broadcasting time as Tamura (1987) pointed out.

AUDIENCES

The average Japanese person watches weekday television for approximately 3 hr per day (NHK Public Opinion Research Division, 1991), which is lengthy by world standards. If consideration is given to the lack of leisure time in Japan, the importance attached to television viewing as a leisure activity is the highest in the world. Audiences peak at breakfast, midday, and evening prime-time hours.

In Japan, many surveys of audiences have been carried out to provide scientific feedback to broadcasters. After World War ll, public opinion polls were encouraged by the General Head Quarters of the Allied Occupational Force as a means of furthering the democratization process. As commercial radio and television broadcasting began, what was mainly expected from public opinion polls was some direct understanding of the audience and of audience requirements. New advances in Western research methods were quickly adopted in Japan. Neilson in 1960 and Video Research in 1962 attached automatic recording devices to television sets in sample households. Surveying by machine advanced and data could be collected continuously throughout the year. With the diffusion of household video tape recorders, surveying of recording and replaying rates also became possible. NHK developed and still uses its own nationwide audience rating questionnaire.

The broadcasting acts stipulate that there must be public participation in broadcasting. Both NHK and commercial broadcasters are required to establish programming councils. However, there has been criticism of the process used for appointing committee members and of the subject matter the committee considers. At both NHK and commercial stations, an audience center has been established to handle queries from members of the public. Independent viewer groups have also been formed to monitor the television stations.

NEW TRENDS IN BROADCASTING

The broadcasting acts were revised in 1989 in order to secure diversity in public debate. Under the principle of eliminating mass media concentration, operation of more than two broadcasting stations by one enterprise was prohibited, opening the way for participation by enterprises other than surface broadcasting stations to be recognized. The turning of satellite broadcasting into a pay medium was recognized. The distinction was made between companies that supply programming for communication satellite broadcasting and those that broadcast programming for surface transmission. This prepared the legal basis for satellite broadcasting.

Thus, Japan has begun an era of two-branched broadcasting: ground transmission utilizing broadcast satellite and direct broadcast satellite (DBS). Broadcasting satellites were launched in 1984 and in 1989 NHK commenced two-channel broadcasting through its DBS service named BS, charging a satellite broadcasting receiver fee. In the case of commercial broadcasting, pay satellite broadcasting began in 1991 with Japan Satellite Broadcasting, which utilizes BS. Thus, BS is a three-channel system. Another DBS system, Communication Satellite (CS), provides six channels including CNN, Star, and pay channels. NHK's satellite broadcasting has advanced smoothly with 4,680,000 subscribers in 1992. However, the diffusion of commercial satellite broadcasting has been slow and the industry has not achieved financial stability.

In the 1990s, so-called "PCM" sound broadcasting, which broadcasts with high sound quality by using satellite relay, launched the multistation age of satellite radio broadcasting. PCM, however, cannot be considered a success because diffusion has been very slow.

Satellite broadcasting covers a wide area and produces good sound and pictures. In order for satellite television broadcasting to develop, problems in preparation of high-quality programming, financing, and broadcasting equipment need to be resolved. With the start of BS, spillover began to occur as Japanese BS can be picked up in such countries as Taiwan and South Korea. In South Korea, criticism is emerging that this constitutes a cultural invasion; in Taiwan, however, it has been warmly received. On the other hand, Hong Kong's Star Television can be received in Japan through CS and thus from now on a new international system is required.

The other new trends in broadcasting emerged in the late 1980s. One is the improvement of the sound and picture quality of the broadcasting. Multiple sound broadcasting is now used by NHK and all commercial stations. In order to improve picture quality, test broadcasting of high precision ("hi-vision") images began in 1987 using NHK's broadcasting satellite. That same year, commercial enterprises began surface broadcasting of clear vision (HDTV).

There has also been an expansion of cable television. Cable television in Japan was born in 1955 as part of a program for areas with poor television reception. Testing of urban-style cable television began in 1987. In 1991, permission was given for the establishment of 143 such systems. The following year, 24 urban-style cable television systems were established and broadcasting began. These systems hope to form a "space cablenet," a network that will use communication satellites to provide multichannel cable television. Demonstrations are being carried out by some stations. In the future, the development of pay service, the introduction of hi-vision, and the actualization of two-way service are anticipated.

In 1992, there were 8.43 million households subscribing to cable television, which translates as 20% of the television-viewing audience (Ministry of Posts and Telecommunications, 1994). Cable television in Japan is moving toward more diversification. However, only 1.87 million households watch programs produced by cable television stations, which are typically carried on a single cable channel. The reasons for the relative lack of cable development in Japan include the supply system for program software, financing, and the networking system's consolidation. Furthermore, the government has made it a policy to carry out cable diffusion on a metropolitan and prefectural basis. Although this has been able to solve the problem of poor-quality television reception in remote areas, it has impeded the diffusion of cable television to the rest of Japan.

CONCLUSION

It may be concluded that broadcasting in Japan has developed at a rapid pace. Due to its occupation after World War II, Japan adopted virtually the same political, economic, social, and mass media system as the United States. (Americans drafted the Japanese constitution). Japan became an excellent Asian example of a country that successfully adopted and developed Western capitalistic, democratic, and cultural styles. These structural similarities to the Western model produce similarities in the development of broadcasting.

The main differences between broadcasting in Japan and the United States is the role of the public sector. The well-balanced competition between the powerful public broadcaster, NHK, and a large number of commercial broadcasters has brought about today's development in Japanese broadcasting. The coexistence of NHK, which relies on receiver fees for income, and commercial broadcasters, which rely on advertising for income, allows two industries based on separate principles to develop their special characteristics. As Nozaki (1990) pointed out, NHK in particular has raised the level of broadcasting in Japan and has carried out the role of maintaining broadcast standards. Because of this, Japanese broadcasting closely resembles Western Europe. With current attemps to deregulate and liberalize broadcasting, however, Japan is adopting policies more typical of the United States.

Compared to the situation in the United States, cable and satellite television has made slow progress. As in many other countries, television is the dominant medium in Japan. In the new electronic age, the influence of television in every country is intensifying but in comparison to other countries this influence is particularly strong in Japan. According to an international comparison of television audiences in five countries carried out by Greenberg, Ku, Li, and Tokinoya (1989), public satisfaction with television is much higher in Japan than in other countries. Furthermore, many studies, including those carried out by Gantz and Tokinoya (1987) and Rosegren (1987), suggest that the Japanese people's interest in information is very high and it is anticipated television's influence will grow even stronger in the future.

REFERENCES

Dentsu. (1993). *Dentsu koukoku nenkan 1993–1994* [Dentsu advertising yearbook 1993–1994]. Tokyo: Author.

Gantz, W., & Tokinoya, H. (1987) Diffusion of news about assassination of Olf Palme: A trans-comparison of the process. *European Journal of*

Communication, 2, 197–210.

Greenberg, B. S., Ku, L., Li, H., & Tokinoya, H. (1989), Young people and their orientation to the mass media. *International study: Comparison among youth in China, Japan, Korea, Taiwan and the United States.* (Study No 6). Lansing: Michigan State University.

Matsumae, N. (1990), Histoire de la fonction culturelle des emissions FM au Japon (de 1957 a 1988), These pour le nouveau doctorat. France: Universite de Strasbourg.

Ministry of Posts and Telecommunications. (1994). *Telecommunication white paper 1994.* Tokyo: MPT.

Nippon Hoso Kyokai. (1993). *NHK Nenkan 1992* [Radio and television yearbook, 1992]. Tokyo: NHK.

Nippon Hoso Kyokai Public Opinion Research Division. (1991) *Nihonin no seikatujikan 1990* [Livelihood time of the Japanese in 1990]. Tokyo: Nihon Hoso Shuppan Kyokai.

Nozaki, S. (1990). NHK shinron [A new perspective on NHK]. *Sogo Jahnarizumu Kenkyu, 132,* 84–93.

Rosengren, K. R. (1987). The comparative study of news diffusion. *European Journal of Communication, 2,* 227–255.

Tamura, M. (1977). Media no keihiteki sokumen [Aspects of management of mass media] *Bunken Geppo, 8,* 23–37.

Tamura, M. (1987). The information environment around the Japanese people. *Studies of Broadcasting, 23,* 7–26.

Tomura, E. (1990). Nihonjin to terebi 1992 [Japanese people and television in 1992]. *Hoso Kenkyu to Chosa, 9,* 12–19

Yoshida, J. (1986), Development of television and changes in TV viewing habits in Japan. *Studies of Broadcasting, 22,* 127–154.

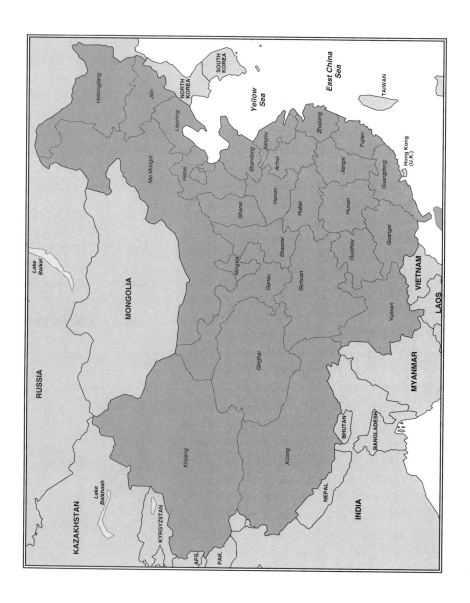

Chapter 13

China

Kenneth C. Petress

This chapter first focuses on how and why China's broadcast history is different from other nations' experiences. Second, the five key dimensions of media systems (control, programming, goals, target audiences, and financing) introduced in Chapter 1 are employed to examine the development of radio and television. Third, Chinese broadcasting's roles in promoting national ideology and education are discussed. Last, the future of Chinese broadcasting is considered.

The Chinese media serve three main functions: (a) to propagate policies (e.g., the one child per family policy, the water conservation campaign, and the stop youngsters from smoking effort), (b) to educate the masses (e.g., secondary education classes in remote rural areas not easily staffed by qualified teachers, technical upgrading for remote factory and research institutes, and for acquainting citizens on a large scale with major shifts in government policy), (c) and to mobilize the masses (e.g., necessary after natural disasters, industrial accidents, or national defense concerns; Lu Keng, 1990).

China has the world's largest population, almost 1.2 billion people (see Table 11.1, chap. 11). Eighty percent of the people are low-income peasants who are scattered over the countryside where traditional classroom settings are impossible. Education Commission Director Li Tieying (personal interview, 1991) pointed out that China's leaders decided in the early 1960s to use radio to reach those people seeking further education not adequately served by traditional teachers. Radio has allowed simultaneous, consistent policy matters to be presented to the masses, especially to the peasantry.

CHINESE BROADCASTING HISTORY

Broadcasting is a Western invention. Inventions are not isolated from their parent culture and they come laden with values and embedded expectations. Such was the case with the introduction of radio and television into China. China had long viewed itself as distinct from other lands and had isolated itself from the rest of the world for centuries. It had demanded that others come to China and pay tribute to its leaders before any international dialogue could occur. China had suffered numerous humiliating experiences at the hands of Western powers since the mid-19th century. This isolation and mistreatment at the hands of foreigners discouraged Chinese broadcasting's emergence.

Some foreign enclaves operated "official" news and religious radio programming, primarily in Shanghai, Nanjing, and Qingdao in the early 1920s (Yang Zheng Quan, personal interview, 1991). These foreign radio transmissions were short lived and sporadic and had little influence on the native Chinese. The Guomintang government (the Nationalist Chinese) established the first Chinese radio station, the Central Broadcasting Station, in the then Chinese capital city of Nanjing, (Wang, 1990). It was used primarily for news. From 1932 to 1936, there were 16 Chinese non-commercial stations: 8 run by provincial governments, 4 by special municipal governments, and 2 controlled by the Communication Ministry. There were also 63 privately owned commercial stations located in major urban areas (Wang, 1990, p. 228). The Japanese invasion and occupation of northeast China from 1937 to 945 curtailed Chinese broadcasting growth. By the end of 1947, there were 41 government-run stations, "48 privately owned commercial stations, and four allied armed forces stations in operation" (Wang, 1990, p. 228).

Because of continuing civil strife, World War II, and Chiang Kaishek's paranoid oppression, developments in broadcasting were slow until the founding of the People's Republic of China (PRC) by Mao Zedong in 1949. Mao had set up a provisional government in Yanan, Shaanxi Province (in the Northwest mountains) in 1936. He and his followers in the Chinese Communist Party (CCP) established their first radio station in 1945: "It was the Yanan Xinhua Broadcasting Station and it broadcast only two hours a day in Yanan" (Wang, 1990, p. 228). The station was moved in March of 1949 to Beijing, the PRC's capital, where the CCP's organization was renamed the Central People's Broadcasting Station (CPBS).

Radio's popularity grew with its accessibility. While the PRC was in its infancy, most radios were imported and thus were expensive and involved foreign currency exchange demands that made radio acquisition difficult. A small number of radio sets were built domestically, but transmission technology was initially backward and China's geographic vastness and impenetrable mountain ranges inhibited broadcasting access to many people.

Chinese leaders "stressed the production of loudspeakers which were cheaper than radio sets" (Wang, 1990, p. 22). Many Chinese county organizations built crude networks in the 1950s: "They used telephone wires at first to relay the signal, preempting phone calls for part of the day to broadcast programs through loud speakers" (Shuer, 1981, p. 328). Eventually, telephone lines were replaced with iron wires strung on wooden poles. Relay stations helped use this technology for work brigades and public gathering spots. County governments, prefecture and provincial units, and ministry allocations contributed to the cost of these wire networks. By the late 1960s, "2,600 cable broadcasting stations with more than 90 million loudspeakers established a broad radio network" (Qiang, 1990, p. 232).

Such loudspeaker systems not only provided greater government access to common citizens, but also guaranteed that the public would pay attention. The intrusiveness of the loudspeakers is hard for Westerners to fathom. These messages were penetrating and could not be ignored. They included routine daily agendas; political notices from local, provincial, and Beijing Party organs; and motivational and safety messages from local work unit supervisors.

At the end of 1962, there were about 4.5 million radios in China, about 1 per 100 people. Radios were still not mass produced in China and imported radio sets were prohibitively expensive. By the early 1980s, radios were being mass produced in China, radios were common and cheap, and the government had begun providing programming that was increasingly popular throughout the nation. Burgeoning controlled commercial advertising had begun and the local and provincial governments began utilizing the airwaves to disseminate information to the listening public.

CONTEMPORY RADIO

Since 1986, per capita radio possession has continued to increase as a result of lowered radio unit cost, virtual universal access to radio sets, and growing popular use of small battery-powered receivers. More people listen to more radio than ever before.

There are no privately owned radio stations in the PRC; all broadcast services are under CPBS supervision (Hamm, 1991). Radio serves as a major instrument "of propaganda for the Party and the government's political aims" (Dennis, Gerbner, & Zassoursky, 1991, p. 111). "Stress is on transmitting official views and policies and mobilizing mass support for national progress" (Mundt, 1991, p. 20). The control of radio is consistent with that of all other information channels in China. Media and education leaders are all beholden to the central government and follow its political orders. Some private citizen dissension and questioning does occur but such individualism is minimal, private, and discrete—never organized, public, or conspicuous.

Noontime soap operas based on popular novels are popular among retired persons, those recuperating from illnesses, and select children who take interest in such programming (May, 1985). Unlike Western soap operas, the Chinese ones do not involve marital infidelity, rape, incest, murder, and drug use: Their plots focus instead on the work ethic, self-reliance, family honor, and adherence to socialist ideals. Chinese socialist propaganda is presented as entertainment, thus making it more palatable.

Music programming includes "Taiwanese dances, Czech music, Japanese and German songs, as well as ethnic Chinese and national minorities' music" (May, 1985, p. 12). "Two radio programs are beamed to Taiwan" and other programs are "designed for the peoples of China's autonomous regions" (Hamm, 1991, p. 2). Radio Shanghai has been allowed certain latitudes in its music selection. Some contemporary U.S. music is played. In a popular 1988 radio-listener poll conducted in Shanghai, Michael Jackson was overwhelmingly judged the most popular among listeners. However, even Shanghai radio music is screened for "pornographic content or expressing sentiments against state policy" (Hamm, 1991,pp. 28–29).

TELEVISION BROADCASTING

Serious consideration of television began in China in 1956. On May 1, 1958, television broadcasting started in the Chinese capital city of Beijing. Several factors delayed China's telecommunication advances including "the withdrawal of Russian science and technology experts" in the late 1950s and Mao Zedong's "policies from 1957 to 1976, when military matters and agriculture and industrial production were emphasized at the expense of telecommunications" (Wang, 1990, pp. 224–226). In 1959, another television station opened, this time in the biggest city, Shanghai, and others soon began in Harbin, Shenyang, Changchun, and Guangzhou. By-mid 1961, 29 television stations and relay centers were operating and more were coming online. Even with this flurry of development television was still scarce among the people partly due to its tremendous expense, its unfamiliarity, poor signal quality, and the lackluster nature of its programming. In 1960, there were only 12,700 television sets, which were used only in public places. Experiments with color began in 1973, but it was 1987 before Beijing became China's first station to transmit in color (Wang, 1990). China's slow television development and penetration was caused in great part by the isolationism of China's political and military leaders who did not want to be seen competing with or coveting the advances of foreigners.

By 1980, television had grown in popularity to one set in 280 households. Television ownership as well as viewing time and interest have increased as other free-time activities have decreased. Attendance at movies, theaters, and sporting events, as well as casual visits to neighbors' homes have steadily declined as television popularity rises. There are now more television sets than radios in the country, with over 200 million sets in use (see table 11.1, chap. 11). Party-leader messages at weekly political indoctrination classes have urged the masses to watch less television, but to little avail.

Most provincial governments support a television station. These stations serve the local region with news, agricultural advice and announcements, education in the local dialect, and cultural shows with programming of particular local interest. Regional stations do not always compete with national network fare; they often simulcast vital national programming, go off the air when crucial national programs are aired, or replay important broadcast shows.

Beijing has two telecasting sources. The first, Beijing Television, is a joint local- and central-government controlled station; the other, Chinese Central Television (CCT), is a three-channel consortium. The first CCT channel is reserved primarily for political information and includes some arts and literature programming. The second CCT channel primarily carries economic and arts programming. CCT Channels 1 and 2 are broadcast nationwide from 8:00 a.m. to 10:00 p.m. CCT Channel 3 is a Beijing arts channel (Dennis, et al., 1991). Shanghai and Guangzhou have two local stations each and many other large cities have one local station. Local stations, like provincial ones, cooperate by simultaneously carrying or replaying vital news from provincial or national stations or by temporarily going off the air when messages of universal interest are aired. Chinese citizens do not have to worry about missing needed news; all information sources—televisions, radios, loudspeakers, newspapers, bulletin boards, and workplace announcements—echo and reinforce vital information. Centralized authority makes this coordination possible.

Chinese television programming is less diverse than the offerings in Western countries but the variety is expanding. Educational shows comprise the major amount of programming in terms of time allocation. Transmitting and interpreting international news is also a major task of television. With burgeoning international tourism, great numbers of students and scholars returning from abroad, and joint economic ventures ongoing in China, the thirst for foreign news has heightened. Foreign news was found to comprise in one third of the total Beijing news programming content, with stories relevant to the United States, the United Kingdom, and Russia receiving the greatest coverage. This survey also reported that 92% of respondents watched television daily (Warren, 1988).

Domestic news stories include, in descending order of coverage, (a) domestic economics and industry (35%); (b) international relations (9%); (c) art, culture, and entertainment (7%); and (d) agriculture and fishing (7%). The remainder was composed of other content topics. The main topics of international stories were international relations (33%), crime and justice (7%), military (7%), and science and health (7%; Warren, 1988). It is apparent from this that emphasis on commercial domestic interests and foreign international relations go hand in hand in China's 1980s "open-door" policy. These foci offer Chinese leaders a way to emphasize to the masses that China is still a power in the world even after the 1990 Tiananmen debacle. Portrayals of Chinese leaders visiting and being visited by foreign dignitaries; images of Chinese diplomats wielding influence in international bodies (the United Nations, World Bank, and ASEAN), and televised images of continued international commerce and trade offer legitimacy to the government and provide proof to Chinese citizens of China's standing in the world.

Most Chinese television news and entertainment programming is produced in Beijing or Shanghai; however, some regional productions do occur in Guangzhou, Harbin, Wuhan, Xian, and Nanjing. Hong Kong supplies a growing amount of telecast production material to China: "We sell many half-finished products to the Chinese, which they complete [edit] according to their wishes" (Sartori, 1986). Some U.S. television programming is sold to China but it is dubbed into Chinese with liberal translating license and severe editing. It is often used to reinforce negative stereotypes of the West and attempts to make the Chinese masses grateful to their leaders for saving them from the "harmful fates suffered abroad" (Gou Hong, personal interview, 1984).

SATELLITE COMMUNICATION

Because of China's past self-imposed isolation and Western nations' unwillingness to openly share sensitive, potentially military-related technology with China, new communication technologies came to China quite late. China launched its first satellite in 1970 but most of its basic functions did not work as planned and those operations that did work lasted only a short time. More improved satellite launches followed. By 1984, a communication satellite involving an Intelsat lease was put in orbit. This allowed long-distance telephone and data transmission improvements. In 1985, a broadcasting satellite and another data-imaging satellite to "promote better land resource management" were launched. Intelsat allocated one half transponder (18 mHz bandwidth) on Intelsat V at C-band frequency (6/4 gHz). "The annual charge for this lease was reported to be U.S. $400,000, which is equal to the annual salary of 500 Chinese workers" (Ross, 1984, p. 8).

China launched three operational communication satellites in 1986, 1988, and 1989, which vastly improved China's broadcasting range and quality. Prior to 1986, many television receivers in China's northern mountain ranges were unable to receive clear signals from Beijing, Shanghai, or Chongqing. Routinely noise-cluttered signals were transformed into crisp, clear transmissions once these satellites were installed. I have personally witnessed some astounding advances in broadcasting strength and quality from 1983 to 1991 on visits to remote rural and modern urban locations in China. Renewed and added Intelsat hookups now "allow direct one-hop transmission between appropriate ground stations anywhere in China" (Ross, 1984, pp. 8–9).

THE ROLE OF IDEOLOGY IN CHINESE BROADCASTING

An ideology is a system of ideals and a "body of doctrines, beliefs, and symbols organized into related and relevant sets of political and philosophic thought" (Gyorgy & Blackwood, 1967, p. 2). Contemporary Chinese ideology resembles, in many ways, that of the former Soviet Union. Such major and familiar concepts as central government control, centralized resource management and allocation, state ownership and control of virtually everything, and one-party rule define the basic Chinese system.

Ideology pervades society, and Chinese broadcasting is no exception. In order to understand Chinese broadcasting, one needs to be familiar with the basic values, biases, assumptions, and philosophy underlying the communications system. The following are several ideological facets that help put Chinese broadcasting into focus.

Images are important to political leaders, and they commonly attempt to control the interpretation of news events (Bennett, 1988). Former U.S. Secretary of State Acheson (1969) said: "The effective public official does not attempt to educate or convey 'objective' images; the official's goal is to represent issues and events in ways that gain support, shape action, and influence outcomes" (p. 375). In these respects, the Chinese Communists and U.S. officials share some common ground. They both use propaganda, the systematic reproduction, paraphrasing, or interpreting of select messages to the masses in such a manner that it (a) belittles, ignores, or threatens those with alternative views; (b) denies, inhibits, or prohibits public access to contrary views; or (c) all of these. Propaganda achieves dominance through exclusivity to communication channels, repetition, saturation, and intimidation. Propaganda is frequently deceptive, incomplete, and vague. Propaganda in the United States, however, is not as institutionalized as in China; it does not constitute the majority of government–people communication, and free speech rights and a vigilant probing press counter much of the government's attempted propaganda. In China, there is a Ministry of Propaganda in Beijing, provincial propaganda offices, and propaganda officials (by that title) in commerce, industry, research, and educational workplaces. Propaganda is not a dirty word in China; it is a respected public service profession.

The government controls *all* media channels (radio, television, billboards, newspapers, magazines, and leaflets); it also controls schools, jobs, permits (to marry, have children, or move to new homes or jobs), retirement, and travel (domestic and foreign). In addition, leaflets are distributed at sports and cultural events and postage stamp portrayals, movies and stage performances, classroom texts and lectures; and work unit party-member-led lunchtime discussions all provide avenues for the saturation of desired government messages. Media control is just one more of life's aspects that is rigidly controlled, so it appears "normal" to Chinese citizens.

Messages are put into simple formats so they can be propagated by slogans, banners, chants, cartoons or comic book pictures designed for the semiliterate and the totally illiterate. Saturation methods are used to combat historical or traditional divergences of opinion and to combat citizen apathy, stubbornness, or isolation. One of the traditional sources of credibility in China is the reverence for age and the elderly Chinese-government leaders have capitalized on this. It is no accident, then, that new government policies, edicts, and proposals get disseminated first to elders (representing families, workplaces, and communities) before being generally distributed. The elders who have advanced exposure to government messages act as opinion leaders and cheerleaders for new government policies.

News is defined quite differently in China than in Western nations. News in China is simply what the government wants the public to know—true, false, slanted, or fabricated. News "leaks" are almost unheard of in China, unlike the virtual information sieve that exists in the United States (Price & Evans, 1988). Chinese national security and domestic tranquility are protected by a noninquisitive press and by severe criminal penalties for anyone daring to violate state secrecy (death sentences for anyone exposing military secrets, lengthy jail sentences for breaches in social policy, and loss of job benefits and privileges for lesser secrecy breaches). Because virtually everyone works for the government, everyone is subject to official secrecy regulations.

Broadcast, theater, opera, movie, and literary rules impose strict limits on explicit sex. As a teacher in China, I vividly recall my students routinely asking me, without prompting or suggestion and without hesitation or embarrassment, whether the magazines and newspapers I brought with me from outside China had been checked by an elder to be sure no "contaminating material may come their way." They have come to believe that depictions of sex and violence are dangerous to their moral well being. Unlike the U.S. media, kissing, fondling, explicit sex, bloody shooting or stabbing scenes, messy accident portrayals, or acts of terrorism are almost never portrayed in Chinese media. Such content is labeled pornography by official doctrine and the penalties for producing, selling, buying, or the transmission of such material include lengthy imprisonment and, in some cases, death. Depictions of violence, however, are briefly used by official propaganda organizations to reinforce the idea of foreign depravity or savagery.

Advertising is permitted on Chinese radio and television. Although Chinese commercials initially appear similar to their U.S. counterparts, they are, in fact, quite different. There is minimal product or service competition for essentials in China; brands do not face off against each other and services are parceled out based on predicted need, demand, and resources. China is poor and most family-disposable income is saved for items in great demand, many of which require government permits (e.g., television, air conditioners, dishwashers, carpet sweepers, or VCRs). Chinese media consumers are faced with few product or service options. The government does use ads to implore people to use certain products (birth control items, new fertilizers, and newly made domestic versions of products previously made overseas) or services (marriage counseling, television schooling, crop management services) but these ads do not pit products or services directly against one another. Comparative ads are unknown in China.

MASS MEDIA AND EDUCATION

When Mao Zedong founded the People's Republic of China in 1949, illiteracy gripped over 80% of its people; drug addiction and dependency ravaged hundreds of millions, and very few well-educated people remained on the Chinese mainland after the communist victory. Mao and several of his close advisors, such as Zhou Enlai and Liu Shiao Qi, were highly educated. They valued literacy and understood the illiteracy menace. China's leaders valued national independence and sought technical aid from the Soviet Union for China's people. To achieve these ends, the masses needed to be educated. The dilemma was how—with massive illiteracy, a paucity of teachers, schools, and teaching materials; and an almost bankrupt economy, could China educate itself? The answer began with radio linked to loudspeakers, a monolithic school for the masses. "Classes" took place during planned workplace periods and during evenings. School took the form of oral education where books were scarce. This was not an ideal system but illiteracy was lowered to 70% in urban areas and 85% in rural regions by 1960, 50% and 70% by 1970, and less than 10% and 30%, respectively, by 1990 (Bao Ziming, personal interview, 1990).

Television took over as the major educational medium in 1986. Specific local stations' programming, blocks of time on provincial and national stations, and dedicated regional television college stations have been authorized to educate the masses. Media education covers a wide spectrum: basic literacy instruction; moral teaching via cartoons and classical and socialist readings and group dialogues, agricultural demonstrations and instructions, remedial and advanced industrial training, safety instructions and warnings, foreign-language (English, French, German, Japanese, and Russian) instruction, mathematics classes, history and economics lessons, and childrearing tips.

All of the more than 300 Chinese college students I have taught in China have admitted they found radio (especially the Voice of America, the BBC World Service, and local foreign-language programs) essential to their learning English. China has recruited thousands of U.S. teachers to China to teach language, science, mathematics, history, and agriculture since 1980. Many Chinese students have attended U.S. colleges for graduate education. The Chinese mass media not only provides needed and valuable education to remote areas, but they also offer quality control and some degree of standardization to instruction. The media have clearly defined education as important and have aided in raising the aspirations of the masses.

Ideology and education go hand in hand and each depends on the other. Ideology is useless if it is not defined for, transmitted to, and reinforced for the masses. Education is vital only when it is valued by the people. Education is the most universal and institutional vehicle for transmitting ideology and ideology provides the surest means of elevating education as a desirable and necessary activity. Such symbiosis was astutely seen by Chinese leaders who utilized that relation to its fullest. China has invested great energy, skill, resources, and manpower to "link the government and the populace, serving as a tool to propagandize, educate, and motivate" (May, 1985, p. 13) the people.

THE ELECTRONIC MEDIA'S FUTURE IN CHINA

China's future electronic media capabilities, needs, and desires are inexorably tied to official leadership policies, China's economic development, and how the PRC deals with Hong Kong after the 1997 takeover. Current top leaders are nearly all elderly, conservative, and appear to be out of touch with the common Chinese citizenry. If future Chinese leaders are similar to present ones, China's future will be one of lagging progress in terms of transmission and receiving technology, programming improvement, and ready-citizen access to programming variety. If, on the other hand, future Chinese leaders assume a more open and permissive view, China may acheive technical and consumption standards equal to the Western world. With such changes, China would probably also encounter Western media problems (i.e., violent content, sex-laden programming, and commercial competition rather than government policy determining programming).

For all the advances in modern China over the past 15 years, China remains economically a Third World nation. Its rural peasants (over 80% of the nation's population) are poor by world standards even though there are a few wealthy farmers. Some industrial improvements have recently been made; however, much of China's infrastructure and industrial output are labor intensive, antiquated, and far less than first-class standard. In order to continue high-cost modernization of electronic media, China's economy must improve. Economic advances have so far been made with minimum political reform. Economic change can only go so far without concomitant political change. Future electronic media innovations are likely to be prohibitively costly and will thus be out of reach for poorer nations.

The PRC will assume sovereignty over Hong Kong from Britain in July of 1997. Hong Kong is one of the world's richest per capita cities (see Table 11.1 in chap. 11) and is much more affluent than mainland China. The population of Hong Kong has adopted Western values and Western capitalism and trades in the developed world's markets. China has promised to allow Hong Kong autonomy from the Communist restrictions and limitations imposed in the PRC for 50 years after the 1997 takeover.

If these promises are kept, China will have an avenue for modern foreign products, up-to-date technology and advances, and the hard foreign-currency flow needed for international trade. If, on the other hand, the PRC government breaks its promises, it will not gain this expertise, trade, and advanced technology because Hong Kong would no longer be the magnet for highly skilled workers, free trade, and foreign cash flow. The answer to how China deals with the Hong Kong takeover lies with its political leaders' stance vis-à-vis political reform and tolerance.

If free or nearly free information flow is maintained in Hong Kong after the PRC takeover, and if tourist and business travel to and from Hong Kong remains intact, undeniable knowledge of what transpired in the 1989 Tiananmen massacre will be exposed via eyewitness accounts and videotape pictures and sounds. This kind of exposure will surely spur challenges to government accounts of that June night in Beijing that are so contrary to what the world witnessed. Exposure to outside journalistic practices and products will inevitably spawn desires for a freer Chinese press and break the government's propaganda monopoly. Even journalists, who now indiscriminantly parrot the government's line, will see their worldwide journalist counterparts as individual creators of and interpreters of information. Such awareness will inevitably change the nature of journalism in China although we can only speculate on the pace and extent of such change.

Geographically, China lies at the center of Asia's emerging economic powers (Korea, Taiwan, Japan, Singapore, and perhaps Malaysia and Indonesia). One half of the world's population lies within a 2,000 mile radius of China's borders. This geographic position offers China great leverage in trade, commerce, and resource access. With its own massive population, it has the potential for significant media demand and purchasing power. China may become a part of a new Asian consortium sharing media and combining economic strength to rival the European Union and the North American Free Trade Agreement countries for talent and products in the future. Emerging technologies may well be made in, marketed by, and predominantly sold to the Asian market.

China, Japan, and Hong Kong now have communication satellites. It is likely that Korea, Malaysia, Indonesia, and Taiwan will soon join the world's broadcasting satellite-using nations. Such access may diminish dependance on U.S.-produced programming and boost domestic Asian programming. China's broadcasting progress, however, is still linked to the current U.S. dominance in broadcasting technology and programming. However, U.S. media executives and producers may soon need to learn how to coexist with an emerging broadcasting giant in Asia.

REFERENCES

Acheson, D. (1969). *Present at the creation: My years in the State Department.* New York: Norton.

Bennett, W. L. (1988). *News: The politics of illusion* (2nd ed.). New York: Longman.

Dennis, E. E., Gerbner, G., & Zassoursky, Y. N. (Eds.). (1991). *Beyond the Cold War.* Newbury Park, CA: Sage.

Gyorgy, A,. & Blackwood, G. D. (1967). *Ideologies in world affairs.* London: Blaisdell.

Hamm, C. (1991). Music and radio in the People's Republic of China. *Asian Music, 22*(2), 1.

Lu Keng, A. (1990). The Chinese Communist press as I see it. In L. J. Martin & R. E. Hiebert (Eds.), *Current issues in international communication.* New York: Longman.

May, S. (1985). Modernation and the media. *China Business Review, 10,* 37.

Mundt, W. R. (1991). Global media philosophies. In J. C. Merrill (Ed.), *Global journalism: Survey of international communication.* New York: Longman.

Price, R., & Evans, M. S. (1988). National security is harmed by the press. In N. Bernards (Ed.), *The mass media: Opposing viewpoints.* San Diego: Greenhaven.

Qiang, X. (1990). Recent developments in Chinese journalism. In L. J. Martin & R. E. Hiebert (Eds.), *Current issues in international communication.* New York: Longman.

Ross, M. C. (1984). China's great leap skyward. *China Business Review, 33,* 8.

Sartori, C. (1986). TV around the world. *World Press Review, 33,* 220.

Shuer, V. (1981). Reports from China: China's local news media. *China Quarterly,* 328.

Wang, R. (1990). Major developments in Chinese telecommunications: An overview. In L. J. Martin & R. E. Hiebert (Eds.), *Current issues in international communication.* New York: Longman.

Warren, J. (1988). Foreign and domestic news content of Chinese television. *Journal of Broadcasting and electronic Media, 32*(2), 219.

India

Goa, Daman & Diu; Dadara & Nagar Haveli;
and Pondicherry; are centrally administered territories.
Parts of Kashmir in Pakistan and China claimed by India.

300 km

0   300 Miles

PAKISTAN

CHINA

NEPAL

BHUTAN

BANGLADESH

MYANMAR

Jammu and Kashmir

Himachal
Pradesh

Chandigarh

Punjab

Haryana

Delhi

Uttar Pradesh

Sikkim

Arunachal
Pradesh

Assam

Nagaland

Meghalaya

Manipur

Rajasthan

Bihar

Tripura

Mizoram

West Bengal

Gujarat

Diu

Daman

Dadra and Nagar Haveli

Madhya Pradesh

Maharashtra

Orissa

Arabian Sea

Bay of Bengal

Andhra
Pradesh

Goa

Karnataka

Andaman and
Nicobar Islands

Tamil Nadu

Kerala

SRI
LANKA

266

Chapter 14

India

Sunil Misra

To understand broadcasting in India, it is necessary to consider the social, historical, and political factors that have shaped it. India is a large country but it has only about one third the territory of its neighbor China or the United States. Its population, which was estimated to be 360 million in 1951, is now over 900 million and if current trends continue it will soon overtake China and become the world's most populated country (see Table 11.1, Chap. 11).

The Anthropological Survey of India has identified 91 ecocultural zones in the country inhabited by 4,635 Castes and communities (Singh, 1992). There are 18 national languages and more than 150 major dialects. Nearly 50% of the people live in poverty and are illiterate. There are many different lifestyles and levels of economic development. Add to this the influence of tradition and conservative outlook and one gets a general idea of the barriers to effective communication.

On attaining independence, India was confronted with massive problems of diverse origin and nature: a large population, a stagnant economy, communal conflicts, caste distinctions, exploitation of weaker sections, and an administrative machinery that was more familiar with governing a subject nation than with its development. These problems were further compounded by the fact that a large majority of people had low aspirations and expectations from life. They had limited mental horizons and, traditionally, had not enjoyed any political, social economic, and religious rights. The foremost task before the new government was to transform this large but inert population from being passive witnesses of the development plans and programs to becoming conscious partners in the process of nation building. This also involved galvanizing social institutions to become dynamic forces that would keep pace with fast- changing technology.

Indian villages have traditionally been described by sociologists and anthropologists as a self-contained universe in which different groups in the social hierarchy are bound by symbiotic relations. Each of the groups is obliged to perform certain group-determined traditional social and economic functions for the others and to receive remuneration according to prefixed norms. The hereditary occupations of these groups are arranged in a hierarchical order, thereby creating status differences. In a way, hierarchical occupational specialization has ensured social and economic protection, eliminated economic competition between different groups, and thus provided opportunities for professional excellence. For centuries, this system has helped to sustain the Indian village communities as close-knit cohesive entities. On the other hand, this has also tended to insulate them from outside influences and thereby made them resistant to change. Every mediated change brings an element of crisis within the group. It involves adoption of a new behavior, evolution of new relationships, introduction of a new kind of specialization, and even emergence of new leadership. The conflicts take place because the established order feels threatened with the new practices and tries to maintain the status quo. The communication strategies for planned change, as such, have to be sensitive to such issues that directly affect people's participation in the developmental effort.

Broadcasting in India has been used by the government as an instrument of social change. Education and motivation for social action is generally difficult to achieve if the programs do not cater to the perceived needs of the people. A dynamic broadcast policy has to be in tune with the dynamics of social change, which, in turn, calls for an equally dynamic system for research and feedback. This developmental use of broadcasting is the focus of this chapter.

The history of broadcasting in India can be divided into three periods. The first, between 1923 and 1947, includes the inception of broadcasting under the British Colonial Administration up to the year India attained independence. The second period, from 1947 to 1976, is marked by the development and consolidation of radio and the beginning of television broadcasting. The modern period, beginning in 1976, is notable for the formal separation of television from its parent organization, the All India Radio (AIR), and the large-scale expansion in the networks of the two media.

THE COLONIAL PERIOD: 1923–1947

Radio broadcasting began as private ventures in 1923 and 1924 when three radio clubs were established in the cities of Bombay (West India), Calcutta (East India), and Madras (South India). The daily broadcasts of 2 to 3 hr consisted mainly of music and talk. These stations had to close down in 1927 for lack of sufficient financial support. In the same year, the government of India created the Indian Broadcasting Company (IBC) that commissioned two radio stations in Bombay and Calcutta. The IBC, like its predecessors, went into premature liquidation within 3 years of its inception because of heavy recurring expenditures and inadequate working capital. Faced with a widespread public outcry against the closure of the IBC, the government acquired its assets and constituted the Indian Broadcasting Service under the Department of Labor and Industries. Since then, broadcasting in India has remained under the government control. In 1936, a radio station was commissioned in Delhi. In the same year, the Indian Broadcasting Service was renamed All India Radio (AIR) and a new signature tune was used. The Delhi station, in the capital of India, became the nucleus of broadcasting at the national level.

Radio broadcasting assumed considerable importance with the outbreak of World War II. By 1939, the entire county was covered by a short wave service and the program structure underwent a change to meet wartime contingencies. During this period, news and political commentaries were introduced and special broadcasts were made for the people on the strategic northeastern and the northwestern borders.

The immediate postwar period witnessed a massive upsurge against British rule. Radio had to be sensitive to the rising aspirations and expectations of the people and at the same time had to serve the interests of its colonial masters. The AIR handled the situation in a balanced manner by being objective in its programming. AIR's transition from the postwar period under British colonial rule to the independence of India was smooth in spite of the instability prevailing in the country.

POSTINDEPENDENCE DEVELOPMENT:1947–1976

This second period is perhaps the most important in the history of Indian broadcasting. Chaotic conditions were created by the transition of power in 1947 and the emergence of a free India, the trauma of the partition of the country, widespread riots between Hindus and Muslims followed by a massive migration of population to and from India and the newly formed Pakistan, and the large-scale destruction of human lives and property. The AIR played an important role by helping to maintain peace and harmony and reduce communal passions. The content of its programs also changed as peacetime responsibilities called for a greater stress on national integration, education, information, and development. The transformation of the AIR from being a mouthpiece of a foreign government to being the voice of a free India was the result of careful planning and a conscious decision to maintain objectivity and present the views of the people. The AIR avoided news that incited communal passions and gave coverage to the efforts of national leaders to bring about communal harmony and peace. It featured regular religious broadcasts that emphasized peace, amity, and nonviolence. By 1976, the number of radio stations in the country grew to 74.

The period is also notable for the introduction of television in India. It started as a pilot project in 1959 under the AIR to assess the effectiveness of the medium in promoting nonformal education and social development. For this experiment, Phillips India, a Dutch corporation, provided all the equipment at a reduced price and UNESCO gave a grant of $20,000 (U.S. currency). The programs were broadcast twice a week for 20 min to audiences in and around Delhi.

To promote collective viewing, urban teleclubs were established by Air for which Phillips India installed television sets in different localities without charge. AIR, in collaboration with the Directorate of School Education and the National Fundamental Education Center in Delhi, carried out a study on audience reactions to the programs. The indicators of assessment included the extent of audience attendance, the extent of recall of the thematic content, and the reaction to the qualitative aspects of the programs. The study by Mathur et al. (1960) showed that the pilot experiment was a success and people demanded extended daily transmission. The government decided to launch a daily 1-hr television service beginning August 15, 1965. This service has grown steadily since then. Between 1972 and 1975, six more television centers were opened in the country, with each center broadcasting for 4 hr in the evening.

A unique experiment in the history of television was the Satellite Instructional Television Experiment (SITE) carried out in 1975 and 1976. This was the first attempt to apply sophisticated satellite communication technology for social education and rural development and to reach people living in remote and backward regions. It was a collaborative effort between the Indian Space Research Organization (ISRO), AIR, and the state governments. 2,400 villages in the remote and backward regions of the states of Andhra Pradesh and Karnataka (South India), Orissa and Bihar (East India), and Rajasthan and Madhya Pradesh (Central India) were selected for the experiment. The government of India and ISRO installed television sets at the community meeting places in the selected villages along with specially fabricated antennae for direct reception. The U.S. National Aeronautics and Space Administration (NASA) loaned its satellite, ATS-6, for a period of 1 year to carry out the experiment. The production centers were established in Cuttack (East India), Hyderabad (South India), and Delhi, which fed their programs to the earth station at Ahmedabad (West India). These programs were then beamed to the satellite for simultaneous transmission to the six states. During this period, an experiment named One Video Two Audio, in which the same programs were carried in two different languages, was also conducted as part of SITE.

A large number of studies were carried out under SITE to assess its impact and the type of social changes that were taking place among the rural audiences. Notable among them were the Holistic Studies of the Village Communities (Agarwal, 1981; Chakrabarti, 1976; Doshi, 1976) and the assessment of the One Video Two Audio transmission experiment (Audience Research Unit, AIR, 1976). The main conclusion of these studies was that television had played on important role in bringing about attitudinal changes. However, 1 year was insufficient to assess the transformation in normative behaviors. The post-SITE period marked the beginning of the large-scale expansion of the television network in the country.

THE MODERN PERIOD: 1976 TO THE PRESENT

This period is notable in the history of Indian broadcasting for two reasons: Television formally separated from the AIR and a massive expansion program for the two media was launched by the government. On April 1, 1976, a new Directorate of Doordarshan (the literal Hindi translation of television) was created. In 1982, a regular satellite link between Delhi and transmitters in other parts of India was established using Indias own satellite, INSAT-1. In the same year, television began color transmission. The rapid expansion of television can be judged by the fact that in some periods in the mid-1980s television centers were being commissioned at the rate of one per day.

AIR also established radio stations in different parts of the country in addition to starting a national channel. According to the latest figures (Audience Research Unit, AIR, 1993; Audience Research Unit, Doordarshan, 1994), there are 564 television transmitters and about 175 radio stations. However, there has been a basic difference between the expansion plans of the two media. Whereas Doordarshan emphasized installing relay transmitters that were linked to the Delhi center, AIR established program originating stations. In terms of reach, the television service covers about 85% of the population (Audience Research Unit, Doordarshan, 1994) and radio reaches about 98% (Audience Research Unit, AIR, 1993) mainly through single channel medium wave stations. The coverage by television is through the interlinking of relay transmitters with the Delhi center. A majority of the television audience is thus able to watch centrally produced programs in Hindi.

Special Features of Current Broadcasting

Both radio and television function as government departments under the Ministry of Information and Broadcasting. As such, both media have to perform according to the policy directives, guidelines, and broadcast codes issued by the ministry from time to time. This has, in a way, strait-jacketed the program fare of both media. It is noteworthy that the programming of radio and television has remained relatively unchanged. This has given rise to a situation in which even those programs that do not enjoy audience patronage are broadcast regularly because they form part of the broadcast policy.

The program staff in radio and television belong to a common cadre with frequent interorganizational transfers. Moreover, most of the functionaries in the television organization originally worked for AIR. The overall result is that both media put out more or less similar program fare. Apart from the interorganizational transfers between radio and television, transfers also take place from one section to the other. Thus, a person who is in charge of external services may be shifted to commercial services; likewise, the one looking after commercial services may be put in charge of staff training. The program cadre in both media, therefore, is composed mainly of generalists.

The spoken word programs of radio and television have to conform to a broadcast code that was developed because of a dispute in 1967 between the director of a radio station and the chief minister of a state over a passage in the latter's speech. In order to avoid such situations in the future, a code for broadcasting was developed by the parliament (Baruah, 1983). The code prohibits (a) criticism of friendly countries; (b) attacks on religious communities; (c) obscene and defamatory programs; (d) incitement of violence; (e) contempt of court; (f) aspersions against the president of India, state governors, and the judiciary; (g) attacks on any political party by name; (h) hostile criticism of the central and state governments; and (i) anything showing disrespect to the constitution of India.

Financial support for the functioning of radio and television is provided by the government of India. Earlier, the revenue earned through the broadcast receiver license fee, the excise duty on radio and television sets, and the earnings from commercial advertising were deposited in the government of India's consolidated fund. The budget for the two media was approved by the parliament on an annual basis. The license fee on radio has since been abolished except for a one-time fee on the purchase of television sets which is still levied. The sources that meet the budget requirements of radio and television are discussed next.

Under the so-called Nonplan Budget, all recurring expenditures for staff salaries, program production, training, replacement of equipment, and so on are met. The budgetary provisions are made along with the sanction of the total budget for the Ministry of Information and Broadcasting.

The government of India set up a planning commission in 1950 to prepare blueprints for development that took an overall view of the needs and resources of the country. The commission provides financial support for the development plans and schemes of ministries and state governments. Its budget is called the Plan Budget and is approved on a 5-year basis. At present, schemes under the Eighth Plan Period are being implemented. To secure broadcasting funds from the plan budget, specific schemes have to be submitted to the planning commission.

In 1975, a so-called Nonlapseable Fund was created out of the earnings from the commercial services for improving the quality of broadcasts and for the development of hardware and software facilities in radio and television. Like all other revenue, the commercial earnings have to be deposited with the government of India and after necessary adjustments 90% of this revenue is provided for development purposes. Normally, the annual financial outlay under the Plan and Nonplan Budgets lapses if not spent within the same financial year but the budget provided under the Nonlapseable Fund can be carried forward to subsequent years. The annual approval for the budget is accorded by the parliament after reviewing the performance of the broadcasting organizations.

All India Radio (AIR)

AIR has four main services: the Home Service, the Commercial Service, the External Service, and the News Service. The Commercial Service is treated as part of the Home Service. All of these services function under the overall supervision of the director general. The staff for the Home, Commercial, and External services is drawn from the Indian Broadcasting Program Service. The engineers have a separate cadre in the Indian Broadcasting Engineering Service. The Home Service has a three-tier structure comprising national, regional, and local stations.

National programs, put out by the Delhi station at fixed hours, are relayed by all the stations. These include the national news and some late evening programs, such as talk shows, discussions, plays, features, sports magazines, and classical, folk, and regional music. All the stations are linked to Delhi through satellite or microwaves. In 1988, AIR started a national channel that covers about 70% of the country's population. The transmission starts at 6:50 p.m. and continues until 6:10 a.m. The program fare includes Indian and Western music, commentaries on business and finance, political commentaries, and hourly news bulletins in English and Hindi.

The regional stations at the state level cater to the different ethnic, linguistic, and cultural zones. The programs are put out in the regional languages. There is, however, practically no difference between the program fare of the national and regional levels of broadcasting except the language of the broadcast. The content and format of the programs at both the levels is almost the same, except that in the latter case the issues dealt with in the programs are of relevance to the region.

The concept of local stations catering to the population at the microlevel is of recent origin. To date, 64 radio stations broadcasting on low-power frequency modulation (FM) transmitters have been established in the country. According to an AIR policy note, the microlevel broadcasting envisage much greater participation by the people in the form of airing people's views, using local talent, outdoor recording, and coverage of local events.

Generally speaking, there is not much difference between the programs put out by the national, regional, or local stations. Radio and television are government departments and have a commitment to development and social welfare that takes precedence over their commercial interests. The programs must conform to policy directives and the code for broadcasts rather than to popular tastes. Almost all the AIR stations broadcast programs for specific target groups, such as women, youth, children, rural audiences, tribal groups, industrial workers, and the armed forces. The studies have shown that these programs enjoy considerable audience patronage. The rural broadcasts and the women's programs have more than 50% listenership among the target groups (Baruah, 1983).

In keeping with its new role, AIR started a number of new services such as farm and home units for rural development, health and family planning units, formal and nonformal education units, and units for science-related broadcasts. For providing effective need-based support, liaison was maintained with the concerned departments in the government and with universities, research institutions, and subject-matter specialists. AIR has launched a few innovative programs to reach its audience. The following merit mention in this connection.

Rural radio forum. In order to promote participatory communication, a nation-wide scheme was launched in collaboration with the extension departments of the state governments. Several thousand radio sets were installed in villages for organized listening. Local extension workers were supposed to participate and discuss important points with the audience. These forums, however, faded out after successful functioning for several years mainly because of the poor maintenance of radio sets, lack of interest on the part of the extension workers, and the considerable increase in domestic ownership of radio sets.

The Yuva Vani service. Translated into English, Yuva Vani means Voice of the Youth. In 1969, the Delhi station started a separate channel for 15 to 30 year olds. The channel was managed by people in that age group. Some of its programs became extremely popular; mention may be made of Firing Line, in which eminent persons including senior ministers were invited to participate in a question-and-answer session with the youth. In recent years, Yuva Vani has experimented with the soap opera format for dealing with development problems of youth. In this connection, the serials titled Jeewan Saurabh (Essence of Life) on conscientious parenthood and Dehleez (Threshold) on population socialization among adolescents deserve special mention. Fan mail and the audience research findings (Audience Research Unit, AIR, 1994) have confirmed that these serials enjoyed considerable audience support. The only criticism of Yuva Vani is that the programs tend to be elitist in nature and content and that rural youth do not get sufficient attention. At present, 71 AIR stations put out programs for youth; however, only the Delhi station has a separate channel for them.

Public participation programs. These programs provide a forum for people to present their views on civic or social issues. A number of radio stations, using different formats, broadcast programs on people's grievances, which include the following:

1. Inviting a senior government officer or a minister to answer questions asked directly by the participants. The questioners include senior citizens, journalists, subject-matter specialists, and academicians.
2. Encouraging people to write about their grievances to the stations, which are compiled and forwarded to the concerned departments. The responses are broadcast over radio. The chief minister of a particular state used to participate in such programs once a month.
3. Making outdoor recordings of civic and social issues.]

A number of studies have been conducted on public participation programs by the Audience Research Units of the AIR at various places such as Jaipur (1977, 1983), Delhi (1983), Cuttack (1991), Jalandhar (1991), Lucknow (1991), and Hyderabad (1993). The findings have confirmed the popularity of these programs.

Language lessons. In order to promote understanding of the languages of different regions, several AIR stations broadcast language lessons. Initially, there was a great demand for such programs. In recent times, however, there has been a considerable decline in the listeners' interest as indicated by audience research studies by AIR at Cuttack (1986), Calcutta (1986), and Ahmedabad (1986). The main criticism has been the classical nature of the language and the pedagogic approach that does not equip an average listener to develop conversational skills. In recent years, AIR has experimented with promoting literacy through radio in the backward Hindi-speaking regions. No feedback is available on this experiment.

Educational broadcasts. At present, 78 AIR stations broadcast programs for students. For this purpose, the central and the state governments have provided radio sets in schools. Programs on different subjects are coordinated with the topics given in the syllabi. The schedule of broadcasts is supplied to the educational institutions and also publicized in the newspapers. The feedback, from studies conducted by the Audience Research Units of AIR in Bombay (1979), Hyderabad (1986), and Delhi (1980, 1986), has not been very encouraging. The main reasons for low utilization have been poor maintenance of the sets, lack of uniformity in course coverage, and a general apathy on the part of school administrations. In this connection, some stations have also experimented with curriculum-based programs. For this, lessons are broadcast on some radiogenic subjects (subjects that can be taught over the radio) in early morning or late evening hours to facilitate home listening. These have proved to be fairly popular. Some of the stations broadcast support lessons for the university students during examination times. Teachers and students have found these programs useful (Audience Research Unit, AIR, Delhi, 1986).

Perhaps the most popular among all the educational broadcasts has been the School on the Air program, which presents selected subjects with special target groups in mind, such as farmers, plantation workers, adolescents, and school children. Once the details of the programs are finalized they are given intensive publicity to encourage registration by target groups. Tests are held periodically and those who complete all the lessons are awarded certificates; those who are particularly successful are given special prizes. Research studies on nonformal education conducted by the Audience Research Units of AIR in Delhi (1977), Trivandrum (1978), and Bangalore (1979, 1987) show that the programs on sugar cane cultivation, rubber plantations, social forestry, problems of adolescents, and human evolution have been successful.

Political party broadcasts. For the first time in 1977 and 1978, prior to the assembly elections in different states, recognized political parties were invited to present their manifestos over radio and television. Such broadcasts have been received well by the people as indicated by popular demand and also by studies by the Audience Research Units of the AIR in Calcutta (1977), Patna (1980), Ahmedabad (1985), and Cuttack (1980). Such programs have become a regular feature whenever there are elections to assemblies or parliament.

Vividh Bharati[1]. This is a light entertainment service that primarily airs Indian film music. It was started in 1957 and converted into a commercial service in 1967. The parliament, however, limited commercials to 10% of total transmission time. The commercials include spots, jingles of 10 to 30 duration, and sponsored programs lasting from 5 to 30 min. The rates for advertising are determined on the basis of the transmitter strength, population coverage, and audience availability in differ-

---

[1] *Editor's note:* India is the world's leading producer of films, many of which are musicals.

ent time slots. At present, 28 AIR stations have a separate channel for Vividh Bharati and two are independent stations. It is primarily a Hindi service but some time slots are provided for regional language broadcasts by the respective stations. Total revenue from commercial radio broadcasting during 1993 and1994 was around $20 million (U.S. currency), about 3% of the country's total advertising outlay.

External Services Division (ESD). This is one of the oldest services in the world. With the outbreak of World War II, AIR started a service in the Pushtu and Dari languages for Afghanistan. Subsequently, services in Arabic and Persian were also started. Since then, external broadcasting has expanded considerably (Baruah, 1983). The main goals of ESD programs are (a) projecting India's life, culture, and the progress made in different fields; (b) presenting India's point of view on matters of national and international importance; and (c)promoting international understanding. The daily broadcasts of ESD average more than 70 hr for 24 services beamed to different countries. These also include two general overseas services in English. The ESD also puts out 66 news bulletins in different languages (Audience Research Unit, AlR, 1993).

News Services Division. Initially, AIR had only one unit called the Central News Organization. In 1948, it was split into the News Services Division (NSD) and the ESD. The news bulletins for the ESD are still the responsibility of the NSD. The sources of news are the news agencies, special correspondents in different countries, and the part-time stringers in different regions. The volume, variety, and complex nature of the output of the NSD can be judged from the fact that every day it broadcasts 88 national news bulletins in 19 languages, 131 regional bulletins in 62 languages and dialects, and 66 news bulletin for the ESD. The combined duration of all these bulletins comes to around 39 hr every day (Audience Research Unit, AIR, 1993).

Doordarshan (The Television Organization)

The television organization has a complex program structure. Until 1975, there were only six program originating centers. Since then, regular television centers have been commissioned in almost all the state capitals to broadcast programs in their regional languages. In this arrangement, the transmitters located within a given ethno–linguistic–cultural zone are linked to the main center at the state capital. Technically, therefore, television broadcasting has a four-tier structure: national, network, regional, and the local levels. For national level broadcasting, all the stations and transmitters are hooked to the Delhi center but for the network programs only the relay transmitters are linked.

National programs are simultaneously broadcast to the entire nation using satellite links. The national transmission starts at 8:30 p.m. and continues until 11:15 p.m. The focus of the national programs is on promoting national integration and communal harmony and presenting the culture of different region. The programs include current affairs, serials and soap operas, plays, music, and feature films. The national programs also include two 30-min news bulletins in Hindi and English.

The network service from Delhi is relayed by all the low-power transmitters. The programs are in Hindi and include music, development, civic and social issues, and health-related broadcasts. The reach of the network service varies with the individual programs and according to the demand from different regions. For example, the routine broadcasts from the Delhi center are relayed by 78 transmitters with an estimated reach of 174 million people. The Hindi feature film broadcast on Sundays is relayed by 337 transmitters and reaches about 452 million people. According to the Audience Research Unit, Doordarshan (1994), the *Friday Chitrahar*, a program of song and dance clippings from Hindi films, has the highest reach among the network programs. It is relayed by 379 transmitters with an estimated population reach of 470 million viewers.

The regional service operates from the television centers located in the capital cities of different states and has a networking facility with the other centers within the state. The program fare is by and large the same as on the national hookup except that it is in the regional languages and of local relevance. Some state capital centers do not have the program-originating capability and are either linked with the Delhi center or to the program-originating center of a nearby state.

The television centers at the four metropolitan cities of Bombay, Calcutta, Delhi, and Madras have a second channel designated the Metro Channels. These carry area-specific programs using local talent. In January of 1993, production of certain programs on the

Metro Channels was given to privately owned companies; later, all of these were interlinked and became a satellite channel. In the same year, four additional channels were added to the Delhi center. These broadcast channel-specific specialized programs that include sports, music, and programs on current issues that are broadcast in different regional languages.

All the television centers with the exception of those in the metropolitan cities have only a single-channel facility. The program fare, therefore, has to be of a composite nature, catering to the varied tastes of audiences in different age groups and of different genders. There is, however, not much difference between the nature and contents of the programs broadcast by national, regional, and local channels except for the language of broadcast. As mentioned earlier, the program pattern is determined by the policy directives issues by the Ministry of Information and Broadcasting.

Regular education programs to support institutional learning are broadcast by different television centers. For this purpose, software is produced by the Central Institute of Educational Technology at Delhi and the State Institutes of Educational Technology in the respective regions. In addition, the television centers in the metropolitan cities also produce programs. In order to transmit educational broadcasts to students in remote and backward regions of the country, the University Grants Commission has launched a countrywide classroom. The programs are syllabus based and are broadcast on the national network twice a day for 30-min on weekdays. The Indira Gandhi National Open University also broadcasts support programs for its students three times a week.

Commercial spots were introduced in 1976 and sponsored programs began in 1984. The first sponsored serial called Hum Log, consisting of 156 episodes and using the soap opera format, was broadcast in the same year. It was tremendously popular and, encouraged by the response, the government vigorously promoted sponsored serials (Saxena, 1993). At present, sponsored programs have a large share of channel time. The serialized plays and soap operas focus mostly on development or social issues, such as women's emancipation, family planning, problems of adolescents, drug abuse, communal harmony, and adoption of modern technology. The studies carried out by media researchers and the Audience Research Units have shown that the serials have considerable audience support, and in terms of popularity ratings, some of the serials equal or even exceed those of films or film-based programs. The gross revenue from commercial sources in the years 1993 and 1994 was around $121 million (U.S. currency) which is 20% of the total outlay on advertising in India (Audience Research Unit, Doordarshan, 1994).

Audience Research in Indian Broadcasting

Public service broadcasting in a democratic structure has to be responsible to both the government and the people. Regular research and feedback assume considerable importance for monopolistic broadcasting organizations because media have to ensure a synthesis between the communication needs, as visualized by policy planners and administrators, and the information needs as perceived by the people (Misra, 1992). India has pioneered this endeavor.

The importance of feedback was realized by AIR during the 1940s when a listener's research assistant was engaged at one radio station to analyze the fan mail. In 1946, listener's research units were created for each of the six AIR stations. In the early 1970s, the service was renamed Audience Research. At present, there are 43 Audience Research Units in the AIR and 18 in Doordarshan. There are also six regional units in AIR under the charge of deputy directors, in addition to one for the Commercial Services. Audience research remained a common service between radio and television until 1982. Both the current organizations are headed by the a director of audience research. However, a common cadre of audience research personnel staff both units.

The Audience Research Units in the two media perform a somewhat different function than similar organizations in countries where broadcasting is mainly a commercial activity under private enterprise and where multiple broadcasting channels are available. In such a competitive situation, the broadcasting organizations are compelled to cater to popular tastes and demands. In India, radio and television have a commitment to development and, as such, they have to maintain a balance between popular tastes and development. In this, audience research plays an important role in identifying the information needs of the people and providing research support to enhance the effectiveness of the programs.

The Audience Research Units in the AIR and Doordarshan make use of all known methods of social research, such as sample surveys, case studies, in-depth qualitative studies, observations, and experimental research. Other methods employed include telephone studies, panel surveys, and analysis of letters. However, because of the nature of the feedback required, sample surveys are most commonly used. The following are the main types of audience research studies conducted in India.

Feed forward studies. These are carried out before a broadcasting station is commissioned. They contain all the relevant information about the area and the sociodemographic characteristics of the population, its development needs, expectations from the new station, general exposure to various mass media, and so on. This information is used in preparing the program schedule of the station.

General listening surveys. These are undertaken mainly to assess audience ratings of different programs, prime-time listening or viewing, and preferred programs. Such surveys are carried out for 8 days (i.e., from Sunday to Sunday). The program ratings are worked out on the basis of the previous day's listening and viewing as recorded on the log sheets of broadcasts of the respective stations.

In-depth qualitative studies. These programs are done to assess audience views on the qualitative aspects of the individual programs, such as the performance of the broadcaster, voice quality, language, thematic content, and relevance of the topic. The audience research findings are then reviewed in the program meetings of the concerned stations and at the directorates.

Weekly feedback studies. These are conducted by AIR station Audience Research Units on the national radio programs. One hundred people, who are supposed to be knowledgeable in the concerned fields are requested a day before to listen to the program and give their comments on its qualitative aspects. The findings of all such studies are compiled and presented in the weekly review meetings at the Directorate General.

Formative research. During the Satellite Instructional Television Experiment, a number of anthropologists assisted production teams by providing information on audience composition and their development needs, aspirations, and expectations. Programs were produced on the basis of this information. Later these programs were pretested by another group of researchers (Mody, 1976). After SITE, several researchers were recruited to specifically undertake formative research for development-oriented broadcasts at program production centers. A number of programs have been produced on the basis of such research. However, this has now been reduced to a ritual, mainly because of the indifference on the part of the program administrators and producers and inadequate financial support (Joshi et al., 1985)

INDIA'S MEDIA FUTURE

For almost 25 years now, there has been a demand for freeing radio and television from government control. However, there appears to be a far greater concern for aspects, such as structure and organization, sharing of assets, the representation of media people in decision making, and formulation of commissions and committees, than for the people themselves. Issues such as the manner in which autonomy will help the individual or will autonomy bring change in the attitudes of the broadcasters to make them more responsible toward their audiences have not been given any consideration. Although talking about the structure of autonomous broadcasting, there has not been any debate on how the system could maintain a liaison with the people for assessing their needs and expectations.

Any pubic service broadcasting organization with a commitment to development has to structure its programs on the needs and expectations of the people. The government of India has created an elaborate research-support mechanism for Indian radio and television. However, in the ongoing debates and deliberations on media autonomy, research and feedback have been totally ignored. It seems that structure and organization have assumed far greater importance than the ultimate consumers of media fare, the people.

REFERENCES

Agarwal, B. C. (1981). *SITE social evaluation*. Ahmedabad: Space Application Center, Indian Space Research Organisation.

Baruah, U. L. (1983). *This is All India Radio*. New Delhi: Publications Division, Government of India.

Chakrabarti, B. S. (1976). *Impact of SITE* (Unpublished mimeograph).

Doshi, J. K. (1976). *Audience profiles*. Ahmedabad: Proceedings of SITE winter school, published by SAC, ISRO.

Joshi, P. C., et al. (1985). *An Indian personality for television: Report of the working group on software for Doordarshan*. New Delhi: Ministry of Information and Broadcasting, Government of India.

Mathur, C., et al. (1960). *Social education through television: A collaborative study by AIR*. New Delhi: Directorate of School Education, National fundamental Education Center, UNESCO.

Misra, S. (1992). *Audience research in India: Retrospect and prospect*. New Delhi: The Indian Institute of Mass Communication, Directorate of Advertising and Visual Publicity.

Mody, B. (1976). *Pretesting programs in SITE*. Ahmedabad: Space Application Center, Indian space Research Organization.

Saxena, G. (1993). *Soap opera: In search of an identity*. New Delhi: Mass Media in India, Research and Reference Division, Ministry of Information and Broadcasting.

Singh, K. S. (1992). *People of India: an introduction*. Calcutta: Seagull Publications.

The Audience Research Units (ARU) of the AIR and Doordarshan carry out a large number of studies which are mimeographed and circulated within the organizations. These studies are meant for internal use. The following were used in this chapter:

ARU, AIR, Hyderabad. (1976). *One Video-Two Audio transmission in SITE*.

ARU, Directorate General, AIR, Delhi. (1993). *Facts at a glance*.

ARU, Directorate General, Doordarshan, Delhi. (1994). *Television India-Update*.

Nonformal Education

ARU, AIR, Bangalore. (1979). *Study of the farm school on the air on rice cultivation.*

ARU, AIR, Bangalore. (1987). *Study on the impact of school on the air on social forestry (for young school children).*

ARU, AIR, Delhi. (1977). *Study of the farm school on the air on wheat cultivation.*

ARU, AIR, Trivandrum (1978). Study of the farm school on the air on rubber cultivation.

Formal Education

ARU, AIR, Bombay. (1979). *Study of the listenership of the educational broadcasts for non-Marathi (language) schools.*

ARU, AIR, Delhi. (1980). *A case study of school broadcasts in Delhi.*

ARU, AIR, Delhi. (1986). *Study of the listenership to University of the Air programs in Delhi (support lessons for graduates or higher level students during examinations).*

ARU, AIR, Hyderabad. (1986). *Qualitative feedback on primary school broadcasts.*

Studies on Language Lessons on Radio

ARU, AIR Ahmedabad. (1986). *Study of the impact of Hindi lessons.*

ARU, AIR, Calcutta. (1986). *Listening to Hindi lessons.*

ARU, AIR, Cuttack. (1986). *Study of listenership to Hindi lessons.*

Studies on the Party Political Broadcasts

ARU, AIR, Ahmedabad. (1985). *Study of the listenership of party political broadcasts..*

ARU, AIR, Calcutta. (1977). *Listenership of party political broadcasts.*

ARU, AIR, Cuttack. (1980). *Study of the impact of party political broadcasts.*

ARU, AIR, Patna. (1980). *Study of the impact of party political broadcasts at Ranchi.*

Studies on public participation programs

ARU, AIR, Allahabad, Bhopal, Delhi Jaipur, Lucknow, Mathura, Najibabad. Raipur, Rohtak. (1994). *Study of Dahleez [Threshold].*

ARU, AIR Cuttack. (1991). *Study of Pravat Parikrama [Morning round].*

ARU, AIR Delhi. (1983). *Study of Aaj Subah [This Morning]*.

ARU, AIR, Hyderabad. (1993). *Study of Udai Tarangini [Morning waves]*.

ARU, AIR, Jaipur. (1977 & 1983). *Study of Khula Aakash [Open Sky]*.

ARU, AIR, Jalandhar. (1991). *Study of Aaj Subah*.

ARU, AIR, Lucknow. (1991). *Study of Aaj Subah*.

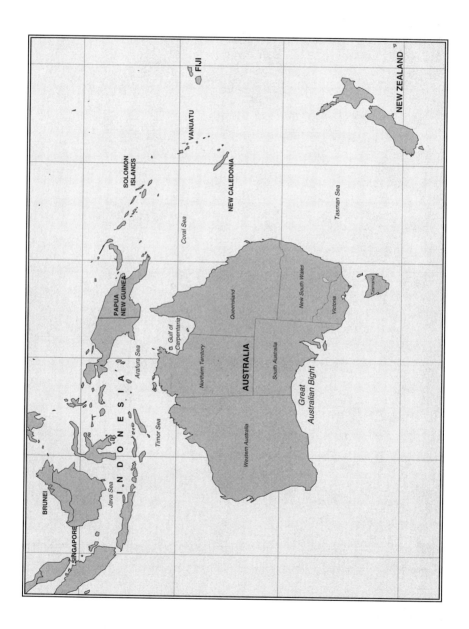

Chapter 15

Oceania and the Pacific

Joseph K. Diemer

An American writer visiting Australia in 1993 observed that people in that country tend to speak very loudly. A simple "G'day" is barked with a volume that the rest of the world finds harsh. The reason, the visitor speculated, is that Australians are overwhelmed by the vastness of their country. He wrote: "Maybe they talk a lot louder because they are so far away from the rest of the world. How else will anyone hear?" (Theroux, 1993, p. 36).

Communicating over large distances is a common theme in Australia, New Zealand, and throughout the South Pacific. From the rugged mountain peaks of New Zealand to the gentle shores of Tahiti, radio and television developed later than in other parts of the world. Once established, however, broadcasting became the South Pacific's most effective tool for linking population centers that are often separated by vast expanses of ocean, desert land, or mountains.

It is a characteristic of the South Pacific that people tend to congregate along the shorelines. This uneven population distribution made it difficult for countries to build effective internal broadcasting systems, as well as to communicate within the region.

Satellite broadcasting provided the region with a giant step forward. Some island countries went directly to satellite reception without going

Table 15.1
Oceania and the Pacific

Country	Population (In Millions)	Growth (%)	Land Area (Square Kilometers)	GNP/Capita (1992 U.S Currency)	Radio Sets (In Millions)	Television Sets (In Millions)
Australia	17.8	0.8	7,682,300	17,070	21.00	8.00
Fiji	0.8	2.0	18,259	2,010	0.45	—
French Polynesia	0.2	2.4	3,652	—	0.11	0.03
Guam	0.2	2.6	544	—	0.27	0.08
Marshall Islands	0.1	4.0	181	—	—	—
Micronesia(Federal States)	0.1	3.0	699	—	—	—
New Caledonia	0.2	2.0	18,285	—	0.09	0.04
New Zealand	3.5	0.9	269,057	12,060	3.10	1.10
Papua New Guinea	4.0	2.3	452,861	950	0.26	0.01
Solomon Islands	0.4	3.7	27,998	710	0.04	—
Vanuato	0.2	2.9	12,199	1,220	0.06	—
Western Samoa	0.2	2.6	2,823	940	0.08	0.01

Note. Population (mid 1994 estimates), population growth (natural increase), and Gross national product per capita (1992) in U.S. dollar equivalents are from 1994 *World Population Data Sheet*, Washington D.C., Population Reference Bureau, 1994. Radio and television set figures are from A. G. Semitt (Ed.), *World Radio TV Handbook*, Volume 49, New York: Billboard Books,1995. Land surface area figures are from *UN Statistical Yearbook, 1991/2*. Because of their small populations, the following have been omitted: Cook Islands. Easter Islands, Kiribati, Nauru, the Northern Mariana Islands, Palau, American Samoa, Tonga, Tuvalu, and Wallis & Fortuna.

through the over-the-air or cable television phases. However, satellite technology may also prove a detriment because it does not encourage local broadcasting production, which is of special concern in the South Pacific because the region is already a heavy importer of American and European programming and, except in Australia, has almost no tradition of making its own programs or developing regional media figures.

Australia and New Zealand are the region's economic powers and are clearly First World developed countries. They are discussed first. The last section of the chapter considers broadcasting in the rest of the region, in much poorer Third World islands (see Table 15.1).

AUSTRALIA

Once described as a "land of magnificent distance," Australia offers a case study of a society that has used the airwaves to overcome geographical factors. Without an advanced broadcasting system, many Australians would have been isolated from their European roots because Sydney is 10,000 miles from London. They would have also been isolated from one another because Australia has one of the lowest population densities of any industrialized countries: Its population is less than New York State's but its land mass is equal to that of the continental United States.

Broadcasting helped Australia conquer its magnificent distance. It also helped the country spread its appealing cowboys-with-cockney-accents culture around the world and gave the country a status above what its 17.8 million population may otherwise warrant.

To accomplish this, however, Australia developed crossbred radio and broadcasting systems that to an outsider appear as strange as the creatures that roam the Great Plateau or pile their skeletal remains on the Great Barrier Reef.

The influence of the British Broadcasting Corporation (BBC) is obvious in the guise of the Australian Broadcasting Corporation (ABC). However, there is also a strong private sector broadcasting element similar to U.S. commercial networks. Not to leave any element out, community groups and universities operate public broadcasting systems not unlike the United States' Public Broadcasting System. here are also foreign language services to meet the needs of minority groups.

Because of Australia's magnificent distance, broadcasting became one of its early national sports. There was little chance of other countries' signals spilling over Australia's borders. Rather, Australians had to actively seek the signals that kept them in touch with the folks "back home," whether back home was Europe, Asia, or the Americas.

In 1919, the first demonstration of wireless technology took place (a broadcast of the British national anthem "God Save the King"). By 1923, there were 37 amateur radio clubs in New South Wales (Thomas, 1980). In 1928, Victoria had the highest proportion of listeners anywhere in the world (Inglis, 1983, p. 9). A private firm took over most of the stations during the 1920s and in 1932 these became the property of the Australian Broadcasting Commission, the forerunner of the modern ABC.

Bringing radio to 40% of Australia's population was relatively easy: They live in the urban areas of Sydney and Melbourne on the southeast coast. Extending broadcasting's reach to the thinly populated outback and to cities, such as Perth in Western Australia, was also not a technical difficulty because Australia has no significant mountains to interfere with signals.

However, bringing quality programming and insightful opinions to Australian listeners sometimes proved too much for the government agency. Almost immediately after being formed, it began suppressing programs that dealt with the status of the Aborigines, the League of Nations, and talk of succession by Western Australia.

Like other elements of Australian broadcasting, the country also developed an unusual way to deal with censorship. A government minister can censor any item or require that any item be broadcast. The minister, however, must report the action to both houses of Parliament within 7 days (Head, 1985).

Dependent on government grants, the ABC became "handicapped by a lack of finance and an oppressive sense of government orthodoxy" (McGregor, 1966, p. 268). The time was ripe for a revival of commercial broadcasting. Commercial stations existed side by side with the National Network almost from the start. By the 1960s, most large towns received at least two ABC radio stations and six commercial stations. Commercial radio was especially popular in urban centers.

Whether the signal came over the National Network operated by the ABC or by the commercial stations, domestically produced programs were rare. Stations could air imported programs for about one fourth the cost of producing their own shows. The same was true with television when it went on the air in 1956.

During the 1960s, as much as 80% of Australian commercial television sion consisted of U.S. imports, whereas the ABC aired British programs. It was possible for Australians to recognize which station they tuned in just by listening to the announcers: ABC announcers spoke with a refined, British accent, whereas commercial station disc jockeys used American accents and glib patter (McGregor, 1966). Ultimately, the commercial stations won the battle as the National Network audience declined.

The government, however, continued to press its agenda to bring radio and television to all regions and different ethnic groups. In 1977, a second government-run system, the Special Broadcasting Service, began offering foreign-language programs to serve the needs of minorities.

In 1983, the ABC assumed its current status as a corporation governed by a government-appointed board. It is free from direct government intervention but it derives funding from license fees and an annual appropriation from Parliament. The system achieved some marked successes, such as strict guidelines for programming aimed at children and regulations that strengthened domestic production of television commercials. News is an ABC strong point. The ABC broadcasts an average of 5 hr of news programs daily and maintains correspondents in major capitals around the world. Its 289 stations also offer music, educational, and children's programs and some even carry sessions from Parliament.

The buzzword for Australian commercial radio and television in the 1980s was "networking." In 1987, the government liberalized its laws regarding media ownership in an attempt to provide more options to viewers. Years of strict regulations aimed at creating competition in each marketplace and in encouraging domestic programming production disappeared overnight.

Australian media leaders looked to the success of U.S. networks. They also sought to take advantage of the ability to reach a majority of Australians without major capital investments: Two thirds of Australia's viewership is concentrated in the five largest markets. The media leaders thus began adding stations to their networks, quickly driving up the cost of those stations.

As ripe as the networking idea appeared, the reality has been sour. A deep recession hit Australia in 1990 and advertising revenue stopped its upward spiral. The fledgling networks found themselves saddled with debt and consequently cut domestic productions, even those that had become popular in foreign markets. The cuts, however, were not enough and several networks went into the hands of their creditors: "The immediate outlook for Australian TV is bleak . The real issue is now who pays the most, the TV industry or the banks, for the corporate and lending madness of the late 1980s" (Turner, 1993, p. 101).

By whatever means the corporate battles are resolved, Australian companies do not appear likely to assume an immediate role among the media giants on the international stage[1]. Like the egg-laying mammals that appear in Australia and nowhere else, the country's mixed broadcasting system may prove to be an evolutionary dead end, a wondrous phenomenon but one that does not translate well to other climates.

NEW ZEALAND

New Zealand faced the opposite problem from its giant neighbor in the north, Australia, in developing an effective broadcasting system. Whereas Australia had to bridge large expanses of flat land (it was once described as "a giant sprawling pancake"), New Zealand is only about the size of the state of Colorado and just as rugged. Mountain chains, such as the "Southern Alps," give New Zealand magnificent scenery and sheep-raising pastures. However, the mountains block clear radio and television transmissions and divide New Zealanders into small enclaves in the valleys and in large cities along the coast.

Because of these geographical impairments, New Zealand developed a series of low-powered radio stations, each serving a small area within the mountain confines. New Zealanders also became accustomed to a strong government role over many areas of everyday life: from health services to care for the elderly. Those two factors—the expense of reaching populated areas and the tradition of state management—made it comfortable for New Zealand to develop a government operated broad-

---

[1] *Editor's note:* Although Rupert Murdoch's money certainly has made an impact.

casting system. The government, in fact, ruled the airwaves until the late 1980s (Levine, 1978).

New Zealand's 3.3 million people live on two large islands and two smaller islands in the South Pacific. It is the most remote of all Western culture nations; even Australia is 800 miles away and the only other nearby land mass is Antarctica.

British settlers came to New Zealand in the mid-1800s to set up a kind of workers' paradise. They embarked on a giant socialist experiment designed to soften capitalism's hard edges by promoting middle-class virtues, such as education and secure employment. To a large degree the experiment succeeded. Despite early wars with the Maoris, the indigenous Polynesian population, and a recent outflow of young, educated workers seeking opportunities in other countries, New Zealand has built a stable, relatively prosperous society. There is almost no disparity between urban and rural incomes and unemployment levels are historically low when compared to most developed nations.

Far removed from their English roots, New Zealanders developed a strong tradition of local theater and vaudeville. When broadcasting arrived in the 1920s, it assumed and has maintained the role of patron of the local arts. The national radio service even provided subsidies to the New Zealand National Symphony Orchestra (Rice, 1992).

In the early 1930s, liberals won the national election and assumed power. The party, however, found it difficult to get its message to the people because the newspapers remained staunchly conservative. That made the new communications medium, radio, especially inviting. By assuming control over the fledgling radio stations, the government could bypass editors and send its message directly to the people via the airwaves.

At first, government control was similar to that exercised by the BBC. In 1936, however, the New Zealand government took a step that was extreme even when compared to other government-controlled systems. It established the post of Minister of Broadcasting. That placed radio openly and directly under the control of the political party in power (Levine, 1978; McLeod, 1968). According to one prime minister, "the government is going to be the master of publicity" (Levine, 1978, p. 428). According to Rice (1992), "the government tried clumsily and at first effectively to control political debate and controversy on the radio and television, and to prevent the appearance of private radio stations" (p. 386).

Although the government wanted to control broadcasting, it did not want to pay for it. Instead of an annual appropriation from Parliament, as is done in Australia and other countries, New Zealand used advertising to provide two thirds of broadcasting's revenue. Advertising proved successful, despite a law in effect for many years that banned commercials 2 days each week. Television license fees provide the remaining funds (Rowe & Rowe, 1967).

Television came to New Zealand rather late. The television channel TV 1 went on the air in 1960, soon followed by a second station. However, television sets were expensive because of heavy import duties and television offered almost no local productions. Perhaps more than any other developed country, New Zealand relied on imports. As much as 75% of its programming came from the United States, Britain, or Australia.

Responding to criticism that broadcasting was insipid, the government tried to appease its citizens. In 1961, it gave up direct political control and established a public body, the New Zealand Broadcasting Corporation (NZBC), to run the daily operations. Curiously, however, the government retained the position of minister of broadcasting. For politicians, it was the best of both worlds. The government could still influence programming but it could deflect criticism to the independent broadcasting entity (Levine, 1978). The result was that few noticed any real change and broadcasting remained noncontroversial and uninspiring.

By the late 1960s, however, pirate stations began appearing offshore. They easily wooed audiences away from the stodgy programming on NZBC and forced the government to take a series of drastic measures. The government finally abolished the ministerial post in 1973 and during the 1980s it authorized private broadcasting systems and dropped its laws against foreign ownership of media outlets. The reforms had immediate effects and gave New Zealanders a range of choices similar to those enjoyed by other developed nations.

By the mid-1990s, more than 90 radio stations and three television networks were on the air. Radio New Zealand's National Network emphasizes news and information but the state-owned system also operates 34 commercial stations geared to local community interests. These stations compete with 43 private radio stations. Similarly, Television New Zealand is a state-owned system that reaches almost the entire population with two VHF channels. It competes with the private network, TV

3, and with a pay television channel called Sky Television.

In recent years, the state systems have dedicated an increasing amount of airtime to the needs of the country's Maori citizens. News is broadcast in the Maori language and 12 Maori radio stations receive public funding. The changes produced a broadcasting system that is livelier, offers more choices, and is more competitive. Although a large portion of the programming still comes from overseas, New Zealand's free press tradition now also extends to the airwaves.

OCEANIA

Oceania is sometimes referred to as paradise, but not by broadcasters. Spread out over thousands of miles of ocean, the islands of Oceania are broadcasting's ultimate challenge. To achieve an effective communication link, radio and television signals must cross vast expanses of the South Pacific. Broadcasters must also deal with mountain ranges; many islands are volcanos sticking up out of the ocean with population centers scattered along the shoreline.

There is also the language problem. Many of Oceania's elite speak English or French but there is no common language shared throughout Oceania. The closest substitute is Melanesian Pidgin, a mixture of English vocabulary and Melanesian grammar and syntax. Pidgin is a widely understood second language but few use it as a primary language (Brookfield, 1972).

Theroux (1993), who paddled around the South Seas in a one-man boat, described the enormity and the remoteness of Oceania: "Being on this boat was like shooting from one star to another, the archipelagoes like galaxies, and the islands like isolated stars in an empty immensity of watery darkness" (p. 151). The boundaries of Oceania stretch from the southeast coast of Asia to the Americas. Many larger islands, however, are located to the east of Australia and receive radio signals from Australia and New Zealand. Some of Oceania's islands are densely populated. Others support only small villages. Hundreds are uninhabited.

There are some common cultural similarities among the islanders. However, on many islands the cities and villages are sometimes so isolated they have little means of communicating with the outside world or even among themselves. Many know little about those on neighboring islands or even on the opposite side of their own island.

Broadcasting has had a lesser impact on everyday life in Oceania than in most other places on earth. In addition to the technical difficulties of spanning the ocean and relaying signals across mountains, in the 1970s there was also a reluctance in some areas to import foreign broadcasting. Many of the island nations had little crime and island leaders feared that Western programs would lead to violence (Mamak & McCall, 1976). However, the proliferation of both audio-and videocassettes has made these objectives moot.

European explorers came to Oceania during the 16th and 17th centuries. Gradually, Europeans began settling the islands and exporting coconuts, coffee, and minerals. Writers have always been fascinated by the subsequent clash of cultures that occurred in the South Pacific. The stories continue today with accounts of how the islanders react to events of the world brought to them via the airwaves. For example, Lockwood (1993) described how Tubuai women on Tahiti in French Polynesia wore long hair for centuries. However, they quickly changed the tradition and cut their hair short to look like Pam, a character on the television series *Dallas* when the show became popular in Tahiti.

Theroux (1993) told of landing on the remote Tongatapu Island Group in 1993. To his surprise, he found Tongans with videocassettes showing Allied military strikes against Iraq that had taken place only days before. The Tongans had bought the cassettes in Fiji from Indians who made them by pirating CNN newscasts. The cassettes were likely an immediate hit on the few televisions available in Tongatapu. In fact, they may have been the only thing to watch. The islands have no over-the-air television system.

Papua New Guinea is the second largest of the countries of the region, behind only Australia. It is almost twice the size of New Zealand and its population of 4 million ranks second. It occupies the Eastern half of the very large island of New Guinea (the other half is part of Indonesia and therefore considered to be Asian). However, it ranks very low in radio and television set ownership (see Table 15.1). The country is poor and its native peoples are diverse with each having their own distinct language. Those living deep in the mountains are among the most isolated people on earth. The government operated a national and several regional radio services, broadcasting in English, Melanesian, Pidgin, Hiri Motu, and some 30 ethnic languages. There is one commercial television station to serve the very few people who own a television set (Sennitt, 1995).

On the high end of the Oceania communications scale are French Polynesia, Fiji, and New Caledonia. Tahiti is the main island of French Polynesia, many of who's people live in the capital city of Papeete. The French Radiodiffusion Francaise D'Outre Mer (RFO) provides the main radio service but "many private FM stations are operating" (Sennitt, 1995, p. 252). RFO also provides one television channel relayed throughout the islands and there is also a private commercial station (Sennitt, 1995). Over the years, the system has become one of the best in Polynesia, although its audience is still mostly in the urban center.

Fiji, with 700,000 people living on 100 islands, broke with the Oceania tradition of government control over broadcasting and has introduced a commercial broadcasting system. In New Caledonia, the French government continues to control radio and television broadcasting by relaying its overseas services, RFO. When the local Kanak people complained that RFO was too French oriented and conservative, the French began training Melanesian journalists and technicians and pledged that RFO would "respect information pluralism and programme diversity" (Chanter, 1991, p. 320). The country now has three other FM radio stations and a private commercial station operating in the capital city, Noumea (Sennitt, 1995).

In other areas of Oceania, however, broadcasting remains relatively underutilized. In the early 1970s, long after most other parts of the world had established radio and television systems, Brookfield (1972) wrote of Oceania:

"The true potential of broadcasting, in generating an informed public with an interest in its own culture and personalities, remains almost totally unexplored. Even in the towns, and most certainly throughout the rural areas of Melanesia, public opinion is thus very poorly informed. The people of different regions know little about one another." (pp. 195–196)

By the 1990s, however, broadcasting's position had greatly improved. Western Samoa, for example, now has one private commercial radio system and two channels run by the government's Samoan Broadcasting Service. Broadcasting is in English and Samoan. One private television station serves the very small telrvision audience (Sennitt, 1995). The advent of satellite transmissions made it easier to receive signals and the new Asian–Pacific News Network localized events more than the Western news agencies.

Nevertheless, many islands remain isolated and have little ability to relate the world's events to their own lives. Again, the modern-day explorer Theroux (1993, p. 217) provided the anecdote. He told of paddling to the remote island of Nguna in the Vanuatu Chain shortly after the start of the Iraqi War. Theroux would monitor foreign news broadcasts via Radio Australia, the Voice of America, or the BBC, whichever would come in clearest on any particular night. He would then tell the islanders what was happening in the Middle East. The Ngunans, who knew of the U.S. operations in the South Seas during World War II, discussed the war news among themselves. They concluded it was quite likely that after victory in Iraq, the American soldiers would come to their island and liberate them from an obscure local chieftain.

REFERENCES

Brookfield, H. C. (1972). *Colonialism, development and independence.* Cambridge, England: Cambridge University Press.

Chanter, A. (1991). The media and politics in New Caledonia in the 1980s. *Journal of Pacific History,* 26(2).

Head, S. W. (1985). *World broadcasting systems.* Belmont, CA: Wadsworth.

Inglis, K. S. (1983). *This is the ABC.* Melbourne: Melbourne University Press.

Levine, S. (1978). *Politics in New Zealand.* Sydney: Unwin.

Lockwood, V. (1993). *Tahitian transformation.* Boulder, CO: Lynne Rienner.

Mamak, A., & McCall, G. (Eds.). (1976). *Paradise postoned.* Australia: Pergamon.

McGregor, C. (1966). *Profiles of Australia.* London: Hodder and Stoughton.

McLeod, A. L. (1968). *Pattern of New Zealand culture.* Ithaca, NY: Cornell University Press.

Rice, G. W. (1992). *Oxford history of New Zealand.* Auckland: Oxford University Press.

Rowe, J. W., & Rowe, M. A. (1967). New Zealand: *Nations of the modern world.* New York: Praeger.

Sennitt, A. G. (Ed.). (1995). *World radio TV handbook* (Vol. 49). New York: Billboard Books.

Theroux, P. (1993). *The happy isles of Oceania.* New York: Putnam.

Thomas, A. (1980). *Broadcast and be damned: The ABC's first two decades.* Melbourne: Melbourne University Press.

Turner, G. (1993). *Nation, culture, text: Australian culture and media studies.* London: Routledge.

Author Index

F

Famoriyo, S., 148, 182
Fletcher, J.E., 109, 118
Foote, J.S., 129, 142
Fox, E., 22
Frederico, M.E.B., 208, 220
Fuhrman, P., 205
Furtado, C., 210, 220

G

Gantz, W., 248
Garrison, B., 188, 190, 195, 197, 200, 205
Gerbner, G., 254, 256, 265
Glover, J., 89
Godbout, T., 79, 89
Gou Hong, 257
Greenberg, B.S., 248, 249
Gross, L.S., 182
Guback, T., 14, 16, 20, 22
Gyorgy, A., 258, 265

H

Hamelink, C.J., 14, 16, 22
Hamm, C., 254, 255, 265
Hardt, H., 19, 22
Harvey, D., 14, 22
Hasselbach, S., 68, 75
Head, S.W., 131, 132, 142, 292, 300
Hellack, G., 69, 71, 73, 75
Herz, D., 208, 218, 220
Herzmann, J., 109, 118
Hollins, T., 57, 59
Hopkins, M., 91, 94, 118
Horlamus, S., 108, 110, 118
Horne, P.L., 32, 45
Hoskings, C., 14, 18, 22
Hunter, B., 151, 182

I

Inglis, K.S., 292, 300

J

Jakubowicz, K., 112, 118
James, N., 16, 22
Jayaweera, N., 12, 21, 23
Joshi, P.C., 284, 285

K

Kalkkinen, M.L., 14, 23
Kandil, H., 121, 124, 125, 143
Katz, E., 133, 142, 169, 182
Kehl, M.R., 210, 213, 214, 220
Kennedy, P., 14, 23
Klieinwachter, W., 75
Kodjo, E., 150, 182
Ku, L., 248, 249

L

Labib, S., 121, 124, 125, 143
Lamb, C., 212, 220
Lekovic, Z., 113, 114, 118
Lent, J., 198, 205, 226, 228, 230, 233
Levine, S., 100, 295, 296
Li, H., 248, 249
Lima, Venicio A.de, 219, 220
Litman, B., 14, 24
Lockwood, V., 298, 300
Lowenstein, R.L., 3, 6, 23
Lu Keng, A., 251, 265

M

Mackay, I., 182
Mamak, A., 298, 300
Marconi, P., 209, 220
Martin, J.L., 130, 134, 143, 159
Martin, L.J., 149, 151, 157, 175, 182
Mathur, C., 271, 285
Matsumae, N., 241, 249
Mattelart, A., 14, 15, 23
Mattelart, M., 14, 23
Mattos, S., 211, 220
May, S., 254, 262, 265
McAnany, E., 17, 23
McCall, G., 298, 300
McGregor, C., 292, 293, 300
McLeod, A.L., 295, 300
McNair, B., 100, 118
McPhail, T.L., 23
Meehan, N., 16, 17, 22
Melkote, S.R., 12, 21, 23
Merrill, J.C., 3, 6, 23, 137, 141, 143, 223, 226, 230, 233
Meyer, W.H., 18, 19, 23
Miall, L., 50, 59

Subject Index

A

Advertising revenue
  Australia, 294
  China, 260–261
  Germany, 69
  government control of, 30–31
  Japan, 241
  time limitations, 6
  United States, 15–16

Afghanistan
  broadcasting systems, 231
  demographics, 224
  television and radio sets, 224

Africa. *see specific region and country*

AIR. *see* All India Radio

Albania
  broadcasting systems, 106–107
  demographics, 92
  television and radio sets, 92

Algeria
  broadcasting systems
    radio, 130–131
    television, 131–132
  demographics, 122
  gross national product, 122
  television and radio sets, 122

All India Radio
  cultural diversity, 275
  expansion of, 272
  local stations of, 275
  programming, 270, 274–275
    educational broadcasts, 277–278
    external services division, 279
    language lessons, 277
    news services division, 279
    political party broadcasts, 278
    public participation programs,
      276–277

    rural radio forum, 276
    Vividh Bharati, 278–279
    Yuva Vani service, 276
  radio development, 270
  services of, 274

Angola
  broadcasting systems, 174
  demographics, 147
  television and radio sets, 147

Antigua
  demographics, 187
  gross national product, 187
  television and radio sets, 187

Arab World
  broadcasting systems
    centralization, 124
    governmental type, countries that
      have
      Bahrain, 136–137
      Cyprus, 139
      Iran, 140
      Israel, 140–141
      Jordan, 134
      Kuwait, 136
      Oman, 137
      Qatar, 136
      Saudi Arabia, 135
      Tunisia, 134
      Turkey, 140
      United Arab Emirates, 137
      Yemen, 137–138
    Lebanon, 138
    mobilization type, countries that
      have
      Algeria, 130–132
      Egypt, 127–129
      Iraq, 129–130
      Libya, 132–133